SECOND-CHANCE MOTHER

A Memoir

DENISE ROESSLE

Red Willow Publishing
www.RedWillowBooks.com

ISBN: 978-1-936539-68-0

Cover design by Carol Yacorzynski

Table of Contents

To every mother who has lost a child to adoption.

Acknowledgements

This book has been as much a long-term project as my reunion.

I have been fortunate to have a community of people cheering me on along the way. There's no way I can mention everyone, but a few must be named: Judy Ranieri, coach extraordinaire, who got me started and challenged me to stay with it; Linda Joy Myers, the wise and inspirational leader of my first writing group; and editor Melanie Rigney, whose feedback lifted my book above the ordinary. I feel lucky to have been a member of several excellent writing groups, both in California and Arizona, as well as to have had many gifted peer readers and professional editors over the years. Thanks to all of you. Without your encouragement and constructive criticism, I wouldn't be here now.

I am more than grateful to those in my PACER (Post-Adoption Center for Education and Research) support groups, who got me through the early stages of reunion by sharing their stories and listening to mine. And to my therapists (now friends): Nancy Verrier and Barbara Shafer. I was a hard nut to crack, but you got through and set me on a path of healing.

A sincere thank you to the childhood friends who were with me during these difficult periods of my life: Diane, Leanna, Linda D., Linda W., and Madaleine. You are truly the family I chose. How can I not mention my late-discovery cousin, Pam, who has become one of my dearest friends?

Most of all, thank you to my husband and best friend, Henry, who loved and supported me through the ups and downs of reunion.

Chapter 1

LOST AND FOUND

He might as well have been dead. Except he wasn't.

I identified with mothers whose children had been stolen from their cribs or snatched out of strollers in shopping malls. Like them, I wondered whether my son was alive and whether I would ever see him again. But I wasn't one of those mothers. I hadn't lost my baby to a kidnapper. I had given him away.

My recollections were as frayed as a piece of cloth worn thin from handling — faded in some spots, like the summer of 1969, a year after high school graduation, when I had fallen in love with the wrong man — and all too vivid in others, like when I was left alone to face the wrath of my parents and swallow the customary antidote for unwed mothers in that era: adoption.

For nine months I'd carried my son, struggling against the urge to bond with the new life that swelled my belly and twisted just below my heart. I entered labor with the anxious resignation of a surgical patient scheduled to have a burdensome growth removed. I rode the pain without complaint until I was given the injection that shut off the feeling from my waist down. Only when his body was pulled from mine and I heard his gurgled cry did the loss take hold.

"Can I see the baby? Is it a boy or a girl?"

The answer came in the whoosh of the delivery room door, as a nurse rushed out with my newborn. Two days later, I slipped out of my room and past the nurses' station, down the sprawling sterile halls to the nursery. I spotted him through the window, in the second row, last bassinet on the right: *Baby Boy Janson*. I memorized every detail of his tiny face poking out of the blue swaddling — the button nose, quivering eyelids, and furrowed brow — certain that this was all I would ever get and all that I deserved. With every cell in my body screaming

"No!" I walked out of the hospital and out of my son's life.

I pushed back the grief until I was as anesthetized as the day I had given birth. I imagined myself becoming stronger when in truth I had merely become more comfortable with the numbness.

I might as well have been dead. Except I wasn't. The proof came in a phone call on an ordinary Tuesday afternoon, almost twenty-six years after I had relinquished what turned out to be my only child.

I was at the computer, putting the finishing touches on a client's newsletter when my business partner, Carol, answered the phone.

"May I tell her who's calling?" I heard her say from across the room.

When I didn't recognize the caller's name, we called out in unison, "Sales dog!" — one of many crack-our-own-selves-up rituals we'd developed during our six years together in the graphic design business.

"This is Susan from International Soundex Reunion Registry," the woman said when I picked up line one.

No bells. "How can I help you, Susan?"

"Are you free to talk?"

"Sure," I said, rolling my eyes at Carol and waiting for the pitch.

"Do you remember registering with us in 1988?"

My heart skipped and my vision blurred. I swung my chair around, slid in close to the desk, and clutched the receiver with both hands.

"I'm happy to tell you that we've matched you with your son," she said. "He registered two weeks ago."

"Oh my God!" The words flew out of my mouth.

"His name is Joshua. He lives in Metairie, a suburb of New Orleans, and works as an auto mechanic. He's been married for a year, and his wife, Marissa, is pregnant with their first child."

I scribbled furiously as she reeled off more details, my

chest pounding so hard I had to strain to hear. "So, what should I do? Write him a letter?"

"We usually recommend a phone call if both parties are up for it."

"Okay... you mean *now*?"

"I still need to call him with the news that we've contacted you, and he's probably at work, too. Are you available tonight?"

My voice squeaked as I tried to disguise my apprehension. "I think so."

"Good. I'll phone him and try to set it up. Then I'll call you back."

"*What?*" Carol said as soon as I hung up the phone. The alarm on her face told me she thought someone had died.

"They found my son."

"*Son?* What son?"

I drew a deep breath and pushed the air out slowly.

"When I was nineteen, I got pregnant. My boyfriend left me and I had the baby and gave him up for adoption."

That's how I always began. Just the facts until I could gauge the person's reaction. Usually I had already weighed the risk, known them long enough that if they were going to say, "I don't understand how a mother could give up her child," they would have by then. Once I decided it was safe, I'd spit out the words in a rush and then change the subject before they could ask too many questions. Before they could judge me.

I'd told my husband, Henry, early on, feeling compelled to disclose anything undesirable from my past before we married. Of my family, only my parents knew — not even my younger sister and brother. There were a handful of friends who were around when I got pregnant and a few I had confided in since. No one brought it up unless I did, and *no one* got the full story.

The memories were buried deep inside me, clumped in the dark like mushrooms growing in manure. Speaking of what had happened gave the emotions too much power, made it hard to breathe. Like now, as I sat in front of Carol, her eyes filling with tears, her face reflecting the mixture of sadness and joy that should have shown on mine.

"Oh, Denise, I'm so sorry! That must have been awful. But now you've found him. I'm so happy for you!"

I looked down and ran my hand across my face, willing the tears to come and failing as miserably as I did at weddings and funerals and every other time when it was appropriate, indeed mandatory, to cry.

I hadn't cried when the father of my son had deserted me, nor when my parents sent me away to wait out my pregnancy, and not even once I realized that I would never look into my baby's eyes, hear his laugh, or watch him grow. There had been no reason for tears. Everyone — the lawyer, the doctor, my parents — had insisted that giving him up for adoption was the best thing for both of us. My child would have a stable, two-parent home and opportunities far beyond those an unwed mother could provide. I would be reborn a virgin, go back to college, meet a nice man, get married, and have children I could keep.

I'd been expected to move on and I had, but I did not forget. Some mornings I would wake from a dream of giving birth and having my baby beside me, his powdery sweet scent filling my nose, the softness of his skin lingering on my fingertips. I'd pull my arms and legs in close and lie there, contented in the warmth of the blankets, until I realized it wasn't real. Then the tears would flow with such force that I thought they would never cease. On those days, I found it harder than usual to rally the capable, well-adjusted young woman who covered for the girl with the shameful secret.

Desperate not to appear heartless, I offered Carol the only viable explanation. "I think I'm in shock," I mumbled. *Later,* I thought. *Once this sinks in, when no one is around, then I'll break down.* Indeed that was the only way I could cry — when I was alone or drunk or half-asleep, and the feelings could sneak up like vengeful ghosts.

"Of course you are," Carol said. "You should go home."

"I've got that newsletter."

"I'll do it. Just go."

"What am I going to do at home? Pace?"

My mind raced as I settled back into work. Susan called back to say that she had arranged for Joshua to phone me that evening at seven California time. Left on my own for four more hours without diversion, I was sure to implode.

"He asked whether I was sure you wanted to talk to him," she said. "I told him you'd been registered with us for eight years."

The year my son turned fifteen, I'd spotted the "Dear Abby" column that I felt sure was a sign. A happily reunited mother had found the child she'd given up through a mutual-consent reunion registry for adult family members separated by adoption. I'd decided it was perfect, clipped out the article and sent for the form. I wouldn't be interfering in his life, only making it easier for him to find me if he decided to search.

As soon as he turned eighteen, I filed the papers. At first I was certain the phone would ring any day, but as the months and years went by, my hope began to wither. *Maybe he's angry,* I thought. *Maybe he's simply not interested. What if he doesn't know he was adopted?* Although I'd kept my contact information with Soundex current — the last change, six years before — I'd started preparing for the possibility that my son was forever lost to me.

But now he was found, the stranger I had given birth to. My love for him fluttered in my stomach, inducing euphoria akin to early pregnancy. I hadn't begun to fathom what it would mean to be his mother, but I wanted the job more than anything else I could remember wanting. Nothing, not even the new round of fears that loomed, could have kept me from embracing that second chance.

Chapter 2

BABY STEPS

Henry looked up from the television when I burst through the front door thirty minutes before Joshua was scheduled to call.

"I was getting worried," he said, glancing at his watch. "You cut it kinda close."

"I didn't mean to. The traffic was awful."

"Are you okay?"

"I guess." My body dropped into the chair across from my husband and cursed myself for not coming home earlier, for choosing distraction over the refuge of my best friend.

"Did you eat?" he asked.

"No. God, no. I already feel like I'm going to throw up."

The look on his face was the one he always got when he was concerned: eyes narrowed, lips stretched, jaw set. I'd seen it every May since we'd been married — from Mother's Day until my son's birthday shortly after — when I slid unconsciously into melancholy. It was the same look he'd given me a year before when I told him I was tired of waiting, and thinking of hiring a private detective to search for my son.

"If that's what you want, I'm all for it," he'd said cautiously. "Just make sure you're prepared for the outcome."

"I need to know that he's all right."

"And if he's not?"

I narrowed my eyes to match his.

"What if he doesn't want to be found? What if he won't talk to you? Will you be able to handle that?"

I stared into my lap and felt my body sag. "I'd be devastated." When I brought my gaze back to meet Henry's, his face softened.

"I'm not trying to talk you out of it," he said. "I just don't want you to get hurt."

Unlike most of the men I'd been involved with, Henry was stable, reliable, and so even-tempered that, even in the emotionally inscrutable state I'd reached by age thirty-one when we'd met, I seemed hysterical by comparison. He was the safe haven that I'd longed for. Still, sometimes I wished he'd say, "Why the hell not? What's the worst that can happen?"

"You're right," I said. "Better to wait."

When I'd phoned him from work to tell him that the registry had called and I would talk to Joshua that evening, I was relieved to hear genuine delight in his voice. "That's great, Deedee. See, your patience paid off."

I looked at my watch for the tenth time in ten minutes and popped up from the chair. "I've got to get ready."

After changing into sweats, I considered pouring myself a glass of wine to calm my nerves, then decided against it. I wanted to be as alert and articulate as I could manage. Just before seven, I went back into the living room and bent down to give Henry a quick kiss.

"Here goes nothin'," I said.

He smiled. "Good luck."

I took a notepad and pen into our bedroom and sat down next to the phone on my side of the bed. I couldn't fathom the courage it would take for Joshua to dial my number. As the minutes ticked by, I was overcome with the need to feel grounded. By the time the phone rang at five after seven, I'd slid to the floor and cocooned myself between the end table and the wall.

The voice was a grown man's, foreign yet oddly familiar. I drew a breath and held it.

"This is Joshua Goldberg," he began, so low it was almost a whisper. "You don't know me, but…"

"You're my son," I broke in, eager to help.

"Hi, Mom."

We exhaled in unison, and then he let out a little laugh. "I hung up three times before I let it ring."

Our first words came out in disjointed bursts, as if we'd both been rehearsing all afternoon.

"I'm sorry it took me so long to register," he said.

"I should have tried harder to find you," I said.

"Thank you for giving me life, for not getting an abortion."

"I wish I could have kept you."

"I want you to know I'm not angry. I'm sure you had good reasons for giving me up."

"I never stopped thinking about you."

Joshua knew that he'd been born in California and he thought it was "cool" that he'd been conceived in Hawaii where I'd gone to high school. He sounded disappointed that he had no siblings, but pleased when I told him that I'd been engaged to his father.

"Oh good," he said. "So you were in love."

"You probably want to know about him."

"Sometime. Not right now."

For the first half-hour, we sounded like two old friends, catching up after having been out of touch — recapping our lives, asking and answering questions. I told him that I was a writer and graphic designer, that I'd been married for fourteen years to a wonderful man who had a grown son, Jeff, and a grandson, Jordan, who would soon have his first birthday. I told him that he had an Aunt Debby, an Uncle Bob, and three teenaged cousins.

Josh had been raised in Brooklyn, the eldest son of Orthodox Jews. His father, Morris, was a textile merchant, and his mother, Judith, a homemaker. He had an adopted brother Jonathan, who was almost four years younger.

It had taken me the full five hours since the registry's call to get used to his name being Joshua. I'd yet to recover from the shock of learning he was an auto mechanic, and not a doctor or lawyer or some other scholarly and high-paying profession that he might never have achieved if he'd stayed with me.

"Do you like your work?" I asked, perhaps a bit too cheerfully in an attempt to hide my disappointment.

"I love it. And I'm really good at it. I've always been good with my hands."

"That's terrific." Who cares what he does for a living as long as he enjoys it? "Are your parents still in New York?"

"No. They're in Miami."

"Do you see them often?"

"Uh, no... not really. We aren't exactly on speaking terms."

While I scrambled for what to say, Josh picked up the slack. "They were pretty strict. And I wasn't exactly the perfect kid."

"When did they tell you that you were adopted?"

"They didn't." He sighed. "I found out by accident when I was twelve after my grandfather died. We were very close. He was the only person who really listened to me. I took his death hard, and I guess I started to rebel — you know, skipping school, sneaking out, talking back.

"My parents sent me to a psychologist, who saw the notation in my records and asked how I felt about being adopted. I didn't get it. I told her, 'I don't need to be adopted. I already have a family.' Once I knew I'd been lied to, my behavior and my relationship with my parents went straight downhill."

I swallowed hard. While I had been getting on with my life — starting a new career and enjoying my first year of marriage to Henry — my little boy's world had been crumbling. "But did they love you?" The words came out too fast.

He paused. "They did their best."

"Oh, Josh, I'm so sorry."

"I never got along with my father. My mother — I mean, the mother I grew up with — she's nice, and things between us were always pretty good. Me and Marissa drove to Florida to see them after we got married. My father was in the hospital and he refused to see me. He was pissed off because I married a *shiksa*. But my mother let us stay at their house and we had fun together for the first time since I was a kid, playing board games and just hanging out."

I was still replaying *the mother I grew up with* when

his silence snapped me back to attention. "That's good," I mumbled before I was sure my response made any sense.

"You know what's funny though? Even before I found out I was adopted, I had a strange feeling that I didn't belong. I didn't look like anybody in my family. I didn't act like anybody. When I was about six, out of the blue, I asked my dad who my real father was. He told me Irving Q. Pullet. You know, the cartoon mascot for kosher chicken?"

I had no idea.

"After I knew the truth, I couldn't stop thinking about you," he said. "I worried that you were in some kind of trouble, that you needed me."

When he told me that he had attempted to find me twice before, I felt a rush of regret for not having searched. The first time was after his brother had been rooting through their parents' papers and saw Josh's original birth certificate. But Jonathan got my last name wrong and Josh's long-distance calls to every Jensen in Southern California yielded nothing. Years later, on an impulse, he took off driving to Los Angeles, determined to go to the hospital listed on his certificate and grill the doctor until he gave up my name. His car broke down in Tennessee and he never made it any farther west.

His registration with Soundex came as a result of his wife and mother-in-law's urging, after they'd watched a reunion show on *Oprah*. "They deserve all the credit," he said.

Henry stuck his head into the bedroom and mouthed, "You okay?" I smiled and nodded. He flashed a thumbs-up before heading back down the hall.

"It feels funny calling you Josh," I said. "I've always thought of you as Erick."

In truth, it felt strange thinking of him by any name. I wondered whether that had been one of the ways I'd kept him at a safe distance.

"That was your birth name," I told him. "Erick Alan Janson."

"Wow."

"When the clerk brought the birth certificate form for me to sign, she said to just leave it blank. She said your adoptive parents would give you a name. But I insisted... even though I knew no one would ever call you Erick."

"How long were you with me?"

My heart quickened as I dredged up the memories. "I was never *with* you, not after you were born. They wouldn't let me hold you. The doctor didn't even want me to know that you were a boy. But I couldn't leave the hospital without seeing your face, so I snuck down to the nursery and looked at you through the window. I remember thinking that you looked like my dad."

"Really? Wow."

"You were only five days old when your parents came for you." The words sounded hollow in my head. "Sandy, the lady I was living with while I was pregnant, went with the attorney to pick you up at the hospital and take you to the airport. She said you were a good baby, that you never made a peep."

"And then what?"

"Your parents flew in and took you home. Six weeks later, I appeared before the judge and signed the papers."

"No, I mean what did you do after?"

"I lived with my parents for a while. Then I took off with my hippie boyfriend and hitchhiked around the country."

"You were a hippie?" Josh exclaimed. "Right on. Me and Marissa had a Volkswagen van for a while."

My body relaxed with the change to a lighter topic and I went on. "We traveled all over the country — Alaska, Florida, Illinois, even New York." Another memory flickered. "You would have been a little more than a year old then. I remember wondering whether every baby I saw on the street might be you. I actually tried to look up your parents in the Brooklyn phone book, but there were way too many Goldbergs."

"Wait a minute," he said. "You *knew* where I was?"

"Well no... not exactly," I stammered. My face burned as if I'd been caught in a lie. "The lawyer said I would get to approve the couple who would adopt you and he showed me a profile of your parents. I knew they were Jewish and lived in Brooklyn. It gave their last name and ages and said your father made thirty-five thousand dollars a year. It sounded like a lot to me. I guess it was a lot in 1970. I figured you'd have everything you'd ever need, way more than I could give you."

I squirmed in the silence that followed, the first since we'd said hello.

I pressed on. "The lady at the registry said they were able to match us so quickly because of how much information I had. Honestly, I was surprised that any of it was true. When I signed the final papers, the judge made it sound like if I tried to find you, I'd be arrested or something, so why would they have told me the truth?"

His voice waned. "I don't know."

I wished I could take back what I'd said. I'd never felt like I had any choice, and I had just given Josh the impression that I'd been an informed participant. After years of feeling like the victim, that I might have been the villain was too much to contemplate, let alone explain. I grabbed the opportunity to steer the conversation back onto a safer subject.

"So anyway, my boyfriend and I ended up in Los Angeles. That's where I finished college — at U.C.L.A."

"I bet you're smart."

"I don't know about that." I laughed. "Did you go to college?"

"I didn't even finish high school. I was in eighth grade when I left home. Or I guess I should say, when my parents sent me away."

A gasp escaped from my throat.

"Don't worry. I'm fine now," he said. "I have a good job, a great wife, a baby on the way. And now I have my mom back!"

His wife of one year had just turned seventeen. "Marissa will have our baby at the same age her mother was when she had her," Josh said proudly.

He was almost twenty-six. I did the math — eight years,

the same age difference as Henry and me. But we'd been thirty-nine and thirty-one when we'd married. Marissa was a runaway when Josh met her in the French Quarter, where he was working as a bartender. She'd stayed with him for a few weeks before he brought her back to her mother, who at first had threatened to have him arrested for contributing to her delinquency, and then let him stay. He and Marissa were married a few months later.

They were living with Marissa's mother and stepfather, who had two small children of their own. I struggled to fend off the Jerry Lee Lewis, poor-white-trash images, allowing Josh to replace them with the encouraging news that he and Marissa were working on getting General Education diplomas.

When I glanced at the clock, I realized that we had been talking for almost two hours. Dozens of questions whirled in my head, but I'd already learned more than I could process in one sitting.

"Josh, it's eleven there. We'd better hang up so you can get some sleep."

He laughed and I heard him turn away from the receiver to call out, "Hey, Marissa! My mom's sending me to bed."

"I don't want to go," I said, not wanting to seem in a hurry.

"Neither do I."

"But we should."

"I know."

"We can talk again soon."

"Tomorrow?"

"Sure."

We agreed to send photos to each other the next day.

"Seeing your picture isn't going to be enough," he said. "When can we meet?"

It was the natural next step. But he'd caught me off-guard. "Um, I don't know…"

"Can you come here?"

"Sure, I guess, but I'll have to figure out when."

"You can stay with us. We have plenty of room."

Susan's words from that afternoon reverberated: New
Orleans is a beautiful city and the weather is perfect this time
of year. If you want, I can recommend some great restaurants.
Her assumption that I would go — and go soon — had struck
me as odd at the time. Now I was beginning to feel ambushed.

"I have a business and a husband," I said. "I can't just drop
everything and go flying cross-country."

"But I need to see you."

"I want to see you, too. I promise, I'll come as soon as I
can."

"I can't wait to meet the whole family, especially your
mom and dad — my grandparents."

"Oh, I'm not going to tell them," I sputtered.

"What do you mean?"

I had to think fast when I heard the hurt in his voice. "You
don't understand. They won't be happy. I can't let them ruin
things for us."

His silence felt like a hundred pound weight thrown across
my shoulders. Finally he said, "This is the happiest day of my
life. Nothing can ruin it."

"I just can't think about them right now, okay?"

"Okay."

"So, we'd better hang up."

"All right. Goodnight, Mom," he said.

"Mom" — the name I'd come to expect no one would ever
call me. My body warmed, like the mornings when I imagined
my baby in my arms.

"Goodnight, Son."

"I don't even know you, but I love you."

"I love you too, Josh." And I did, with an intensity that
blazed beyond maternal instincts.

Henry looked at me expectantly when I emerged from the
bedroom. "How'd it go?"

"Good," I said, grinning wide. "*Really* good."

For the next hour I delivered the highlights of our
conversation. In the retelling, the impact of the more horrific

details diminished, and the enormity of what was happening registered.

"Oh my God, Henry! I've found my son!"

His blue eyes grew teary and his lips trembled faintly around his wide smile.

"This is weird," I said, "but I feel as if I already know him."

"I don't think that's weird."

"He said his hair is light brown and his eyes are green. I forgot to ask whether he has a cleft chin. I thought he might look like me, or my brother. Maybe his father. But it never occurred to me that we might have a million other things in common. I think we're a lot alike."

"Oh no, not that," Henry joked.

I laughed, until I remembered Josh's invitation.

"He asked me to come there. He wants to meet me."

"Of course he does."

"What's wrong with me? Why am I hesitating? I should already be on the phone to the airlines. This is my son, *my only child.*"

"You just talked for the first time. Cut yourself some slack, Deedee."

"That's not all. He wants to meet my parents."

"Uh-huh."

"I can't tell them about this. They'll freak out."

"I don't see how you can keep it from them."

"Well, I will. I have to."

Henry shot me the look. "You're forty-five years old. It's well past time you stopped caring what your parents will say."

"I know, I know." I shook my head as if that would clear it. "This is happening so fast, I can't think. I wish I could just slow everything down."

I was nowhere near ready to sleep. After Henry went to bed, I dug through my boxes of photos, choosing the ones that best represented different periods in my life.

I barely recognized the girl in my 1968 high school

graduation picture, looking innocent and hopeful in the requisite black sweater and pearl necklace. She wasn't the same girl as the hippie chick in the picture taken almost three years later; something in her eyes betrayed the façade of her carefree smile and fringed purple poncho. In the photos from our wedding in 1982, Henry and I looked young for our years — and normal, aside from my curly perm that had seemed like a good idea at the time.

It was almost midnight when I sat down to write a letter to send with the pictures. There was so much to say and I wanted it to be perfect. I cringed, remembering how I'd hesitated when he'd asked to meet and then blurted out that I wouldn't tell my parents. He said he didn't blame me for giving him away. But how could he not, especially with all he had been through as a result?

Dear Joshua,

Words can't express how happy I am that we've found each other. I've dreamed of this day for a long time. I wish I'd done more to find you, instead of just dreaming and waiting. But that doesn't matter now. Our waiting is over! I am so grateful for this second chance to be your mother.

I need for you to understand that things were very different when I was growing up. "Good girls" didn't have sex before they were married. But if they did and they got pregnant and the boy wouldn't marry them, they certainly didn't keep their babies. I loved your father very much. I was already four months along when he left me, and I had to tell my parents. They were so angry and ashamed. My father arranged everything — found the lawyer, sent me to California to hide out until you were born. I was technically an adult, but without a husband, a job or family support, I didn't feel like I had a choice. There was nothing I could do but go along. Please know that I've always loved you and I've thought about you every day. I would have kept you if I could.

I only wish you'd had a happier childhood. I always imagined you having a better life than you would have had with me. Everyone said you would.

I hope you aren't thinking that I don't want to meet you. I do! I feel that waiting for your birthday would make it even more meaningful, the first one we'll share since the day you were born.

I can't wait to see your pictures! Mine are enclosed.

All my love, Mom.

When the letter was finished, I fell into bed and closed my eyes. But I didn't sleep. I hovered in a fitful shallow place just below consciousness, exhausted yet afraid that if I loosened my grip, the day's events would turn out to be another dream.

Chapter 3

WAKE-UP CALL

When the phone startled me awake the next morning, I had to think about where I was and why my heart was pounding as if I'd already consumed a whole pot of coffee.

"Good morning, Mom!"

"Josh, Honey, it's…" I squinted at the clock. "Five-thirty."

"Oh, sorry. I forgot about the time difference."

"Is everything okay?"

"Everything's great! I just wanted to hear your voice again."

I heard myself giggle like a teenager asked out on her first date. "It's good to hear yours, too."

"What are you going to do today?"

"Uh… go to work. Aren't you?"

"I called in sick," he said. "There's no way I'll be able to concentrate today. I'd probably end up dropping a car on my foot. Anyway, I was thinking we should send our pictures by overnight mail, so we'll have them by tomorrow. Is that okay?"

"Sure," I said. "So, we'll talk again tomorrow, after we get them?"

"I hope I can wait that long."

After I hung up, Henry rolled over. "How do you like your new Joshie alarm clock?"

I groaned and crawled back under the covers. I tried to will myself into a couple more hours of sleep, but my mind had already engaged in a Ping-Pong game of annoyance at being awakened and guilt over feeling annoyed. Guilt won. *You're someone's mother now*, I thought. *Soon you'll be someone's grandmother. You can't just lie here.*

As useless as I felt, I went to the office. I needed the distraction of tasks, the comfort of my routine. I thought about calling my closest friends, the ones who knew about my son, to tell them we had been reunited. But the news was too fresh. "I found him" would lead to questions that I wasn't ready to answer.

Josh phoned early that evening before I got home and talked to Henry.

"He thanked me for taking care of you all these years," Henry said. "I told him you're a strong, capable woman, that you don't need taking care of."

I smiled, wondering if it were true — whether I had actually become that woman or had fooled even my husband, the man who knew me better than anyone.

As early as my teens, I had mastered the art of convincing family and friends that I was okay when I wasn't. Easing their concerns eased my own; if they believed I had things under control, it became so. The night I'd left Hawaii to wait out my pregnancy, I'd cracked jokes to wipe the worry from my friends' faces. Every letter I wrote from California reassured them that I was all right. After Joshua's birth and relinquishment, my proficiency improved to the point that *even I* wasn't sure what I was feeling.

Anticipating the arrival of Josh's pictures, I found it easy to pop out of bed on Thursday. I was surprised when Fed Ex brought them to my office mid-morning, noting that he had paid for early delivery, while I had figured that afternoon delivery was good enough since he wouldn't get the package until after he got home from work.

He'd sent four times as many pictures as I had. There was only one of him as a child: *Ten years old with my brother Jonathan at summer camp in upstate New York,* he'd written on the back. They wore matching striped t-shirts, Josh's arm slung around his brother's shoulders. His hair was pale blond, like mine had been in my youth, and he had the Janson cleft in his chin.

In the other photos — his wedding to Marissa, the two of them with her family, one where Josh was standing over a barbecue, holding up a charred hotdog — his hair was darker, a reddish light brown, and wavy like mine when I let it dry naturally. Even when he smiled, his green eyes revealed a seriousness that mirrored my own.

Another picture, taken on a beach, revealed tattoos on his bare chest and arms — not trendy basketball tattoos, but large colorful illustrations, more suited to a member of Hell's Angels. I quickly banished any thought that made him less than perfect.

A picture I hadn't noticed before slid from the stack. When I bent down to retrieve it, I felt the air knocked out of me. Josh was seated at a table, his head twisted toward the camera as if he'd been summoned. He looked irritated, distant. It was his father's face. His body was John's, too — stocky and muscular. I couldn't prove it, since any pictures I'd had of his father were long gone. But the image I held in my hand was an exact match for the one that lived in my memory.

I'd forgotten how much I'd loved John. How he'd swept me away on that June night in Waikiki. I was with my girlfriends, walking along the strip after seeing a movie. I could still feel the warm night air, picture the bright lights from the hotels and nightclubs against the velvet-black sky, and almost smell the plumeria and ginger flowers mixed with the aroma of grilled steaks and fish that poured out of the restaurants.

John had pulled up on his motorcycle, looking tanned and blond and hunky. He'd looked straight at me, flashed a broad smile and said, "Want a ride?"

I'd never been picked out of a crowd before, and the invitation was too intoxicating to resist. "Sure," I said and hopped onto the back of the seat. I wrapped my arms around his sturdy middle and off we went, leaving my friends standing there in amazement while we cruised up to the end of the strip and back.

I'd also forgotten how much I'd hated him — for betraying me, casting me aside and walking away unscathed. And most of all, for making me feel worthless. I shoved the pictures back into the envelope and unfolded Josh's letter.

Dearest Mom,

It's been ten minutes since I spoke to you on the phone and I miss you already. Thank you so much for sending me to bed. I'm delirious. I could have talked to you all night. I've got half a mind to hop in my truck and head your way, but my wife won't let me.

We've waited for this moment too long and now that we're whole and together again I want us to have no secrets between us. I know you can't lift me up in your arms (you'll get a hernia), but this is the most important day in my life and I want us to do everything together. Thanks for being my mom and never giving up.

A chill shook me. I hadn't been his mom, and I'd as good as given up on finding him.

He signed it, I love you always. Your son, Joshua.

At the bottom he wrote: P.S. I really hope you can make it over here ASAP. We've got so much catching up to do.

And then, something I hadn't seen since junior high:

2 Good

2 Be

4 Gotten

When I got home, Henry presented me with a baby congratulations card. *It doesn't get much better than this!* he wrote, and signed it *Step-Daddy-O.*

More than anyone, he knew how important this was to me. He also knew the pain of having a child missing from his life. Just the previous year, we had reconnected with his son Jeff, who had been estranged from us for nearly a decade after our efforts to keep him off drugs and in school failed. Despite Henry's confidence in how he'd handled the situation, there were days when the loss was crushing — not knowing where his boy was, whether he was okay, whether he would ever see him again — and he had broken down in my arms.

Henry's eyes misted when he read Josh's letter. Watching him, I felt the same discomfort I had with Carol. Not a dry eye in the house, I mused. Except for mine.

"This is great," he said. "Jeff's back, and now Josh. I can't wait for the daughters to call."

"You mean Janice and Judy?" I joked. "I just hope they give us a few months to recover from the sons."

"You're beautiful," Josh said when we talked later that evening.

"No, *you're* beautiful," I said.

"No, *you* are."

"*You* are."

"Wow, our first fight."

I loved Josh's hearty, uninhibited laugh and the quick sense of humor we shared. That commonality enhanced my connection to him.

"Do I look like you thought I would?" he asked.

"You look a lot like your father," I said softly.

"I was worried about that. I'm afraid that whenever you look at me, you'll be reminded of him and hate me."

"Oh, Josh. I could *never* hate you. And I don't hate your father."

I'd been relieved that he wasn't ready to hear the details, but I knew it would come up eventually and wondered how much I would tell him. "Besides, I see a lot of my family in you." I felt a stab of regret, realizing that I hadn't included any pictures of my parents, brother and sister, or Jeff and Jordan. I shuffled through his pictures. "So, what's the deal with the hot dog?"

"That's my favorite food."

"You're kidding! You aren't going to believe this, but when I was pregnant with you, I craved hot dogs with mustard. That's all I ate for the first few months."

"Man, that is weird."

"So… tattoos?"

"Yeah," he said. "Actually, I have quite a few."

"Of what?" The only person I knew who had tattoos was my friend Leanna's father. He had an anchor with the name of his ship on one arm and an eagle on the other from his time overseas in the Navy.

"A dragon, a tiger, flowers."

"When did you get them?"

"I got some of them in Brooklyn when I was still a kid, and some of them when I was in Israel. That picture at the beach was taken in Sinai."

"What were you doing in Israel?"

"Enlisting in the Israeli Army."

"*Why?*" My stomach rolled as I visualized my son alone in a foreign land, at war, in danger.

"Because that's what all good Jewish boys do."

"Your parents wanted you to go?"

"Yeah. I was trying to make up with them. It didn't work."

"How long were you there?"

"About three years," he said.

There were a million questions I could have asked. What was the situation in Israel at that time? Had he seen combat? Had he killed anyone? Instead, one of Henry's jokes flew into my head: *Like Adam said to Eve, "Stand back, I don't know how big this is going to get."*

Josh filled in my silence. "I traveled around for a while before I came back to the states. That's when I took the auto mechanics course. I love Volkswagens. I have a VW logo tattooed on my stomach."

I forced a laugh.

"Do they bother you? The tattoos, I mean."

I hoped he couldn't hear the angst in my voice. No way in hell would tattoos be acceptable in my parents' fine, upstanding world. "No, not at all."

As if he'd read my mind, he said, "Now that I'm older, I regret getting them. But it's really expensive to have them removed."

How much? I wanted to ask. But I opted for, "Marissa's a beautiful girl. And her family looks very nice."

"Henry looks really nice, too."

"He is."

"Listen, Mom, I want to ask you about something. Did you call the registry back to report on how things went?"

"Yeah, yesterday. Did you?"

"Yeah, but Susan wasn't there. I talked to some guy named Tony. What do you think of this? He said I should slow down and be careful not to get overwhelmed. How can I help but be overwhelmed? I'm so happy that I found you."

"I think you mean overjoyed."

"It's the same thing, isn't it?"

"Not really. Overjoyed is happy. Overwhelmed is... well, like too much at once."

"Is that bad?"

"It can be hard," I said. "You know, to sort through it all."

"Are you overwhelmed?"

"A little. But you're right. How can we not be? This is a big deal."

"So, it's okay?"

"I think so," I said, and then to myself, *I hope so.*

"Have you thought any more about coming here?"

"I still think your birthday would be the best time."

"But that's two whole months away."

"I know, but it'll give us time to plan."

I'd expected Josh to argue, and when he didn't, I shuddered at my own reluctance — that even after seeing his picture, I couldn't commit to meeting him. For years, I had fantasized about being found, hearing a surprise knock at the door and opening it to a moment of instant recognition. We would be immediately comfortable with one another; we would be mother and son. In my mind's eye, it had always been that easy.

Josh didn't call on Friday, and what should have been a welcome respite was interrupted by surprising pangs of withdrawal. On Saturday, a beautiful bouquet of flowers arrived, with a card that read, *Just because I love you. Your son, Joshua.*

"That son of yours is making me look bad," Henry teased when he came in from working in the yard. Finding me slumped on the sofa, staring at the bright mix of snapdragons, daisies and mums, he said, "What's wrong?"

"Me," I said. "*I'm* wrong. I should be bouncing off the walls with glee. This is what I've always wanted, and I can't get happy. Shit, I can't even get sad!"

"Is there anything I can do?"

"Not unless you can make me cry."

"Don't be so hard on yourself. This is a lot to handle."

"It hurts so much," I moaned. "I know I'd feel better if I could get it out."

My chest was a swollen mass of grief, joy, anger, remorse, and a dozen other unidentifiable emotions, fidgeting like restless children waiting for roll call. And then I remembered: during the last few months of my pregnancy, I'd spent hours listening to the most maudlin songs in my record collection, wallowing in self-pity.

I got out my old records and played them over and over, hoping to trigger the tears. The Carpenters: On the day that you were born, the angels got together and decided to create a dream come true. And the Five Stairsteps: O-o-h child, things are gonna get easier. O-o-h child, things will get brighter. I put on B. J. Thomas' "Rock and Roll Lullaby," which had come out years later and become my anthem for what should have been: She was just sixteen and all alone when I came to be. So we grew up together, my mama-child and me.

Lying frozen and tearless on the sofa, I thought about my mother. I saw her face and realized with a start that I had never seen her cry. I racked my brain: I could picture Mom delighted with a handmade Mother's Day card, disappointed if my grades fell short of her expectations, furious that I'd gotten pregnant, but never sad. *Mothers are supposed to cry*, I reasoned. Especially for their children: when they've been hurt like John had hurt me, if they were lost and then found, or if they've been through the horrors that Josh had.

How many people have seen me cry? The possibility that I might have become the woman I had spent most of my adult life resenting sent a shiver through my spine. My desire — no, my *obligation* — to be a better mother than she had been provided all the push I needed. I jumped up from the couch and went to find Henry.

"I'm going to New Orleans," I told him. "I have to see Josh."

"Whatever you want," he said. "Do you want me to go with you?" It was a generous offer, since Henry despised long-distance travel to anywhere other than a tropical beach.

"Thanks, Hon. But I think I should do this on my own."

Josh was thrilled when I called and asked if I could come the following Friday for Easter weekend.

"She's coming!" he shouted to Marissa. "My mom's coming!"

"I told you she would," I heard her say.

"I'm worried about something," I told him. "I haven't cried yet. That can't be normal."

"I haven't cried either," he said. "Maybe it's because all I feel right now is happy. But I don't think there's anything wrong with us. I think we're just saving the best cry for last. Once we meet, I'm sure it will all come out."

When he put Marissa on the phone, she proclaimed her certainty that finding me would "heal the hole in Josh's heart." The prospect of having a chance to right my wrongs and make a difference in my son's life made me forget the hole in my own.

Chapter 4

SIGNS

I'd never had a problem with flying, but that day my body was twisted into one giant white knuckle.

Once I'd made the decision to go, anticipation provided the energy I needed to book my flight, buy presents for everyone, and pack and unpack a dozen times. The night before, as I closed my suitcase, I felt a familiar trickle and rushed into the bathroom. My period had started even though it wasn't due for more than a week.

As I rifled through the vanity drawer for a box of tampons, I caught my reflection in the mirror: eyes with the glassy daze of someone startled out of a dream, surrounded by the puffs and creases of exhaustion.

"Now there's a face only a son could love," I said to my haggard image.

At the airport the next morning, I assured Henry that I was fine and insisted that he drop me out front and go on to work. I hoped he wouldn't sense the mounting panic in my hug or see it in my eyes when we kissed goodbye. As soon as he pulled away from the curb, a wave of nausea rushed over me and I wished I could call him back.

After checking my luggage, I went back outside. I found an empty bench and lit a cigarette. The tears I had worked so hard to set free a week before welled in my throat and stung my eyes. I tried to focus on the people rushing past, the chirping of the crosswalk signal — anything to keep from crying in public. Despite the chill of the early morning air, I stayed on that bench until I had just enough time to buy a pack of tissues at the gift shop and get to the gate.

"Be sure to secure your own oxygen mask before assisting your children," the flight attendant warned as she demonstrated the safety equipment.

Her words startled me and I realized she was right. My son was counting on me. I had to get a grip. After take-off, I moved away from the other passengers on the under-booked 747, claiming an aisle seat in an empty row. Once I was alone, any hope of getting that grip vanished. I let myself cry, silently soaking tissue after tissue.

The trip from San Francisco to New Orleans would take eight hours, including a stop in St. Louis. Whenever the flight attendant approached, I pretended to be engrossed in the airline magazine, grunted my beverage order, and declined the snack. After the third trip to the restroom, I gave up trying to make my face look smooth and my nose sound clear. I couldn't concentrate enough to read and finally took out the blank journal I'd brought along. As if on autopilot, my mind drifted to the red-eye flight I'd boarded on New Year's Eve twenty-six years before...

Even at four months pregnant, I was still able to wear the gray and white coatdress Mom had sewn for me to take to college a year earlier. The airplane cabin was dark except for the emergency lights and a sprinkling of overheads, but I didn't sleep. I hoped I wouldn't wake the snoring businessman beside me each time I switched on my light to take another look at the gifts and notes that my friends had pressed into my hands at the airport. These were all I had to ground me, to keep from feeling more alone and punished than I already did.

Arriving in Los Angeles the next morning, I'd scanned the crowds for a stranger: the short balding attorney, who held a cardboard sign that read *Janson* — and my fate — in his hands...

Later today, I wrote in my journal, *I'll search the terminal for a different sign, and a different stranger.* My sense of my son was fierce and primal, yet I was so worried I wouldn't find him that I had asked Josh to bring a sign that read "Mom."

Weeping again, I chronicled everything I could remember from the summer I'd gotten pregnant...

We were girls waiting to become women — over eighteen, but girls nonetheless — not yet fully-formed, and on our way to grownup lives that we could not quite envision. Raised on *I Love Lucy, The Donna Reed Show* and *Father Knows Best*, we were plunged into the era of free love, leaving us suspended somewhere between "I Want to Hold Your Hand" and "Why Don't We Do It In The Road."

Birth control was irrelevant, since we weren't supposed to be "doing it" in the road or anywhere else. We knew about condoms, since almost every boy in high school bragged about carrying one in his wallet. All we knew about "The Pill" was that it was only prescribed to married women. Abortion was no more than a concept, a dangerous last resort performed overseas, or illegally in the back rooms of sympathetic or unscrupulous doctors.

But none of that mattered. We wanted to be in love. When our boyfriends said "It's okay because we love each other," we believed. As for any consequences, like catching some embarrassing disease or getting pregnant before we were married, surely that would never happen to us.

I'd been so excited to return to Hawaii in June 1969 after a miserable freshman year at a women's college in Missouri. While I was away, my father's employer had relocated my family from the islands to Anchorage, Alaska. I'd seen all I cared to of that frigid, untamed place while visiting them over Christmas break, and I begged my parents not to make me join them there. They agreed to let me return to Kailua, live with my best friend Leanna's family, and transfer to the University of Hawaii in the fall. Leanna and I had been inseparable since meeting the summer we turned fifteen. Her house became my second home, and the Daniels my chosen family.

Living out from under my parents' watchful eyes gave me the illusion of independence, despite that they were paying my school expenses and sending Mr. and Mrs. Daniel a monthly check for my room and board. Leanna had never had a curfew, and finally neither did I. No one questioned what I was wearing, where I was going, or with whom.

I fancied myself grown, when in fact I was lost, adrift on

an ocean of uncertainty and indifference, waiting for a beacon
to show me the way. When John appeared that July, I was ripe
for rescue.

Unlike the long-haired rebel boys I'd been drawn to during
high school, he was clean-cut, well-mannered and confident.
He was a United States Marine, a "real man," Leanna said.
Everything about him screamed military — from the firm set
of his jaw and short-cropped hair to the muscles that bulged
beneath the chest and sleeves of his polo shirt. He wasn't tall,
but he presented large, with an intensity that made him seem
older than his twenty-two years. I liked the way my body fit
neatly into his when he put his arm around my shoulders, how
secure and settled I felt when I was with him.

We'd only been dating for six weeks when John proposed
during an especially hot make-out session in the back seat of
the cavernous Buick he'd borrowed from a friend.

"I know it's wrong to be doing this before we're married."
He pulled away with a groan. "But I can't help myself. I love
you, Denise. Would you consider marrying me?"

He threw the life preserver and I grabbed it. We would
have a small wedding in December, when my family visited
Hawaii for Christmas.

I wasn't concerned when he admitted that he'd been
married before — was still, in fact — to his high school
sweetheart in Delaware, who had cheated on him while he
was deployed to Vietnam. I tried not to fret when he refused
to tell his parents about our engagement until after his
divorce became final in October. I ignored the signs when
our occasional spats escalated into personal attacks on my
smoking, the way I wore my hair, and my not being amorous
enough during lovemaking.

When he suggested we take some time away from each
other, I told myself it was a break, not a break-up. He would
miss me and come running back. I was still waiting two weeks
later, when I realized — my head thrust over the toilet after just
a whiff of scrambled eggs — that I couldn't remember when
I'd had my last period.

Leanna went pale when I returned from my doctor's appointment and presented her with a pair of pink and blue bubblegum cigars.

"Don't worry," I told her. "John and I will work things out."

I had confidence in him. He was a Marine, after all, a man of principle. He would do the honorable thing and marry me.

He didn't. By the time I realized that no amount of coaxing and pleading would change his mind, I was almost four months along.

I hadn't anticipated ever having to confess my pregnancy to my parents. But with John out of the picture, I had nowhere else to turn. Afraid to tell them over the phone, I decided to write a letter. Too proud to admit my mistake, I took a defensive stance.

I'm not sorry, I wrote. Sure, I regretted that I'd gotten pregnant, but I was not sorry for having sex. It's a natural part of being in love, I told them. Besides, I was an adult and could make my own decisions about what to do with my body. If I'd expected my parents to be displeased in the first place, I had no idea the fuel that little gem would add to their fire.

"You've gotten a little too big for your britches, young lady," my father said when he called. "You will take back your words right now, and apologize for your brazen attitude and your shameful behavior."

He didn't raise his voice; he'd never had to. His disappointment had always been enough to break me.

"I'm sorry," I said.

"I wish you'd told us sooner," Dad said. "We could have sent you to Japan for an abortion and end this whole mess."

Abortion? The word made me shudder. As shaky as my relationship with John had been near the end, I hadn't envisioned any outcome other than having the baby. Japan was the closest place to Hawaii where abortions were legal.

"We'll have to wait to deal with this until we get there," Dad said. "Who else knows?"

"Leanna, Linda, Monica, Diane… most of my friends."

"Are you out of your mind, Child?"

"I was supposed to be getting married, Dad. They're my friends. They understand."

"And the Daniels?"

"I haven't told them."

"From this moment on, you are forbidden to tell anyone else. Especially Debby and Bob. They don't need to see such a bad example from their older sister."

As their arrival approached, I grew nervous about coming face-to-face with my parents. But I also knew that with my sister and brother along and all the plans they had to get together with old friends, they would be compelled to act as if nothing was wrong. The trick, I figured, was to avoid getting stuck alone with Mom and Dad.

Leanna came with me to meet them at the airport. I wore a short flowered sundress, gathered above the bust, that I'd purchased months before. At that point, I weighed about one hundred and ten pounds and was nowhere near showing.

"You look pregnant," my mother hissed when I leaned in to hug her. "What are you thinking, wearing something like that in public?" She told me we would shop for a panty girdle the next day, which I would wear until they could get me out of town.

It wasn't long before the other A-word — *adoption* — came into play. Like abortion, the idea was alien to me, an option that hadn't crossed my mind. When their initial plan to send me to a Florence Crittenton Home for Unwed Mothers on the mainland proved too costly, Dad called a lawyer friend and got the name of an attorney in Los Angeles who arranged private adoptions.

I would fly to California, Dad explained, where I'd live with an uninvolved family — people who were willing to provide room and board to "girls in trouble" in exchange for light housework and babysitting. Once the baby was born, it would be placed with adoptive parents on the opposite coast, who would pay all of the legal fees and medical expenses related to the pregnancy and birth.

"Because both parents have to be Caucasian, the attorney wants you to bring a picture of you and John," my father said. He cleared his throat and added that because this particular group of attorneys focused their practice to helping Jewish families, we should understand that the child would be raised as a Jew.

Mom glared at me, tight-lipped. "Look what you've driven us to!" she said. "We have no option but to give that child to heathens."

"Then don't do it. Let me stay here."

She lifted her chin and laughed.

Dad shook his head. "It's obvious that you can't be trusted on your own."

"Okay, so I'll come home."

Horror flashed across my mother's face. "And have our neighbors find out?"

No one had cared what *I* wanted. They never even considered helping me keep my baby. *And you never brought it up,* I accused myself. *At least not then, not when it counted.*

As my trip to meet my son neared its end, I made one more notation in my journal: Please let me recognize his face right away. Let our first embrace be as healing as I need it to be. Let him not care that I look a mess, or that I'm dizzy under the weight of these feelings that have been buried for so long.

When the plane began its descent into New Orleans, I made my way to the restroom for one last attempt at fixing my face. My legs felt like rubber; my stomach quaked.

"Ladies and gentlemen, welcome to New Orleans International."

Oh, God, I can't breathe.

"We'll be at the gate in just a few minutes."

I'm going to be sick.

"Please remain seated until the plane has come to a complete stop."

I don't think I can stand up.

Once the plane rocked to a halt, the other passengers were up and in the aisle, grabbing their carry-on bags, jockeying for position. Three rows from the back, I stayed in my seat, gathering my strength. Finally there was just a handful of us left, and I forced myself to my feet.

Up the aisle and past the flight attendants. "Bye-bye, thank you for flying TWA." Out the door, into the boarding tunnel. *Keep walking,* I ordered myself. I could see the exit, people moving about in the terminal. I stepped out into the open, stopped, and scanned the waiting room.

My gaze landed on him immediately, leaning against a wall directly across from the gate, between a very pregnant Marissa and her mother Nina, who was holding a video camera.

Josh didn't look nearly as much like his father in person. He had John's thick, muscular build, but his face was fuller and softer. His gaze met mine and we smiled: the same smile, the same crinkles forming around our eyes. As he walked toward me, everything around us dissolved, like a soft-focus movie scene. I dropped my carry-on to reach for him and we folded ourselves into a hug.

I felt his tears on the back of my neck. I cringed at the absence of my own and tried to will them back, so afraid that without them, he wouldn't see how much this moment meant to me. But they would not come.

"I can't believe I'm here," I said, stepping back and taking his face in my hands. "Look at you. You're so handsome!" I turned to Marissa and Nina, who had joined us. "This is my baby!" The four of us hugged, grinning and giggling like lunatics.

Marissa was a striking young woman, nearly as tall as Josh's five-nine, her full face showing off flawless skin, and long brunette hair that accentuated her large brown eyes. The grace with which she carried her seven-months-pregnant belly gave her an almost Madonna-like quality. Nina too was tall and blond, with charming traces of her native German in her speech. Even though I knew she was only thirty-four — more than ten years my junior — I'd pictured someone less attractive and more motherly-looking. Suddenly I felt old as well as short.

Just outside the security checkpoint, Josh collected the "sign" he'd brought along but had not been allowed to take to the gate: Charlie, he called him — a four-foot-tall helium clown, holding a balloon with the letters *I love you Mom*.

We walked arm in arm to the baggage claim area, our conversation coming in gushes and lags.

"I got my hair cut today," he said, running his hand across his head. "I wanted to look my best for you."

"You look great."

"How was your flight?"

"Good. Long though."

"You must be tired."

"I should be, but honestly I can't remember feeling more wide-awake."

I tried not to stare and could sense Josh doing the same — stealing glimpses and then looking away. I felt a little like I had at the nursery window, noting that he must have cut himself shaving and that he had somehow escaped the large Janson ears. A long-sleeved pullover covered his tattoos. I wondered when I would see them, whether he would show me or I'd have to ask. I glanced down at his feet and blushed as a strange, new-mother impulse came over me: to remove his sneakers and count his toes.

Tucked with Josh on the back seat of Nina's Jeep Cherokee, I began to relax. From the highway to Metairie, he pointed out various sites: the restaurant where he and Marissa had their wedding reception, the oil-change shop where he worked. I looked and nodded even though it was too dark to see. As we neared Nina's, the homes got larger and more lavish, set on wide, tree-lined streets. We turned into a curved driveway in front of what seemed to me more of a mansion than a house, and I was embarrassed for having envisioned them as poor white trash.

The inside was grander still, with shiny hardwood floors, crystal chandeliers, and a circular staircase leading to the second floor. The guesthouse where Josh and Marissa stayed was bigger than most apartments I'd rented before I was married, and it opened up onto a lush yard with a pool and hot tub.

We hadn't been at the house more than ten minutes — just long enough to introduce me to Nina's husband Max and their toddler sons, Jacob and Leon, and stow my bags in one of the several extra bedrooms — when Josh rushed me back to the guesthouse. His eyes burned with purpose.

"The reason I understand what you went through," he blurted, "is because I gave up two sons of my own."

My heart raced as he explained about getting married when he was eighteen, right before going overseas to join the Israeli Army. How one child later and with another on the way, his marriage began to crumble and his wife's parents intervened, urging them to divorce and put the boys up for adoption. He pulled out a picture of a tow-headed toddler smiling shyly at the camera.

"So, this is my grandson," I spoke in monotone.

"That's Sammy. Samuel Joseph, named for my grandfather." His voice held a hint of pride, even though he hung his head as he spoke.

There was no time to absorb his news before Nina called us in for dinner. As hungry as I was, I had trouble eating much and pushed the salad and lasagna around my plate, hoping no one would notice. It was after nine by the time we finished. Max and the boys went to bed, and the four of us lingered at the dining room table.

Marissa's air of confidence made it hard to grasp that she was just seventeen — two years younger than I had been when I got pregnant. That is, until she spoke.

"Josh and I are going to be friends to our children," she

said, eyeing her mother. "Not uptight parents with a bunch of stupid rules."

"You just wait, Marissa. Motherhood is hard work," Nina said, and then turned to me, "Of course, it's worth every minute."

"I have presents," I said, remembering the packages stashed in my luggage. It had been easy to choose gifts for the others — a silver heart necklace for Marissa, a fuzzy teddy bear for the baby, San Francisco sourdough bread for Nina and Max, colorful Hawaiian print hats for the boys — but I'd obsessed over what to bring for Josh. Nothing seemed quite right or suitably momentous. I dug out the beaded baby bracelet my mother had given me years before. Even though she swore it had been mine, it was blue and more likely my brother's. The beads in the middle read *J-A-N-S-O-N*.

"Was this mine?" Josh said, staring at the bracelet.

"My mom says it was my baby bracelet," I said self-consciously. "But it's blue. Anyway, that was your last name when you were born, and I want you to have it."

"Thanks." He grinned. "This is really cool."

I'd also brought him a small gift book: Eat Dessert First (and Other Ways to Take a Recess from Being a Grown-up). Inside I had inscribed I missed your precious growing up years, so please stay a kid for a little longer.

"Don't worry." He laughed. "I'm in no rush to grow up."

"Yeah," Marissa echoed. "We're going to grow up with our kids."

Josh handed me a jewelry store box. Inside was a tiny gold charm with engraving, but I couldn't make out the words.

"It's beautiful," I whispered, straining to focus through bleary eyes. "I'm sorry… I can't read it."

"Number one Mom," Nina said.

My heart leapt.

Josh said softly, "Not only my first mom, but number one in my heart."

"Thank you, Sweetie. I love it."

I would have sat there all night, my eyes and ears trained on my son. Still, I was relieved when around midnight Nina suggested that we turn in. I needed to sleep, but once my body touched the sheets, my mind went into overdrive. I couldn't stop thinking about my grandsons.

It didn't make sense. Josh had been married. Marriage was supposed to fix everything; it would have fixed everything for me. Even if John and I had divorced later, I would still have had our son. Letting Joshua go was supposed to give him a good life, but it hadn't. And what about his sons? What if their lives weren't any better? How could Josh have let this happen? How had I?

Chapter 5

FRENCH QUARTER

The next morning I woke to the sounds of Jacob and Leon playing. As dazed as I was after a restless night, I bolted out of bed and hurriedly made myself presentable. I didn't want to miss a single minute with my son.

Josh wasn't up yet, and I sat in the kitchen drinking coffee and chatting with Nina and Max. Nina told me about the day Josh got the call from the registry.

"He said 'I've found my mommy.' Not 'mom' or 'mother.' He said 'mommy.'"

I couldn't tell whether she found this sweet or strange. I was still deciding when the usually quiet Max broke in.

"That boy needs a mother," he said. "He's had a wild life and gotten himself into a lot of trouble. He needs you more than you know."

I wasn't sure that I wanted to know what he meant. But before I had an opportunity to ask, Josh came through the back door from the guesthouse, looking like a little boy who had just rolled out of bed — sleepy-eyed and rumpled in a t-shirt and sweatpants. He walked straight over to hug me and said "Good morning, Mom." At that moment, nothing else mattered.

After breakfast, Nina brought out a cake frosted with the words, "Welcome Back Mom," which she'd intended to serve the night before. Jacob and Leon's eyes lit up.

"This is a special day," she said. "That makes it okay to eat cake for breakfast. Let Josh's mom have the first piece, boys."

"Thanks, Nina. I really appreciate you making me feel so welcome."

"So what should we do today?" She addressed her question to Josh and Marissa. "I'm sure Denise would like to see some sights while she's here."

Marissa's face lit up like a kid begging to go to an amusement park. "Let's go to the French Quarter!"

"That won't be any fun for the boys, Marissa, " Nina scolded. "How about the aquarium?" She turned to me. "We have a fantastic one here."

Sightseeing wasn't what I had in mind. Desperate for one-on-one time with my son, I put aside any concerns about offending them and forced myself to speak up. "Would it be okay if Josh and I went off by ourselves for a while?"

"Yeah," Josh said. "That's a good idea."

Marissa frowned, transforming her face from glowing mother-to-be into pouty teenager. At her age, I would have acquiesced to any adult's request. It annoyed me that she could not understand my need, as well as Josh's, to have some time alone together. But she was my son's wife and I was determined to like her.

"We'll do something as a family tonight," Josh assured her.

"And I want to take everyone out to eat tomorrow," I said to Nina. "For Easter brunch, or whatever you'd like."

Once we'd showered and changed, Josh and I headed out in his pick-up truck. I assumed we would make small talk until we got into New Orleans, but Josh launched into the details of his childhood. The intensity in his face and the way he gripped the steering wheel made him seem possessed, as if driven to get it out.

"Losing my grandfather and finding out I was adopted sent me over the edge," he said. "I was so angry. I hated my parents. I rebelled against everything, refused to go to school, stayed out all night. So they put me in a hospital."

"Hospital? What kind of hospital?"

"A mental hospital. For testing."

"So, what happened?" I muttered. "Was there a diagnosis?" I pulled my jacket tight around me, as if it could shield me from any distressing news.

"There was nothing wrong. But my parents didn't care. They didn't want me back. I spent the next nine months in hospitals and group homes."

"But they couldn't do that without a reason."

"There is *nothing* wrong with me," Josh growled.

I was too stunned to speak. How could his parents have sent him away like that? Something must have been very wrong. I wanted to believe Josh. I wanted to believe that his tests were normal. But he'd only been twelve years old. How much could he have understood? What if there was a serious problem, one for which he'd not been treated?

The realization that I might have been to blame hit hard. I thought back to the drugs I'd taken the summer he was conceived — mostly pot, and twice LSD. Once when John and I were fighting, I'd dropped a tab of acid, hoping to take my mind off my problems. The experience had been so terrifying that I'd begged Leanna to take me to the emergency room. Realizing that I probably would have been arrested, and no doubt scared to death, she drove me around in her car until I calmed down.

I tried to recall exactly when that had been, whether I could have been pregnant at the time. As soon as I'd known I was carrying a child, I'd quit everything including cigarettes. But what about the tranquilizers the obstetrician prescribed when I couldn't sleep? Once those stopped working, he gave me sleeping pills and instructed me not to take them more than twice a week, even if I had to go sleepless in between. Was it possible that those had hurt my son?

Josh drove the next mile or two in silence until we reached the French Quarter. He cruised up and down the narrow streets, looking for a parking space.

"Okay, I'm just trying to understand," I ventured. "How could the Goldbergs get away with not taking you back? Parents can't just dump their kids."

"They went to court and filed a PINS petition."

"A what?"

"It stands for 'person in need of supervision.' If you can prove your child is beyond your control, the state intervenes."

"And were you beyond their control?"

"Yeah, pretty much."

"But you saw them again. I mean, when you were still a minor."

"They visited me a few times. I'd make up reasons why I needed money and they'd usually give me some. Then I'd escape and be on the run for a while. Usually I got picked up and sent back to the home. Sometimes one of the rabbis I knew would help me out and find me a place to stay, but mostly I was on the street. I learned to live by my wits."

He was not quite fourteen when he'd gotten his first tattoo, took his first drugs, and started running with a gang of street kids. The wits by which he said he had lived sounded to me more like crimes and cons. As a new series of unsettling images invaded my head, Josh found a parking space and put his story on hold. I pushed back my questions and followed him onto Bourbon Street.

We made the rounds of his personal landmarks: the strip club where he'd worked for a while, the exact spot in front of the pool hall where he and Marissa had met. Weaving in and out of the Easter weekend visitors, we stopped now and then to listen to the street musicians or check out the odd little shops selling voodoo paraphernalia and tacky souvenirs. Finally, we let a barker lure us into a little upstairs dive for lunch and continued our conversation over Cajun shrimp, Po' Boy sandwiches, and rum and Cokes. I savored the taste of the alcohol, letting it warm my body and sooth my head.

"There's one more thing I have to tell you," he said sheepishly.

I braced for whatever was coming.

"I didn't just bartend at that club. I danced, too."

"You were a *stripper*?" I laughed, relieved at the triviality of this latest disclosure.

"Exotic dancer," he corrected me. "Hell, yes! They make big bucks." He'd taken up bodybuilding while he was in the hospital, after one of the counselors pointed out that he had the ideal physique for it. "I figured I might as well do something with my time. I haven't kept it up lately," he said, patting his slight paunch. "But not that long ago, I was as tight as a drum."

"Hey, we all do what we can," I said. "I once worked as a poop-scooper in a dog kennel."

"Yeah? And what else?"

"I've been a hotel maid, a school picture photographer, sign-maker in a department store, switchboard operator — nothing near as glamorous as an exotic dancer. After college, all I could get with an English degree was secretarial work. Then I married Henry and went back to school to learn graphic design."

"That's really something — that you and Henry have been married so long," he said. "Where'd you meet?"

"In a bar." I paused, waiting for the usual reaction, but it did not come. I'd forgotten I wasn't talking to someone who might judge me.

"How come you didn't have kids?"

I shrugged, as unsure of the truth as I was uneasy with the subject. "We were older by the time we met. Henry's son was a teenager, almost out of the house."

"All I've ever wanted was a big family," he said. "To be married, have a bunch of kids, and a home of my own."

"Well, you're on your way."

"Yeah." He turned his head and stared out the window as if envisioning something from his past. "Did I tell you that I was building a house once? Last year, Marissa and I got sick of the city and just took off. We ended up in Alabama, found this great spot out in the middle of nowhere, and started paying on a lot. I picked up a little work as a mechanic and spent every other waking hour working on the house. I got most of the materials free. You'd be surprised what people throw out."

"Where did you live? I mean, while you were building it."

"We camped out. But then Marissa got pregnant and winter was coming, so we came back."

"What about the house?"

"It's about half-finished. We're still making payments on the land. Maybe we'll move back out there when the baby's older."

As we talked, we discovered a number of parallels in our lives. Where we couldn't find them, we created them, declaring even the smallest coincidences to be significant. There was his innate talent for construction, and the fact that he'd been conceived in the framework of a custom beach house John and I had happened upon in our late-night search for a place to make love. In addition to the hot dog connection, we discovered that both he and my brother hated mayonnaise. Josh had been raised in Brooklyn, and I married a man from Brooklyn.

"Can I ask you something?" he said.

"Of course."

"How come you and my father didn't get married?"

"We were supposed to, but he changed his mind."

"After he knew you were pregnant?"

"Yes."

"Do you hate him?"

"No. Well, I guess I did at the time." My teeth clenched. "I realize now that we weren't a good match. It wouldn't have lasted."

"So, you said I look a lot like him."

"I thought so, but now that I've seen you in person, I think you look like me, too. Do you think so?"

"Yeah. I see it." He smiled and I smiled back.

"Are you going to search for him?" I asked. "It's okay with me if you do."

"He wasn't in the registry. Which probably means he doesn't want to meet me."

"Not necessarily. He might not know that registries like Soundex exist. Besides, he has no idea what happened to me — where I went or whether I kept you or not. He doesn't even know you're a boy."

"I'm afraid of what I would do to him for hurting you." Suddenly his eyes were full of rage.

I reached over and put my hand on his. "Believe me, Josh, it's ancient history. There's nothing to be done."

After lunch, we walked down to the river and along the promenade, where I snapped pictures of Josh with every statue and interesting building. We got lost coming back to the Quarter and ended up going blocks out of our way before making it to Bourbon Street. With sore feet and parched throats, we collapsed in the Fat Tuesday Daiquiri Bar.

"I've been thinking about your sons," I said cautiously.

"I think about them all the time." He looked down at the floor.

"Is it okay to talk about them?"

"I'll talk to you about anything," he said, bringing his gaze up to meet mine. "I told you, I don't want us to hold anything back."

"Tell me about their mother."

"Rebecca. We'd only known each other a couple of weeks. I was leaving for Israel, and I was so scared. I had this awful feeling that I wasn't coming back, and I didn't want to die alone. The day she turned eighteen, we went to the courthouse and got married so she could come with me."

I couldn't help but think about the similarities to John, who had married his girlfriend right out of high school before joining the Marines and shipping out to Vietnam. Then, three years later, he had asked me to marry him just weeks after we'd met. Josh had only known Marissa a short time before he married her. Was a proclivity for hasty marriages as genetic as the aversion to mayonnaise?

"Rebecca's parents were really pissed," Josh added.

"Because she was so young?"

"That too, but mostly because we were from different sects."

"But you're not even Jewish," I said. "Not technically. Isn't that right, that a person can only be Jewish if their mother is?"

"I was converted as a baby."

"Do you feel Jewish?"

"I guess. It's all I've ever known."

"So, what about that poster?"

I was referring to the eight-by-ten matted print Josh had sent me the first week we'd been in touch, with gold and black calligraphy that read, *And we know that in all things GOD works for the good of those who love Him, who have been called according to His purpose... He who did not spare His own SON, but gave Him up for us all — how will He not also, along with Him, graciously give us all things? Romans 8:28,32.*

It had been more than a little spooky — not just Josh's assumption that I was religious, but also the reference to giving up a son. Was he likening himself to Jesus? Was he trying to reassure me that I had done the right thing? Had he come to embrace Christianity after being raised a Jew?

"I saw it and thought it fit us. I got myself one too. I figured whenever we looked at it, we'd think of each other."

A painful memory emerged. After I had given birth and signed the relinquishment papers, I'd rejoined my family in Anchorage. I'd worried that my parents would lecture me about what I had done. But no one said a word — not until I told my mother that I needed to see a gynecologist. During my last appointment in Los Angeles, the doctor had said I should have a final postpartum examination three months after the delivery. He'd also urged me to look into birth control, although I didn't mention that to Mom.

"No way," she said. "Your father knows too many important people in this town. Doctors don't know how to keep their mouths shut, and people just love this kind of gossip. His reputation would be ruined."

"But the doctor said I have to," I said, taken aback by how far she would go to keep the secret. "Besides, doctors are sworn not to tell about their patients."

"Forget it!" she snapped. "End of discussion." But that wasn't the end. "I can't believe you allowed your child be raised by Jews. You know he'll never go to Heaven if he doesn't believe that Jesus is the Son of God."

I wanted to scream at her that it was she and Dad who had made that decision. Instead, I turned away and retreated to my room. I decided that if God were so vengeful that he would punish me for being in love, or my son for being adopted into Judaism, I was finished with religion once and for all.

When I'd received the poster from Josh, I resisted the urge to stuff it in the back of a closet. Because it was a gift from my son, I placed it on the guestroom bookcase, where I wouldn't see it often.

Josh startled me out of my thoughts. "Right? Do you think about me when you look at it?"

"I think about you *all* the time."

His smile reassured me it was okay to press on.

"What about your parents? How did they feel about you getting married?"

"They'd been pissed off for so long, it didn't matter."

"But you said you joined the Israeli Army to make them happy."

"Trust me, nothing about me could make them happy."

"When was Sammy born?"

"About a year later."

"In Israel?"

"No. New York. Rebecca wanted to go home to have the baby. But we went back to Israel after."

Less than two years down the road, she became pregnant again. By then their relationship had almost completely deteriorated. Josh had a serious drug problem, cocaine mostly.

"It was everywhere in Israel," he said. "Rebecca had no idea. She was so innocent. I managed to keep it hidden from her until the very end."

When they'd returned to New York for Rebecca to have their second baby, her parents had stepped in. They wanted their daughter back and her young slate wiped clean. Judah was given up for adoption as a newborn, and Sammy, by then two-and-a-half, was relinquished several months later.

"I did my best to prepare him." Josh's eyes glazed over,

reminding me of my own zombie-like state in recent weeks. "I told him, 'You're going to have a new mommy and daddy, really nice people who will take good care of you.' He seemed to take it in stride until the time came to deliver him to the adoption agency's office.

"I hugged him and told him I loved him. I remember walking up the stairs, while Sammy screamed 'Daddy! Mommy! Come back!' I can still hear his voice. It was the hardest thing I've ever had to do."

There was nothing to say. We both turned and stared at the list over the bar that boasted more than one hundred daiquiri flavors.

"I know what it's like to lose a child," I said finally. "If I could spare you just one thing, it would be this."

"Someday, we'll search for them together," Josh said without looking at me.

"Yes. We will."

Chapter 6

BREAKABLE

Josh, Marissa, and I returned to the French Quarter that evening. They said they wanted to show me the "real" New Orleans. Little did I know that meant a female impersonator show, then mind-numbing music in a heavy metal bar, and several shows and a table dance at the Unisex World-Famous Love Acts club where Josh had once worked. I pasted a smile on my face and pretended I was having a wonderful time. I wanted to know my son, even the parts that unnerved me. I waited for the night to be over, planning to sort it out later.

On the way home, after breakfast at the Déjà vu Café, they declared that I had passed the "cool mom test." Cool had changed a lot since I'd been in my twenties; nonetheless, I reveled in their approval.

We didn't get to bed until almost four and I awoke just a few hours later with a long-buried memory pounding in my head…

"The judge is going to question you," the attorney had said, coaching me as we drove to the courthouse to sign the final adoption papers. "It's important that you don't hesitate, that you answer clearly and decisively." We would be alone in chambers, he told me, with only the judge and his stenographer. It wouldn't take more than ten minutes.

Sitting in front of the judge's massive wooden desk, I felt neither clear nor decisive. I felt weak and pathetic under his stern gaze, and I tried not to twitch as he asked the same questions over and over.

"Are you giving up this baby of your own free will?"

"Yes, Your Honor."

"Do you swear that you have not been compensated, either in cash or goods, as an inducement to relinquish?"

"Yes Sir, I swear."

"Do you understand that once these papers are signed, the adoption will be final and you will have no further right to this child?"

"Yes, Your Honor."

"And do you promise never to interfere in his life in any way?"

"Yes."

I signed my name and it was over. Even though by then he'd been gone for almost two months, as I stood to leave I realized that my son officially belonged to someone else…

Well, he's yours now, I thought as I rolled away from the morning light that streamed through the window. A full-grown man, on whom you've had no influence other than abandoning him.

Voices wafted in from the living room and I heard the kids squealing over their Easter baskets. I checked my watch: nine-fifteen. I pulled the pillow around my head and wondered whether I could get away with pretending to have overslept, and then decided against it. I dragged myself out of bed and into the bathroom, hoping a shower would wake me up.

The hot water melted my determination, like ice cubes crackling in boiling tea. I looked down at my naked body, still reasonably trim and fit for forty-five years, and recalled my first shower after Josh's birth. Standing in the tiny hospital stall, I had stared at the hanging sac that had been my pregnant stomach and collapsed into tears, feeling damaged and empty.

This is all I've been left with, I'd thought then.

The same thought flashed in my head that April morning. I pressed my palms against the shower wall, lowered my body to the floor, and sobbed into the tiles.

I wished I were home, taking my time waking up, with my cats curled up next to me, eating breakfast with Henry, lounging around until it was time to get ready for Leanna and Jerry's annual Easter gathering. I wished I were anywhere else — on familiar turf, a place as gentle as plastic Easter grass, where I wouldn't be afraid that one wrong step could break me.

As I dried off and dressed, I thought I had the tears under control, only to start weeping again. I reapplied my mascara four times and doused my red eyes with drops. After I managed to go five minutes without crying, I stepped out to join the others.

Nina stared at me with a questioning look that made it unbearable to hold her gaze. "Look what you've done to your poor mom, Josh," she said. "She's exhausted!"

Nina had Easter baskets for Josh and Marissa too, and a box of candy for me. I thanked her, apologized for getting up so late, and asked whether they'd decided where to go for brunch.

On our way out the door, she pulled me aside and asked, "Are you okay?"

"Sort of," I replied. "Just tired."

But the heaviness returned at Mulate's, the downtown Cajun-style restaurant we decided was casual enough to accommodate small children. As long as I stayed focused on my food and didn't look at Josh, I managed to ward off the tears.

It was a radiant day, sunny and warm, and after our meal, we joined the crowds at a street fair near the French Quarter. Somewhere between the balloon artist who made hats for the kids and Jackson Square, Josh came up beside me and my dam broke again.

"Mom, are you all right?" he said, putting his arm around me. "You're so quiet today."

"I think I'm losing it," I wailed and let my face fall against his chest.

"That's okay," he said. "Go ahead and lose it if you need to."

"I feel like my heart is breaking."

We stopped and sat on a park bench, letting the others go on ahead.

"You were so happy," he said after a few minutes. "Did I do something wrong?"

"No," I gushed between soggy breaths. "I'm still happy. And I'm sad too. That I wasn't there for you and all the problems you've had."

"It's all right. We're together now." He put his arm around my shoulder, comforting me as I had him the day before in the daiquiri bar. "I think the best thing is to forget the past," Josh said softly. "The only thing that matters is that we found each other. I think from now on we should only look forward."

He made it sound so easy. I dabbed at my eyes with my shirtsleeve and told him he was right. That's what we would do. We stood and hugged, then dashed to catch up to the others. Marissa took our picture in front of General Jackson's statue, with Josh wearing Jacob's balloon hat.

Since my plane didn't leave until evening, we had most of Monday. We spent an hour in the morning, using up what remained of my film: pictures of Josh and Marissa, Josh and me, Josh alone. He took off his shirt and posed while I documented the dragon, the tiger, and the naked lady with a *Be My Girl* banner. His forearms were decorated in vines with flowers, only half-filled-in with color.

Josh said, "When people ask why they aren't colored in, I tell them, 'Everybody knows how cheap Jews are. I left them that way so I wouldn't have to buy coloring books for my kids.'"

"What an awful thing to say!" But I laughed, because he did.

Josh's tattoos would become my symbol for unconditional love. Accepting him in spite of them made me feel more like a mom, better than my parents who so readily judged others.

We went through his stack of photographs and those I had brought along, and each picked out ones we'd like to have. I shuffled through his snapshots of Sammy, trying to choose one or two, but Josh insisted I take several.

"I can see how much you care about pictures," he said. "They'll be safer with you."

I stared at the one of Sammy at about two years. He was

dressed in blue flannel pajamas and a stocking cap that covered most of his head, sitting on a miniature easy chair. His tiny, trusting face burned into my heart. There were no photographs of Judah. A new wave of sadness engulfed me as I realized how much having even one picture of my son — some proof that he existed — would have meant to me all those years. Surely the hospital took pictures of all the newborns. Why hadn't I thought to ask for one?

When Josh opened an old briefcase and brought out the boys' adoption papers, a gasp escaped my lips. I had nothing from his relinquishment, no copies of anything I'd signed in the judge's chambers. Seeing the loss in black and white made me too woozy to read the mass of fine print.

"The agency said I can find out where they are once they're eighteen," Josh said.

"Really?" I said with more than a trace of skepticism.

"That's what they said."

"How old are they now?"

"Sammy would be almost seven, and Judah, four."

He handed me their original birth certificates and again I felt cheated.

"Do you have yours?" I asked.

"Not the one with you on it."

"Can I see it?"

I studied every line. There was nothing to indicate that he'd been adopted. Everything on it was true — the date and time, the hospital and doctor — except for the names. Morris and Judith Goldberg had been inserted where John and I had once been, as if they had flown from New York to California to deliver their child. Any sign of me had been erased.

What if he hadn't found out he was adopted? He would have never thought to look for me. And if I'd found him, he might have told me I had the wrong person.

Josh sprung to his feet.

"I want to play something for you," he said. "It's a song that has always meant a lot to me. I thought about you whenever I heard it. It got me through a lot of rough times."

He put a tape into the cassette player, but as soon as the song began, he realized that he'd have to translate it for me. It was in Hebrew, sung by Shimi Tavori, a popular Israeli artist. For the next thirty minutes, Marissa sat at the stereo controls playing the tape in snippets — starting and pausing and rewinding — while Josh transcribed the words in English.

When he was finished, he handed me the paper, started the song from the beginning, and sat down across the table from me. I looked at the sheet. The title was "Imma," Hebrew for mother.

"You have a good soul
A warm heart full of love
You're good and gentle
And you always understand
You organize and prepare
And always buy presents
You want to know what's happening
And I don't always answer
Every night you sit
And tell me wise things
You don't close your eyes
You wait patiently, always there
I see everything you do
It's pleasant, yet I don't show it
But God knows.
Mother, I love you
Mother, thank you with all my heart
When I'm hurt, your heart is broken
You try to console me by saying it's nothing
You don't ask too many questions
And you forgive everything
When you're in pain, you don't show it
Even if it's very hard for you
There are days that you feel sad
Sometimes even angry

But you immediately reconcile
And your face lights up
Sometimes I am wrong
And I don't always admit it
But God knows.
Mother, I love you
Mother, thank you with all my heart."

I couldn't look at Josh while the song played, even when I heard him start to cry. Without moving my eyes from the words, I reached across the table and squeezed his arm. He put his hand over mine, and I could feel him shaking. Once the music stopped, I moved around the table and put my arms around him.

"I'm so sorry, Baby," I whispered, and we cried together for the first time.

With just an hour before we had to leave for the airport, I went to pack. Josh came into my room holding the helium clown that had spent the past few days in a corner of the family room.

"What about Charlie?" he said. "I think he wants to go with you."

I laughed. "I doubt the airlines will let me bring him unless I buy him a seat."

"You can just pack him."

He pulled off the plastic clip on Charlie's back and squeezed its middle. We stared in silence as the balloon slowly began to deflate. Then Josh put his mouth over the air valve, took a breath, and said in a high-pitched helium voice, "Take me with you, pleeeeeeease."

I giggled, grabbed the valve from his hand, and inhaled. "I love you, Josheeeee."

"I love you, Mom-meeeee," Josh squealed after taking another hit.

We both knew how hard it would be to say goodbye, to be separated again. Waiting near the gate, we fidgeted, cracked jokes, and tried to make each other laugh. But the strain was palpable.

"I can't live like this, so far away from you," he mumbled.

"I know. I don't know how I'll stand it either. But we'll talk as often as we can."

"Not good enough." He shook his head. "I have to figure something out."

I put off boarding until the last possible minute, hugged Josh, then Marissa, and then Josh again.

"Tell the pilot to be careful," he told the gate attendant. "I don't want anything to happen to my mom."

I walked through the tunnel without looking back. Josh said they were going to wait until the plane took off. From my seat I searched the tinted airport windows, trying to catch a glimpse of them, until the plane roared into motion and backed away from the terminal.

Chapter 7

IT'S A (BIG) BOY

Back at home, I felt exhilarated and dizzy, as if I'd stumbled off a four-day roller coaster ride. Henry listened patiently while I recounted the details of my trip late into the night.

"Josh is *so* sweet. And sensitive. And handsome. Did I tell you that he has my eyes?"

"Three times now." Henry laughed and rolled his eyes.

"Oh yeah." I slapped my hand against my forehead. "What a relief to be home. It was wonderful, but so intense. I wish I'd had more time alone with Josh. He was so genuine in those moments, so forthcoming about his life — not like it wasn't unnerving to hear about all the bad things that happened to him."

Josh and I continued to talk on the phone three or four times a week. We joked about how long it would take us to "get normal" and go a whole week between calls. I knew we couldn't keep the pace forever; eventually, Josh would become like every other grown son and have to be nagged to call his mother once a month. But I wasn't ready for that. Three days was as long as I could go without hearing his voice; more than that and I became as anxious and irritable as a junkie in need of a fix. Once we talked, I felt peaceful again, satisfied and full, like after Thanksgiving dinner.

My moods rose and fell depending on how Josh sounded on the phone. His joys and problems became mine. When he proudly reported how many cars he'd repaired that day or how much overtime he'd earned, I echoed his enthusiasm. If he had a bad day at work or a fight with Marissa, my heart ached. Sometimes he asked for my advice, and I gladly gave it.

"You're the only woman he really listens to," Marissa had said when I was there.

"Well, he can't have been listening to me for more than two weeks."

"He's been listening to you in his head for years."

Her words put a flame to the kindling of my maternal instincts. *If only he lived closer,* I thought, *I could have a real impact on his life.* I wanted to be there for the day-to-day stuff, to hear his plans and dreams, and help him through the rough spots. I fantasized that he would move to California, pictured him right across the street, and then realizing that was excessive, changed it to across town.

Somehow I knew it wasn't to be — not yet, anyway. Maybe after the baby came, once they had saved some money. At least Josh would be here for his birthday in May, and I'd have him to myself for a whole week. I'd offered to fly there instead, since Marissa would be within a few weeks of her due date by then. But after her doctor confirmed that she was not likely to deliver early, Josh insisted on traveling to California as planned.

With his visit still more than a month off, I turned my attention to my role as "new mother." I had never met anyone in my situation; my girlfriends were my only models, and by then most of their children were in their teens. I began by compiling a "brag book" of pictures from my time with Josh, and started a scrapbook with our first cards, letters, and photos. I decided that the occasion called for some sort of official announcement. I went to work on the computer and came up with the perfect balance between serious and silly — It's a BIG boy! — centered over my favorite picture of Josh that I'd taken in New Orleans.

Joshua Mayer Goldberg
Born: May 24, 1970
Found: March 26, 1996
Length: 5'9"
Weight: 180 lbs., 8 oz.
Ecstatic Mom: Denise Roessle

Before I could mail them, I had to make some phone calls. In addition to my business partners, Carol and Julie, I'd told Leanna and a few other close friends about finding Josh prior to my trip to New Orleans, but there were others who deserved to hear the news first-hand.

Sandy, the woman I had lived with during the last five months of my pregnancy, was at the top of the list. I had landed with her by chance, when the home that the adoption attorney had planned for me fell through at the last minute. Sandy was someone he knew socially; she had never before taken in a pregnant girl. A divorcee with two young daughters, she had the space and could use some help. She agreed to meet me…

When the attorney turned off Sunset Boulevard into Bel Air Estates, I thought we must be on the tour route of the stars' homes. Each house was more splendid than the next, and the one where we were headed stood regally at the top of a long, steep driveway.

Standing at the entry after Mr. Lawrence rang the doorbell, I became as edgy as a waif at the orphanage door. Poor little knocked-up girl, ready to run, but desperate not to have to.

"Arthur," Sandy said as she opened the door. She leaned close so Mr. Lawrence could plant a kiss on her cheek, then took my hand. "You must be Denise. Please come in."

She was the tiniest woman I'd ever met — less than five feet tall and probably not a hundred pounds — and the classiest. With big brown eyes and a glowing smile, she reminded me of a platinum blond Jackie Kennedy. Sitting across the living room from her amid the massive oil paintings and marble sculptures, I felt smaller than she, even though I topped her by at least four inches and twenty pounds. In quick, nervous gestures, I smoothed the rumples from my dress, leaned forward, then sat up straight and folded my hands in my lap. She smiled and held my gaze as she took a cigarette from an ornate box on the glass coffee table, put it between her lips, and lit it with a heavy crystal lighter.

"I understand you're from Hawaii." She exhaled a long stream of smoke. "What a beautiful place to live."

"Yes." I smiled. "It is."

"Were you born there?"

"No, I was born in California... San Diego, actually. My family moved to Hawaii when I was in high school."

"And your parents? They're in Hawaii?"

"No. They live in Alaska now. They moved there over a year ago, for my father's job."

I struggled to maintain eye contact, mesmerized by the steady motion of her hand as she moved the cigarette from her mouth to the crystal ashtray and back.

"So when are you due?"

"May twenty-fourth."

"And are you feeling all right? Have you seen a doctor?"

"I took her to meet Dr. Levy in Beverly Hills this morning," Mr. Lawrence interjected. "He examined her and said everything's fine."

"That's good."

When Sandy looked back at me, I sensed something new in her eyes. Was it empathy? Sadness? What could such a beautiful, wealthy woman possibly have to feel sad about?

"I'd be happy if you'd stay. I think you'll love my girls, and I have a feeling they're going to love you."

Mr. Lawrence brought my luggage from the car and left. Learning that I'd spent the night on the plane, Sandy showed me to my room and suggested I take a nap. Her nine- and ten-year-old daughters, Patty and Jackie, were with their father for the New Year's holiday and would be home that evening. I fell asleep the second my face hit the pillow. When I awoke, two giggling little girls — brown-eyed beauties with long dark tresses — were at my bedroom door, eager to sneak a peek at their new housemate.

Sandy's lifestyle was unlike any mother's I'd ever met. She didn't work, but neither did she stay home much. In addition to an active social life with multiple suitors, she had an active legal life and made regular visits to her attorney to tend to the aftermath of what had been a messy divorce. At thirty-six, she was ten years younger than my mother.

Other than answering the door and babysitting, my duties were negligible. Because of my "delicate condition," Sandy limited my chores to dishes, laundry, dusting, and vacuuming. She insisted on mopping the floors herself, and anything more physical, like window washing, she hired out.

On weekday mornings, she rose early and got the girls off to school, then retired to her bedroom until almost noon. By then I had been up for hours, showered, dressed, and scrambling for ways to appear useful. Finally, she would emerge, hair coifed into a bouffant flip, fully made up and flawlessly dressed in a stylish mini-dress or pantsuit for the day's rounds. She was always home by five and made dinner for the girls and me, even if she had a date that evening and wouldn't be dining with us.

When Jackie and Patty were in school, I busied myself with my meager duties and daytime television. Once the things my parents had shipped arrived — my typewriter, record player, records, and photo albums — I turned my room into a refuge. I spent hours writing cheery letters to the friends who knew my situation, and gloomy poetry to vent my despair. Checking the mailbox became an important part of my routine. Each weekday afternoon I inched my increasingly cumbersome shape down the steep driveway, hoping for some connection to the life I'd left behind.

"How are you doing?" everyone asked. My father called every few weeks with the same question. My mother didn't come to the phone. Instead, she wrote chatty notes about the weather in Anchorage, how people there attended church woefully underdressed, and her increasing proficiency on cross-country skis. Mr. Lawrence asked when he checked in monthly, and more often as my due date approached.

"Fine," was my standard answer. It was the one they wanted, and the one I desperately needed to be true.

Sandy inquired regularly how I was feeling and whether I wanted anything special from the market. She tried to engage me in conversation when she drove me to my doctor's appointments. Despite her kindness, I was reluctant to consider her a friend. She was one of "them" — the attorney, the doctor, my parents, and whoever else jumped in to shepherd me through this process that I did not want or trust. I would be polite, and nothing more.

"So where's the baby's father?" Sandy asked one day.

"I guess he's still in Hawaii."

"What does he do for a living?"

"He's in the Marines."

"Why didn't he marry you?" Her eyes narrowed. "Was he already married?"

"No. Well, he was getting a divorce. We were supposed to get married, but he changed his mind."

"He left you?"

"Uh-huh."

"Men are such bastards," she said, tossing her head. "You don't think he'll change his mind and try to find you?"

She sounded a bit wary, and I wondered whether Mr. Lawrence had asked her to keep an eye out for anything that might threaten our arrangement.

"No. I don't know how he could."

"Do you love him?"

The question caught me off-guard. The last time I saw John, it hadn't mattered whether I loved him — only that he no longer loved me.

"I did. I don't know now."

"Well, I hope someday he realizes what he's lost and ends up a bitter, lonely old man."

As my belly grew, so did my need for a friend. Once Sandy whittled down her list of beaus to just one — Allen — she had more time, which we spent together — shopping, going to the movies, and taking the girls to the beach. Sometimes she shared details of her life: a mother who treated her with contempt, an early true love that her parents had driven away, her tumultuous marriage to the girls' father. Years later, I would reflect on the twist of fate that brought us together and the inexplicable camaraderie that kept us in each other's lives long after I left her home…

In the years that followed, Sandy was the only friend who had no qualms about broaching the topic. Every now and then, she asked whether I still thought about my son and whether I had considered searching. When I was filling out the registry form, I'd called on Sandy to provide the name of the hospital and other details that had sunk too deep in my memory. For the next eight years, she inquired regularly whether I'd heard anything.

"Guess what?" I said when I phoned her to announce our reunion.

"You found Erick," she stated matter-of-factly.

"How did you know?"

"I was sure it would happen. I just didn't think it would take this long."

"His name's Joshua."

"Well, he'll always be Erick to me."

"He's coming here for his birthday. Do you want to come up and meet him?"

"I wouldn't miss it for the world."

My news came as a surprise to most of my friends — even those who had known about my pregnancy and the adoption — since I hadn't revealed my hopes for finding him. Some said they had often wondered how I was coping over the years.

"You deserve this!" they exclaimed. "He's so handsome!" when I showed my pictures. "I see so much of you in him." I drank in every ounce of their joy as I told the story again and again.

When they asked about Josh's adoptive parents, I explained how they had deserted him when he developed problems as an adolescent and that his relationship with them had not improved since. I was the only mother he had now, I told them, and I was ready and willing to fill that void in his life. Everyone agreed he was lucky to have me.

I left out the most distressing details. Other than informing

Henry, I kept the part about Josh's sons to myself. That one thing was still too painful to say out loud. And regardless of what people thought of me for giving away my son, I couldn't bear for anyone to think poorly of him.

It was harder to tell the good friends I'd never confided in. I worried that they'd feel betrayed, or at least excluded, that I had not revealed this important piece of my life to them.

Madaleine, a close friend since junior high, was one of those who got caught in the web of secrecy when my parents demanded that I tell no one else. She wept when I called her with my news. "That must have been so hard for you, watching my girls grow up when you had a child of your own somewhere out there."

Her comment made me pause. For nearly twenty years, I had watched my friends raise their children and been an "auntie" to them, all without so much as a twinge. Had I unconsciously compartmentalized my friends' children, assigned them a separate space in my heart, like meat, potatoes, and salad on plastic picnic plates?

I didn't feel the same anxiety about belatedly informing my brother and sister. They were fifteen and sixteen when I'd gotten pregnant — according to Dad, too young to understand, and not to be trusted to keep the secret. Following my parents' directive, I'd written to them from Sandy's as if I were away at college. I did so without guilt. Growing up, we'd been more like roommates than siblings — much less allies — connected only by meals and shared bathrooms.

"I had a feeling something was going on back then," Bob said after I told him.

"You did not!"

"I did, too."

"Is that why you gave me a package of diapers for Christmas when you guys came to Hawaii?"

"I did not."

"Yes, you did. Dad said he gave you and Debby money to buy presents for everyone and sent you down to Woolworth's.

You also gave me an ashtray with a naked woman lying on her stomach, with the words, 'watch your butt.' You thought it was hilarious. Mom and Dad nearly choked."

"I don't remember that."

"I do. That was right before they sent me to California."

"I can't imagine what you went through. But this is great, Denise. So, I'm an uncle." Officially, he was the only one of us three who had children. "Tell me about my nephew."

I excluded anything that might sour his enthusiasm.

Debby leaped to a different conclusion when I said I had something important to tell her.

"You're pregnant," she blurted.

"No." I laughed, and wondered for a minute whether everyone was still waiting for Henry and me to have kids. "But I was once."

I was still putting off telling my parents, and turned instead to Leanna's mom and dad. They had known John, welcomed him into the family, and celebrated our engagement. Even though my father had ordered me not to tell them about my pregnancy, I felt as if I had to. My confession had been as painful as with my own parents — but out of love and esteem, instead of fear…

"I have some bad news," I said to Mrs. Daniel as she placed freshly laundered clothes in Leanna's dresser. "John and I aren't going to get married after all."

"Oh, Honey, I'm so sorry," she said, turning to look at me with genuine concern. "Are you doing okay?"

"Not really. I'm pregnant."

Her blue eyes glassed up and her freckled face turned white. "Are you sure John won't change his mind, that there isn't some way you can patch things up?"

"No. I don't think so."

I explained how my father was checking into maternity homes on the mainland, that their plan was for me to have the baby and give it up for adoption. Mrs. Daniel turned another shade paler.

"Oh, this is just awful" she said. "There's got to be another way."

It never occurred to me to solicit the Daniels' help. Even if I had, it was unlikely that they would have gone against my parents' wishes...

Twenty-six years later, as I sat across from Mr. and Mrs. Daniel in their living room, I was struck by how little had changed in the three decades I had known them. I glanced around at the brocade-covered sofa and chairs, dark wood tables with curved legs, and clusters of knick-knacks, and smiled as I realized that, with a few exceptions, everything was the same as it had been in Hawaii. Valeria's bright smile, Willard's soft chuckle, and the warmth of their hugs were a constant I had only begun to appreciate.

Tears rose in their eyes when I said the words: "I have my son back."

"This is wonderful news!" Valeria cried.

"When can we meet him?" Willard said.

"Next month, when he comes here for his birthday."

"I always wondered what happened to him and how you were feeling," Valeria said. "Leanna said you never talked about it."

"That's true. I couldn't."

"Well, that's over now. And we couldn't be happier for you."

Bolstered with an armload of positive reactions, I prepared to tell my parents. They were in the middle of a move from Spokane to Tucson, and planned to spend one night with us in California on the drive south. Although I dreaded it, I decided that telling them in person was the right thing to do. Their travel plans were tentative and I anxiously waited for news of their arrival date, all the while rehearsing what I'd say and how I'd deal with their reaction. After a series of uncanny delays, Dad called to say that they would have to forgo their visit and drive straight through to Arizona.

I took this as a sign that I was not meant to tell them in

person. But even in my relief, my need to have it done burned. Dad always took the lead when they called. As much as I had resented his running interference for my mother in the past, this time I was grateful that I would only be dealing with him.

They were still on the road when Dad reported in again. While he related the latest from their journey, I gestured to Henry.

"This is it," I whispered, with my hand over the mouthpiece. My stomach churned and my hands became clammy.

"I've got something to tell you," I said after Dad finished his stories. "I was going to do this in person when you guys came here."

"I'm listening."

"Remember back when I got pregnant and had a baby?" I actually believed this was possible — that they might have wanted so badly to forget, that they had. "Several years ago, I signed up with a reunion registry. About a month ago, my son registered. And they matched us. We've found each other."

"My goodness. I don't know quite what to say." He sounded surprised, but not upset. "I had no idea that was possible."

"His name is Joshua. He lives near New Orleans and I went there to meet him at Easter. He's married and in a couple months, I'm going to be a grandmother."

"A grandmother." He cleared his throat. "That's really something."

"This is important to me," I said, just as I'd practiced. "I've wanted to find my son for a long time. I'm very happy and I need you and Mom to be happy for me."

"Well, of course you're happy."

I was certain I detected a trace of joy in his voice. With a hitch in my throat, I asked, "Do you want me to tell Mom?"

"Uh, gosh," he stammered. "She's taking a bath right now. I'll tell her later."

The release I felt at being delivered from that task

confirmed that I'd been crazy to think I could have told my mother in person.

"See?" Henry said, after I hung up and recounted the conversation. "Your dad was bound to be glad. He comes from a close family. He has to have wondered what happened to his grandson, and to think finding him is a good thing."

It was more than I dared hope, but I let myself believe.

Two weeks passed with no word from my parents. Every time the phone rang, my heart leapt in anticipation and then plunged again in disappointment. As optimistic as I'd been, I was losing hope that they would respond with the acceptance I needed.

Finally, one Sunday afternoon, Dad called. Mom had developed a sinus infection, he said, and wasn't up to coming to the phone. Then he launched into ordinary chitchat — how they were getting settled in their new home, escrow problems with the house in Spokane, and the nice weather in Tucson. I listening dutifully, waiting for him to get around to asking how we were doing. He skirted through the conversation without a word about Josh.

"Ignore it and it will go away," I blustered at Henry later. "That's my parents' approach to every problem. Why did I think things would be any different this time?"

It wasn't the first time I'd felt forsaken by my father. I had been in my seventh month when he visited me at Sandy's during a business trip to Los Angeles...

After shopping for a few necessities, he took me out to dinner. Jackie and Patty were at their father's for the weekend and Sandy was having friends over for cocktails. Dad and I were parked in her driveway, saying goodbye in the dark of his rental car, when I burst into tears.

"I'm so sorry... for letting you down," I gulped. "For everything. It hurts that you're so afraid that people will find out, that you're ashamed of me...."

He reached over and touched my shoulder. For a minute, everything was quiet.

"You're my daughter and I love you," he said softly. "I'd be proud to be seen anywhere with you. I'd walk down Sunset Boulevard with you right now if that would prove it to you."

"Then don't make me do this," I sobbed. "Let me come home! Let me keep my baby!" I buried my face in my hands.

"This is the way things have to be. You may not see it now, but trust me, it's for the best."

I was still wiping away my tears as he walked me up the steps to the house.

"Oh Baby, what's wrong?" Sandy said, when she opened the door. Turning to my dad, she said, "Come in, Cliff. You look like you could use a drink. Somebody, Irving, get this man whatever he wants."

I never explained why I was crying, what I had asked my father, or what his answer had been. Sandy led me back to my room and sat me down.

"I know what you need," she said, and then disappeared. When she returned, she had a glass in her hand and my dad in tow. "Here, love, drink this. It'll make you feel better."

The vodka and orange juice warmed my tummy and calmed my jangled nerves. Longing for the escape of slumber, I said goodbye to Dad. Sandy went back to her party…

Confronting my father that night had been a spontaneous act. I hadn't planned it, nor had I expected a different response. When I'd first arrived at Sandy's, I fantasized about finding a way out of the adoption arrangement. I looked up the number for County Social Services and considered calling to inquire about assistance. I made a list of friends my parents didn't know, people I might run to. I watched TV game shows.

My favorite was *Queen for a Day*. The contestants were ordinary women, each with a sad story — a fire in which they'd lost everything, a husband out of work, a handicapped child. One by one, they revealed their troubles and what they wished for most of all, the thing that would repair their lives. Once the studio audience selected the winner with their applause, the "queen" was draped in a royal cape, crowned with a sparkling tiara, and presented with a huge bouquet of roses. She smiled broadly through her tears, as beautiful young models with no problems unveiled her bounty.

That's it, I thought. *I would go on Queen for a Day.* Surely my story was tragic enough. The viewers would see how helpless I was, how trapped by circumstance. I'd tell them how much I longed to keep my baby, that I'd be a good mother if only I had the means. I could almost hear their applause, feel the crown on my head and the roses in my arms.

I watched for the contestant phone number, but it never appeared. Finally, I looked up the production company and called.

"Gosh, Darlin', we aren't taking contestants anymore. We haven't filmed in over a year. Those are reruns you're watching."

As I drifted into sleep after my father's visit, whatever courage I'd exhibited that night dissolved. With less than two months until my due date, I was resigned to my fate. Perhaps I had been all along.

Chapter 8

MOTHER MATERIAL

The knot in my stomach tightened as I scanned the rack of Mother's Day cards.

As usual, I'd waited until the last minute to buy one. I took a deep breath and opened the first card that caught my eye: *A mother is love.* I put it back and grabbed another: *For all the wonderful things you do.* And another: *I'm glad you're my mom.*

One by one, I rejected them. Even the humorous cards expressed too much, a lightness that my mother and I had never shared. I rushed out of the card store, confused and clammy. My mother's words echoed in my ears:

If you're smart, you won't have kids.

I could still see us standing in the kitchen: Mom at the sink, her rubber-gloved hands in the dishwater, me leaning in the doorframe behind her. I was twelve, old enough for her to dispense advice on life, like "Go to college and get a career so you'll have something to fall back on," or "It's just as easy to fall in love with a rich man as it is a poor one."

If you're smart, you won't have kids. It wasn't the first time I'd heard those words. But this time the meaning seared my brain like a branding iron. She wished she hadn't had us; she hated being a mother.

For twenty-six years, I'd dreaded the month of May, feeling obliged to honor the woman who not only regretted my existence but had been instrumental in the loss of my only child. And then his birthday, two weeks after Mother's Day. The memories that I was usually strong enough to deflect dragged me into that dark place where I hated myself for obeying my mother and giving him up for adoption.

But this year was going to be different. I would receive a Mother's Day card that wasn't from my husband or the cats.

My son would call, as he had every Sunday for two months since we'd found each other.

Back in the store, I chose a card with a photograph of bright wildflowers: *Wishing you a beautiful Mother's Day.* After all, there wasn't anyone I wouldn't want that for.

Josh's call didn't come until mid-afternoon on Mother's Day. His voice was unusually soft and solemn.

"I got some bad news this morning," he said. "I tried to call the mother I grew up with and found out that she died two months ago."

"Oh my God, Josh!"

He went on. "My father asked me why I was calling. When I said I wanted to wish my mother a happy Mother's Day, he said, 'You don't have a mother anymore.' I asked what he meant and he told me, 'She's dead.' Just like that." Josh's voice broke ever so slightly and I heard him clear his throat.

The frustration I'd been feeling toward my own parents evolved into a raging anger toward all parents. "Why didn't he contact you?"

"He said he didn't know how to reach me, which isn't true. And you know what else? He said he didn't want me coming down there and embarrassing him in front of their friends with my non-Jewish wife."

His father had managed to reach his brother, whose whereabouts were supposedly unknown, and Jonathan had attended the funeral. Josh sounded crushed.

You son of a bitch. I wanted to kill Morris Goldberg. Whatever Josh had done, he didn't deserve this. I struggled my way out of the anger and tried to comfort my son. "Oh Sweetie, I'm so sorry."

Josh continued, "The weird thing is the timing. She died on March sixth, right around the time I sent for the registry forms. If my father had called me, if I'd known that she'd died, I might not have registered and we wouldn't have found each other by now. I might have thought it was a sign and felt too guilty to look for you at all. So maybe things do happen for a reason."

I didn't ask him what he had planned on saying to her or whether he planned to tell her he had found me. It no longer mattered.

That evening, my rage toward Morris and my sadness for Josh gave way to relief. From our first conversation, Josh had bestowed upon me the coveted title of "Mom." However desperately I wanted it, I wondered whether I deserved it.

I had given birth to him, but I had also given him away to strangers. Judith had been his real mother. She was the one society had deemed more fit to parent than an unwed teenager, the one who saved my baby from being a bastard. Just six years my senior, she'd swooped down to catch the child I had dropped and, together with her lawfully wedded husband, carried him off to an idyllic life in a real home, where she got to hold him, feed him, hear his first words — everything I had given up and could never get back.

Secretly, I was glad that she was gone. Even after learning that she too had deserted him, I was intimidated by her existence. With Judith in the picture, I was certain I'd never be more than second best.

Josh clearly wanted a mother — needed one, in fact — and now the job was all mine. For the first time since we'd met, my love for him gave me strength, made me believe that I could fix his problems and make up for lost time. Simply having me in his life would heal all of his pain. Never mind that he was a grown man or that we were virtual strangers, with nothing in common but a handful of genes and no history past the nine months he'd spent in my belly.

I had no other children and he had no other mother. It was perfect.

The only cloud left hanging over my sunny scenario was my parents' silence. They had relegated the fact that I'd had a child to the Closet of Never Happened and clearly did not want that door opened. But it was my door, a piece of my life that they had stolen from me.

"I'm sick and tired of their bullshit," I told Henry. "I don't

care if they never speak to me again. I will not let them treat
my son like a dirty little secret."

"Good for you," he said. "It's about time."

A week after Mother's Day, I wrote Dad and Mom a letter,
just as I had when I'd confessed my pregnancy.

It's been more than a month since I told you about Josh, I
wrote. It hurts me that you've said nothing. I realize that it may
be difficult for you to revisit what you probably still consider a
shameful family secret. But I need you to face the reality that
I had a child, who is now back in my life, and be supportive of
our reunion. He is, after all, your grandson.

Dad called a week later. He spoke openly enough that
I was sure Mom was gone from the house, or at least out of
earshot.

"I want to apologize for not getting back to you," he said
in a contrite tone. "We've been so busy dealing with the new
house and your mother's medical problems, we just haven't
had a chance to give it any real thought."

"I don't understand what there is to think about," I said.
"You've had twenty-six years to come to grips with this."

"You've got to understand that this is a reminder of a
terrible time for us. We can't help but think that we failed you
somehow, that we must have done a crummy job as parents for
things to have gone so wrong."

"That was a long time ago, Dad. I turned out fine, and
personally I think you should be proud."

"Yes, but it was a long, bumpy road getting there." His
chuckle rankled me.

"This is happening with or without you. But it would be
nice if you wanted to be involved."

"What do you mean by involved?"

"Well, for *example*," I said, too frustrated to keep the
sarcasm from my voice. "Would you like to know something
about him, maybe see a picture?"

He asked a few polite questions — Josh's full name, where
he lived, and when his and Marissa's baby was due — and then

said he guessed it would be "okay to send some photos."

I let go an audible sigh, telling myself to be patient. Once my parents saw Josh's face and he became real to them, they would be unable to maintain their resistant stance.

"I'm concerned about how Bob and Debby will take this," Dad said. "Are you planning to tell them?"

"I already have. They're fine with it — thrilled, in fact."

"I see. Well, I hope you haven't said anything to the folks out in the Valley."

"No." It hadn't occurred to me to tell my father's relatives, who still lived in the Central California farm community where he had been born and raised. I hadn't been in regular touch with my uncles, aunts, and cousins for years. Although Henry and I now lived only two hours away, I hadn't seen them since a family reunion a few years before.

"Good. Because I think it would kill your mother if they found out."

Kill my mother? A chill stabbed at my heart before the heat of my mounting anger could melt it.

Dad picked up the slack of my silence. "You must know that your mother and I love you very much."

"I know," I said, with little conviction.

After we hung up, I repelled my irritation before it could evolve into anger. Even as a girl, the power of that emotion frightened me. I was certain that if I unleashed it, everyone and everything I cared about would disappear in its wake.

My parents had done their best for their children, I reminded myself. We had lived in nice houses in good neighborhoods and gone to first-rate schools. We'd taken all the lessons — music, dance, art — gone to camp, belonged to clubs. Dad worked hard, steadily climbed the business ladder, and provided well for his family. Mom was always there when we got home from school. She kept an impeccable house, sewed our clothes, baked chocolate chip cookies, and served dinner promptly at six.

Ugly images interrupted my ruminations:

The disapproving looks my Republican parents gave me when they found out I'd written a condolence letter to Mrs. Kennedy after President Kennedy was assassinated. Bob near tears at sixteen when the used truck he'd bought broke down before he got it home. "I can't do anything right," he'd said, worrying what Dad would say when he found out he'd picked a lemon.

Debby, whose learning disabilities and emotional fragility held her captive in the role as our "family problem," kept getting fatter and more depressed until she was barely functional.

There was no love without conditions. There was merely approval. We performed to the best of our abilities, worried when we missed the mark, and mourned our failures.

I'd been so ashamed when my mother came for Leanna and me after our first high school dance. What should have been one of the most exciting nights of our young lives had turned into the worst. No one had asked us to dance, but I couldn't tell Mom. I would have been a failure; she would have called me a "wallflower." So I'd lied.

"Did you have a good time?" she'd asked.

"Yes," I said, turning to nod persuasively at Leanna in the back seat.

"Did you dance?"

"Yes."

"Who did you dance with?"

"Nobody you know, Mom."

The next day, Leanna told me that her mother had heard her crying and come into her bedroom to see what was wrong. She'd told her mom that no one had asked her to dance, and her mother had comforted her, told her not to worry, that she was a wonderful person, a beautiful girl, and the boys just couldn't see it yet.

How I had wished for such a mom. Someone who wanted the truth, whatever it was, who could recognize my pain and tell me everything was okay even if it wasn't. A mom who loved me for who I was, even when I wasn't what she hoped for.

I cursed myself for telling my parents about Josh. I felt as exposed as I had been when I returned to their house after my pregnancy.

From the day I'd arrived, getting out was my sole mission. I got a job, enrolled in college part-time, and started making friends. But what I thought I needed was a man. Between the dating service my parents encouraged me to join and the men I met at the dance clubs, I had lots of chances, but I was drawn to the marginal ones. Anything better was somehow too good for me.

Six months after coming home, I met the man who would facilitate my escape. Don was exactly what I wanted — an honest-to-goodness, long-haired, hippie freak, the exact opposite of the respectable, clean-cut man who had ruined my life the year before. What began as a summer hitchhiking adventure turned into a five-year relationship.

For the first several years after giving up my baby, my friends were still young enough that I wasn't thrown into situations where I'd have to watch their pregnancies advance, or "ooh" and "aah" over nurseries decorated in pastel stencils. When that time eventually came, I managed to avoid holding their newborns, feigning nervousness about dropping them. The tiny, floppy ones hit too close to home. Once they became toddlers — walking and talking — I regained my composure.

When people asked why I'd never had children, I usually responded that I just hadn't met the right guy until it was too late, which was at least half true. Again and again, I fell in love, moved in, broke up. I lived in fear of getting pregnant without a husband, and subjected my body to the most surefire forms of contraception — hormone-loaded pills, and then IUDs that looked like prehistoric sea creatures.

I was thirty-one when I met Henry. By then, it had dawned on me that while I had diligently protected against pregnancy, I had also prevented myself from being with anyone capable of having a committed relationship. I'd had it with deadbeats and opened my mind to the possibility that I deserved better — someone responsible, trustworthy and kind. Henry had all of that, plus intelligence, wit, dreamy blue eyes, and great legs. Within a week of meeting him, I was madly in love. And to my amazement, so was he. We were engaged five months later and married in three more.

We agreed to wait a year or so before discussing children. Jeff, Henry's sixteen-year-old son from his first marriage, had lived with him part-time for a year after the divorce and full time after Jeff's mother died of cancer less than two years later. He was honest about his hesitation to start a second family.

"You know I love kids," he said. "When I was younger, I wanted more."

At forty, he wasn't sure he had the energy to give the one-hundred percent he'd given Jeff, to come home from work and chase balls and help with homework, attend dance recitals and soccer games.

"But if having a baby is something you feel strongly about, I'll go into it wholeheartedly."

Our parenting styles with Jeff reflected the enormous disparity in our own upbringings. Henry was soft, trusting, and lenient. I was rigid, suspicious and strict. He reasoned and I enforced. I was so sure I could whip Jeff into shape, keep him in school and away from drugs with rules and supervision. No matter how much I had resented my parents' approach to childrearing, I unconsciously followed their example. I cringed every time I heard my mother's disciplinary words coming out of my own mouth, but I couldn't stop. And it did not work. It only drove a wedge between us.

Ultimately, it was my decision not to have more children. "I've been thinking," I told Henry. "We're probably too old to start a family."

Who knows how long it might take me to get pregnant, I reasoned, and if we were going to do it at all, I didn't want to have an only child. If we had two, it was possible that Henry would be in his sixties before our kids were out of high school. What I kept to myself was that after three years with Jeff, I was convinced that, like my mom, I was simply not mother material. Her example had destroyed my ability to parent, to love a child wholeheartedly as he deserved. Quietly, gracefully, I had accepted my destiny. A few years later, when the FDA took the last long-term IUD off the market, I underwent surgery to have my tubes tied and put motherhood out of my mind.

Chapter 9

BIRTH DAYS

The first contractions roused me in the dark hours of the morning before the baby's due date. Having grown used to the steady stretching of my abdomen during the previous few weeks, I didn't recognize the cramps as labor. It was midmorning before I realized that the pains were coming and going in rhythm and decided to time them. They were about ten minutes apart.

I called the doctor's office and was told to call back when the contractions were five minutes apart. Sandy made the waiting into an event. Since it was a Saturday, we spent the day lounging with Jackie and Patty on her king-sized bed, watching TV and snacking, checking the clock, and writing down the times as the contractions came and went. Around four, I phoned the doctor to report that I had reached the five-minute mark. Sandy left the girls with a neighbor and we headed for the hospital.

I may as well have had "unwed mother" stamped on my forehead. Everyone from the admitting clerk to the nurses seemed to know that there would be no celebration connected with this delivery. No joyous "It's a boy!" No nervous daddy in the waiting room and no beaming new mom.

The five-bed labor room felt more like a basement science lab: windowless, cold and sterile. Fortunately, I had it to myself and, after I was gowned and shaved, Sandy was allowed to stay with me in between the routine pokes and prods. The nurses were attentive but indifferent, sometimes smirking at my naiveté.

"How long before the baby comes?" I asked.

"Oh, it'll likely be a while," one of them answered, winking at the nurse who was noting my vital signs on the chart. "Best to just lie back and relax while you still can."

In 1970, there were no machines to measure contractions or monitor the baby — just timing and periodic pelvic checks. During the first exam, when I complained to the on-call doctor that I could not spread my legs any further apart, he came back with, "Obviously you can, or you wouldn't be in this condition."

My face burned as I scooted down the table and forced my knees sideways.

After I was given an enema, the pains intensified and I got a taste of what real labor would be like. At my monthly check-ups, the obstetrician had weighed me, done a pelvic exam, and pronounced me healthy and on schedule. He hadn't offered any information, and I hadn't asked any questions. No one except Sandy had offered labor and delivery advice.

"If the pain gets too bad, kick the doctor in the face," she'd said. "That's what I did when I was in labor with Jackie, and they gave me more drugs."

Sitting next to my bed, Sandy fed me ice chips and let me take drags off her cigarette — my first taste in six months. The smoke helped break up the antiseptic hospital smell. I was still only five centimeters dilated four hours later when she left to check on Jackie and Patty.

Staring at the huge clock on the wall across from my bed, the big hand clicking slightly back before lunging forward to the next minute, I thought about my mom and wondered if she was thinking about me. I'd called my parents earlier in the day to let them know I was in labor and would probably be going to the hospital soon.

"I hope you don't have as hard a time as I did with you," Mom said. "Forty-eight hours of horrible pain before they decided to do a Cesarean." There was a note of concern in her voice that I hadn't expected.

"I told the doctor what you said, that he should check my pelvis width since you had to have Cesareans, and he thinks I won't have any problems."

"Oh, of course you won't. I'm sure everything will go fine. Call us as soon as you can."

My mother was at her warmest when we kids were sick. She'd bring us ginger ale with a straw, or Campbell's tomato soup with a pat of butter melting on top. She'd feel our foreheads and rub Vicks on our chests. If she went out to the store, she'd always bring back a new comic or coloring book to keep us from getting too bored in bed. When I had cramps with my period, she would fill a hot water bottle and wrap it in a towel for me to hold against my stomach.

I tried to picture her, how soft she seemed in those moments. But all I could pull up was the way she looked during Christmas in Hawaii, pinched and rigid.

By the time Sandy returned, the contractions were relentless. We didn't talk much and finally the nurse sent her to the waiting room. With each new wave, the pain gripped me with such force that I thought my insides would heave out onto the bed. Between surges, I wondered whether this was normal or I should call for a nurse. But before I could reach the button, I was swept away again.

Just after two a.m., a rush of liquid came from between my legs.

"I think I peed the bed," I told the nurse.

"Is that what it felt like? No, your water just broke."

Water?

"You're ready to deliver."

A different doctor appeared, explaining that my regular obstetrician was off-duty for the weekend. He turned me onto my side and injected something into my lower back. The pain evaporated. I let my body melt into the welcome numbness.

Two orderlies transferred me to a gurney and rolled me down the hall to the delivery room, where a new set of nurses, masked and gowned top to toe, moved me onto the table. I watched as one of them strapped my feet into the stirrups, and I saw the doctor step into position before another nurse pulled a white curtain that blocked my view to the lower half of my body. The overhead fluorescent lights glared.

"I'm going to do an episiotomy," the doctor said.

A what?

"Don't push."

I didn't know what "push" meant.

"There's the head. Forceps."

One of the nurses came from behind the curtain and stood near my head.

"Almost done," the doctor said. "How are we doing up there?"

"Fine, doctor," the nurse answered.

I turned my head to look up, but her face was silhouetted in the harsh light. I felt her hand on my shoulder. *Not fine,* I wanted to say. *Alone. Fading. Dead.*

I willed myself to feel something — even pain — some signal of my baby's arrival. Then came a gurgled cry.

The nurse at my side said, "It'll just be another few minutes while the doctor cleans you up and puts in some stitches."

"Is the baby okay?"

Bustling and whispering from the other end of the room filled the silence.

"Did I have a boy or a girl?"

I heard more whispering, louder this time, and then the doctor said, "Christine, please take the infant to the nursery."

Nurse Christine removed her hand and disappeared back behind the curtain.

Once I'd been transferred to the recovery room, Sandy was beside me, insisting that the nurse reveal the baby's sex.

"I have a bet with a friend," she said. "How are we going to know who won?"

The nurse exhaled noisily. "A boy."

"I knew it," Sandy said. "Now I can collect my five bucks."

"Is he healthy?" I asked.

"Yes." The nurse paused and then added, "Seven pounds, eleven ounces, nineteen inches."

Instead of being returned to the maternity ward, I was

moved to a post-op wing, away from the nursery and the new mothers. Because of the saddle block — the anesthetic that had been injected into my spine — I would have to lie flat for the next twenty-four hours to avoid bringing on a severe headache.

"Get some rest," the doctor said. "I've ordered something for the pain you may have once the anesthesia wears off, and medication to dry up your milk."

"I still want to see my baby," I said, with as much force as I could muster.

"That's not a good idea," he said with a solemn glance as he scribbled on my medical chart. "It will only make it harder to give him up."

Harder than what? Nothing about the experience had been easy, and as my body emerged from the numbness, I knew the hard part was just beginning. I wished there was a saddle block for my heart.

Finally, twenty-six years later, Josh and I would spend his birthday together. I could look at him, touch him, and celebrate him all I wanted.

His flight was thirty minutes late and I felt as if I would spin off the planet. My period had started unexpectedly that morning, and between the hormonal gyrations and weeks of anticipation, I couldn't sit still. I paced from the waiting area where Henry sat calmly reading the newspaper to the flight status monitor, and rushed to the window whenever a plane rolled into view. By the time his face appeared in the mob of arriving passengers, my pulse had approached warp speed.

"There he is!" I called to Henry, while waving furiously in Josh's direction. When we hugged, there was still electricity, but the charge was not so alarming as it had been before. It was more like two pieces of a puzzle sliding naturally back into place.

As I'd prepared for his visit, I'd been haunted by a childhood memory of an eight-year-old friend announcing to me that she was adopted.

"I have a birthday and an adoption day," Susie bragged

during a sleepover. "So I get *twice* as many presents as other kids."

Oh boy, was I jealous.

"My mommy and daddy chose me out of all the little girls." She was "special," she said, and I believed it.

I was determined that Josh would have the best birthday ever and, above all, that he would feel special. Nothing about this visit would be ordinary. I'd planned it down to the finest detail. I wished that I had twenty-six gifts to give him, that I'd had the faith and foresight to have bought one every year and stashed them away for this occasion. I thought about buying them anyway, choosing something appropriate for each age I'd missed — a stuffed animal, a truck, a model airplane, a football, and so on — and presenting him with a mountain of packages.

Finally, I decided on a wristwatch in an elegant blend of gold and silver. The volumes I wanted inscribed on the back wouldn't fit, so I settled for *Joshua, 5-24-96, Love, Mom.* I took great care in making up his room, bought all his favorite foods, re-inflated Charlie the clown — this time with a *Happy Birthday* balloon — and armed myself with plenty of film.

Having my son under my roof roused maternal feelings I'd never suspected I had. Sometimes when he called out "Mom" from the next room, I refrained from answering, just to hear him say it again. Being able to hug him each night before he went to bed and waking in the morning knowing he was sleeping in the next room made me feel both blissful and vulnerable, like a young mother who has just brought her newborn home.

I found myself wishing I didn't have to share him with anyone, but meeting Henry and the other important people in my life was one of the reasons I'd wanted him to come to California.

The next day, Sandy and her latest husband, Don, flew in from Los Angeles.

"Is this the *baby*?" she called out, triggering Josh's blush.

"Oh, you're as precious as I remember!" After they hugged, she presented him with a rattle and a teddy bear.

When she referred to herself as his godmother, he turned to me, confused and asked, "Was I baptized?"

The question caught me off guard. I realized that, even after my accounting for our lack of time together after his birth, he still envisioned having had a history with me.

"No. Sandy just gave herself the honorary title."

"He looks like a Josh," Sandy said, giving up her previous intent to call him Erick.

"Actually, he's more of a Bubba." I laughed.

Despite growing up in New York City, Josh had a redneck bent that I had found disconcerting at first, and then amusing. I'd threatened to call him "Josh-Bob," but had since decided on "Bubba."

We spent a lazy afternoon in our back yard, the three guys chattering and laughing while Sandy and I gazed from Josh to each other, alternating between giggles and sniffles. That evening we went to dinner at our favorite steakhouse, where Sandy insisted that the waitress bring "the baby" a children's menu and coloring book.

Josh glided into the role and reveled like a child-star in our undivided attention. He wasn't the only one who regressed. The next day, when we went to Pier 39 in San Francisco, I got Josh to ride the merry-go-round with me. Side by side on our carousel horses, we waved and called out to the others each time we came around. We posed together for silly pictures at the photo booth. Sandy and I joined Josh on the bumper cars, plowing into each other and screaming like nine-year-olds, while Henry and Don stood on the sidelines shaking their heads.

The night before Josh's birthday, I stayed up late to decorate the dining room with balloons and crepe paper. I arranged his gift, and the stack of birthday cards from Aunt Debby, Uncle Bob, and several of my friends, on the table. The next morning, when he stumbled out from his room, wrapped in a blanket, his surprise met my every expectation.

"Happy Birthday, Dearrrrr Josh-eeeee," I sang.

"Wow. No one has ever decorated for me before."

"I can't wait! Open your present!" I held my breath as he pulled the wrapping from the box.

"It's beautiful, Mom," he said, caressing the metal with his fingers and eyes. "This is the best present anyone has ever given me." He slipped the watch onto his wrist. "I promise I'll never take it off."

We spent the day at the vintage automobile museum, where I took his picture with the Bentleys, Rolls Royces, and Ferraris. On the way home, I picked up the birthday cake I'd ordered from the bakery.

"There's no question what I'm wishing for," he said as I lit the candles. His face scrunched up like a child's, concentrating on his wish and sucking in enough air to extinguish all the flames in one puff. "You wanna know what I wished?"

"You can't tell or it won't come true."

"I wished that we could live closer together so I can see you every day."

"I want that too," I said, coming around the table to hug him. "Maybe someday we'll get our wish."

Saturday was the barbecue I'd planned for our friends to meet Josh. Mrs. Daniel brought a homemade birthday cake. Some people brought gifts, ranging from a California T-shirt and other souvenirs, to mementos like a shell from Kailua Beach where he had been conceived. Josh seemed comfortable in the spotlight and I felt a motherly glow as I showed off my handsome son.

I'd wanted everyone to like him and accept him into the fold, as I had with their children. I was hypersensitive to what my son lacked — a history with these people, a typical childhood, social and educational opportunities — but I needn't have worried. Josh had a knack for reading people, zeroing in on what they would respond to, and saying exactly what they wanted to hear. In response to "I hope we'll see more of you" and "It would be great if you could move to California," he said "I hope so too" or "God willing" or "Whatever my mom wants," depending on who he was talking to. He was the most skilled and colorful chameleon I'd ever met. For an instant, I wondered how much of that talent he had used on me. The idea that I couldn't be sure whether I was seeing the real Josh or someone he had invented to please me was too disturbing to consider. I credited his flair to genetics — in particular to my father, the diplomat, who had an innate ability to interact with people from all walks of life and win them over.

On his last day, Josh and I met Leanna and Jerry and their teenaged sons, Scott and Chad, at a family fun arcade with miniature golf, a batting cage, and bumper cars, then went to McDonald's for lunch. Even though they were no longer children, watching my best friend's boys play and laugh with mine made me feel peaceful and whole. During the ride home, Josh fell asleep in the front seat beside me and I could hardly keep my eyes on the road from sneaking glances of him.

The days and nights clicked by as fast as my camera's shutter, and the time for his return home came way too soon. Waiting at the same gate where he'd arrived, we both grew unusually quiet. When boarding began, I urged him to stay until the last call. But he insisted on going as soon as his row was announced, as if eager to get past the goodbye. One last hug and he was gone.

"I can't leave… not yet," I said to Henry, and slumped into a chair in the waiting area. Once the plane pulled away, the tears came in a torrent of grief far more primal than this departure.

I remembered the day Sandy had accompanied Arthur Lawrence to deliver my baby to his adoptive parents at the Los Angeles airport…

"They'd better be good people," she'd said before she left. "Or I swear I'll grab Erick and bring him home."

I had been terrified that she might do it, and at the same

time afraid she might not. Jackie and Patty were in school that day, and for the nearly three hours she was away, I lay on the sofa staring at the ceiling, my stomach churning.

I'd carried my baby to term, taken reasonably good care of myself, and delivered him into the world. I'd picked parents with means. I'd ignored the doctor's advice and gone to see him. I'd given him a name. I had done what I was supposed to do, and what little I could for my child and my own peace of mind. Still, I felt weak and insignificant. I was angry with Sandy for thinking she had the right to decide not to give my baby to those people, when I did not.

My gaze flew to the front door when I heard Sandy's steps on the walkway. She was alone.

"How'd it go?" I'd asked breathlessly.

"Erick was such a good baby," she said. "He didn't cry, just slept the whole time." Car seats weren't required in those days, and Sandy had held him for the entire ride. *Held him.* My breath caught and I tried to ignore the flicker of envy that ran up my arms.

"The parents seemed nice," she said, settling into a chair across from me. She and Mr. Lawrence were at the gate when their plane arrived, and apparently they were scheduled to turn around and fly back to New York that same day. The man was dressed in a suit and tie; the woman had shiny black hair, wore a fashionable suit and a large hat. Sandy said she reminded her of Elizabeth Taylor. The father held back and didn't say much, but the mother's face lit up at the sight of the baby.

As I listened, I'd gritted my teeth and promised myself never again to let things get so far out of my control...

Who was this hysterical mother weeping in an airport, this girl underneath the confident, even-keeled woman I'd spent years cultivating? Even with my loving husband beside me, holding my hand, I felt utterly alone — abandoned by my former self, not yet introduced to the person I was becoming.

I spent the afternoon putting our house back in order, taking down the birthday decorations, and straightening up the room where Josh had slept. When I stripped the bed, his smell was still so strong on the sheets that I held them to my face and breathed him in. I left the bedding in a pile and came back to it several times over the next few days.

Once all the physical evidence of his visit was gone, I had to depend on the pictures I had taken to keep that week alive. As I added them to my scrapbook, I realized how little we still knew about each other. There were easy questions — the things a mother should already have known — like what his childhood birthdays were like, if he'd had a favorite subject in school, how old he was when he'd first fallen in love. And much harder ones, about his parents, his time in Israel, and Rebecca, that died on my tongue because I feared the answers.

Josh hadn't gone deep either. Mostly he'd entertained us with stories about growing up Jewish, embellishing them with a credible Yiddish accent. Admiring the shiny new watch on his arm, he'd mused about never having a Bar Mitzvah or receiving the customary watch his parents would have given him on that occasion.

He spoke about his past relationships, women he'd spent time with during the five years between Rebecca and Marissa. Henry's and my fourteen years together seemed to him an eternity.

"I've always had bad luck with women," he said. "But I'm determined to make things work with Marissa. I chose her because she's young and I'll be able to mold her."

Henry and I shot each other a glance. I decided to try my hand at offering motherly advice.

"When you love someone, it has to be for who they are, not for who you want them to be. If you try to *mold* Marissa, she'll only end up resenting you."

"Okay, maybe 'mold' was the wrong word. I do love Marissa. I just meant that she's still innocent. She doesn't have all kinds of crazy expectations. She looks up to me."

I hoped there was something worth looking up to. Josh had some excellent qualities: he was bright, hardworking, affectionate, and amiable. And yet, the more time I spent with him, the more I sensed some less desirable traits: a recklessness, immaturity and self-absorption that reminded me of Marissa.

I didn't mind his penchant for country music, and in small doses I could endure his repertoire of Jeff Foxworthy redneck jokes. But the racial slurs got to me. The first few times he used the word "nigger," I ignored it, thinking it might have been fall-out from our watching the movie *Pulp Fiction* the night before, in which all the characters, black and white, used it in every other sentence. Finally, I had to speak up.

"You keep saying that word, and I can't help but wonder whether it's because of the movie or you talk like that all the time."

"I don't see what's wrong with it," he said. "They call each other that."

"There's a big difference between saying it as a joke with someone you know, and using it to describe an entire race of human beings. It's derogatory."

He engaged me in a series of "well, buts…" that ran the gamut from Jewish doctrine on the chosen people and the inferiority of other races — as well as gentiles of any color, for that matter — to questioning our acceptance if Jeff had brought home an African-American girlfriend. After an hour of around and around, I called a halt.

"You have a right to your opinion," I said. "Nonetheless, I find that word offensive, so please don't say it around me or my friends."

"Okay," he said. "No big deal."

It was the first time I'd set a boundary with my son — and the last time I did so without fear of losing him again.

Chapter 10

LITTLE REMINDERS

"Congratulations, Grandma! It's a girl."

On June thirteenth, three weeks after Josh's birthday, Naomi Ruth was born. She was just ten minutes old when he called to give me the news.

"Oh, Josh, that's wonderful! I'm so excited! So, the delivery went smoothly? Tell me everything."

"Marissa did great. They gave her some good drugs, but she was right in there, breathing and pushing and yelling at me." He paused for our simultaneous laughter. "I even got to cut the cord."

Picturing Josh beside Marissa — coaching and comforting her, taking turns holding their newborn — sparked a flash of jealousy unbecoming of a grandmother.

"Who does Naomi look like?"

"Right now she looks like a little old man, bald and wrinkled. But she's got the makings of a supermodel. Twenty inches long."

"Longer than you were. I bet she'll be tall. How much does she weigh?"

"Seven pounds, fifteen ounces."

"Bigger than you, too. But just by a few ounces."

"This is the happiest day of my life," he said. "Other than finding you, I mean. Oh, what the hell, let's just say they're tied."

Thanks to ultrasound, Josh and Marissa had been fairly sure they were having a girl. I'd hoped it was true, for all of our sakes. At first, I'd wished for a grandson, and even fantasized that they would name him Erick in honor of the boy child Joshua was meant to be, until I realized that he might look too much like the face I remembered from that nursery window, or become a painful reminder for Josh of his lost sons.

I wondered whether Josh had been in the delivery room when Sammy and Judah were born, if he and Rebecca had seen and held Judah, or if the doctor had whisked him away, telling them it would "only make things harder." Somewhere in the midst of this beginning, did Josh feel the tug of an old ending? I couldn't bring myself to ask, not so early in our relationship, and certainly not while he was celebrating this new phase of his life.

I wondered about Rebecca, the only woman I knew — even though I didn't know her — who shared my experience. Had she had more children? Did they ease her pain, or was the joy of birth forever entangled with grief? Josh hadn't seen her or heard anything about her life since their divorce five years before.

Nina had attended Naomi's birth. I knew that if I lived nearby or had expressed the desire, Josh would have invited me to be there, too. The thought unnerved me. A few years earlier, one of my closest friends had asked me to come to the hospital when she went into labor with her first child. I stayed for four hours, twitching at the thought of what I would witness, what I might remember, until her labor subsided and they sent her home. When she returned two days later, in the middle of the night, this time for real, I was grateful to have been spared.

Josh did his best to keep me involved, calling regularly with updates and sending pictures. Other than in the hospital pictures, where she indeed looked like a little old man or an extraterrestrial, Naomi was a beautiful baby. I dug out my own baby pictures, searching for a resemblance and finding none beyond our coloring. Josh didn't have any of his baby pictures, so I settled for the snapshots of Sammy that Josh had given me during our first visit. I studied my grandson's face floating above his body, which hung loosely in his father's arms as if he were already slipping away.

He would turn seven later that year. I wondered whether I would see Sammy in Naomi as she grew. Probably not, I guessed. As best as I could tell from the pictures, Naomi looked like Marissa, with her big eyes, soft cheek lines, and delicate mouth. The realization left me feeling both delighted and deprived.

Every thought of my granddaughter reminded me of what I had missed with my son. I longed to see her, and yet I was petrified — in a different way than I'd been scared of holding my friends' babies. I was afraid of what I might feel, or that I might not feel anything.

Although Josh didn't say so, I worried that he might be hurt that I hadn't already jumped on a plane, or at least talked about when I could come. Henry hadn't said anything to discourage me from going, but neither had he offered it. After what we'd paid for the two trips — mine to meet Josh, and his to come here — I was nervous about bringing it up.

"We've already spent a lot of money," I told my friends when they asked whether I was going.

Their advice — that it would be best to give the new parents a month or two to settle in — validated my hesitancy. I set my sights on Christmas. By then, Naomi would be six months old, past the fragile infant stage.

I hadn't talked to my parents in almost a month, and I decided to call them with the news. This time, entitlement displaced my anxiety.

"I just became a grandma," I said when Dad answered. "That makes you and Mom great-grandparents."

Dad chuckled. "As if I didn't already feel old."

"Her name's Naomi Ruth."

"Oh, they picked a Jewish name."

"It's a *biblical* name, Dad."

"Well, that's just great. Congratulations."

"She's a beautiful baby. I'll send you some pictures. Speaking of which, did you get the pictures of Josh I sent?"

"Why, yes we did."

"Isn't he handsome?"

"He has tattoos."

"Yeah…" Of all things, I thought. Why couldn't they look past the imperfections and focus on the good?

"Sheesh," Dad said.

He made excuses for Mom not coming to the phone. After we hung up, I felt the same rush of anger that had inspired me to confront them back in May. By now, my rage had evolved into determination. Once again, I got the shove I needed to step up to the plate.

I lectured myself. I refuse to be like them, so motivated by fear and prejudice that they cannot be there for their children, and now their grandchildren. I will embrace my son, for whoever he is. I will love him and support him, no matter what. I will be a grandmother to Naomi, starting right now.

"I think I'll go in August," I told Henry. "If it's okay with you."

"Of course it's okay. You need to see your granddaughter."

"That will give me enough time to get a good fare."

Mom was the last person I expected to be calling when the phone rang a week later. I could tell she had something on her mind and I waited while she chattered about the weather, her aches and pains, and not having to cook because my father was away.

"So, you're a grandmother," she said finally.

"Yes," I gushed, relieved that she had opened the door. "A little girl. I'm going to see her in a few weeks."

"I feel sorry for the children," she said, as if she hadn't heard me. "They aren't to blame."

"What do you mean?"

"I don't know why you insist on dredging up the past."

"Mom, Josh is my son. Naomi's my granddaughter. I love them."

"I guess it's just the way I was raised," she sputtered into the phone. "It's like *The Scarlet Letter*. You know there's no way you can avoid going to hell."

Before I could respond, she said she had something on the stove — apparently something that she had just said she didn't have to make since my dad was out of town — and hung up quickly.

Me and Hester Prynne — two shining examples of fallen women, doomed to wear embroidered "A"s on our chests for all to see. I shook my head as I related the conversation to Henry.

"They were adamant in their belief that giving my child away would solve everything. So how come they, and God according to them, are still punishing me? What does my 'A' stand for — adoption?"

I went into my next visit with Josh with even greater expectations than I'd had for the first two. But from the minute I walked into Nina and Max's house, I knew I was headed for disappointment. The collective excitement I'd enjoyed five months previous was gone. Only Josh made me feel welcome. He presented me with a mug he'd had personalized with Naomi's hospital photo on one side and *I Love You, Grandma* on the other, and then showed me his new tattoo: a large heart on the side of his calf, with two banners that read *Marissa* and *Naomi*. Despite his outward exuberance, he seemed weary and distracted.

Marissa came dragging out of the guest bedroom, her hair uncombed and her clothes disheveled, grumbling about having to make up my bed. "Hey," she said in my direction and slumped onto the sofa.

"Marissa," Josh said. "Go get Naomi. My mom wants to see her."

"She's sleeping."

"That's okay," I jumped in. "Don't wake her. I'll go in and peek at her in a bit."

I'd seen my girlfriends within days or weeks of their children's births, and I understood that just two months into new motherhood Marissa might be a bit tired and moody. Still, I was surprised that she couldn't bring herself to pretend even a bit of appreciation or delight as she opened the pile of baby gifts I'd brought from my friends at home.

The sight of her slammed into my romantic notion of what my life would have been like if I'd married Josh's father and kept my baby. Before John had changed his mind, I'd used my very first credit card to purchase an expensive velvet lounging outfit with a tented top and an elastic waist. I envisioned wearing it on Christmas morning, sitting with my adoring husband, newly wed and anticipating the birth of our baby in May. Shortly before leaving town, I'd returned it to the department store.

Marissa had what I had been denied — a husband and her child — and she didn't appreciate it. My heart welled with such resentment that I almost wished I hadn't come.

But then there was Naomi — a perfect little angel, her lips puckered like a kiss between two chubby cheeks, her head covered in barely visible fuzz. Standing over her crib watching her sleep, again I felt my heart pounding, this time with love unlike anything I'd experienced before. She was real, and she was mine. Nothing could change that. At that moment, I realized that the doctor had been right. If I had seen my baby, I never could have left him.

I stroked the side of her face with my hand, and she blinked three times before revealing her immense blue eyes.

"Hey, Naomi," I cooed.

"Do you want to hold her?" Josh said.

"Yes."

As Josh lifted her and placed her in my arms, my body radiated with warmth, thawing the hard, icy layers that had protected me for all those years. Tears welled up in my eyes, catching me off guard. I felt my body stiffen, the chill of old fears returning — not that I would drop her, but that I might lose her.

Go away. Leave me alone. Not this time.

I turned to Josh. "She's beautiful."

"I know," he said, beaming.

Since he had to work most of that week, I would spend more time with Marissa. Although Nina welcomed me, she was preoccupied with her two toddlers and her own four-month pregnancy, as well as her frustration with her grown daughter.

The tension between them hung in the air like the New Orleans humidity. "She's so lazy and inconsiderate," Nina complained to Max the next morning at breakfast. "The guesthouse is such a pigpen that even Josh is fed up. And they're hardly saving any money toward getting their own apartment."

I overheard so many heated conversations that I felt like an intruder, and other than for sleeping and showering, I kept my distance from the main house.

"Here you go, Grandma," Marissa would say each morning after Naomi was fed. "She's all yours."

When she wasn't attending GED classes, Marissa preferred watching television to hanging out with her baby and mother-in-law. For that, I was more grateful than annoyed. I spent most of the next three days in the guesthouse, lying beside Naomi on a blanket on the floor, watching her sleep, talking to her softly, and studying the changes in her face. When she was awake, I carried her around the backyard, bouncing her in my arms and singing, "Isn't She Lovely" and "You are the Sunshine of my Life." I fumbled with diapers and changed her into different cute outfits, cherishing the brief time I had with her and musing about all the fun things we would do together when she was older.

My third day there, I offered to help Marissa clean and straighten up their quarters. "Working together, we can get it done quickly," I told her. "And think of what a nice surprise it will be for Josh." By the time I'd finished washing the dishes, dusting and vacuuming, she was still sorting the piles of laundry, exclaiming over each item of clothing that she hadn't seen in weeks.

"Please tell me you didn't do all this yourself," Josh said when he got home.

"No," I lied. "Marissa did a lot."

The next day, Nina asked whether we wanted to drive over to the new Wal-Mart. We had lunch at the McDonald's Playland inside. Then, with Nina's five-year-old Jacob in

tow and her two-year-old, Leon, and Naomi stashed in
their respective shopping carts, we spent more than an hour
wandering through the housewares and children's clothes.

"We could really use some new towels," Marissa
exclaimed, looking at her mother expectantly. "This would be
so cute on Naomi," she said, turning to me.

Nina didn't take the bait, and although I considered it once
or twice, I followed her lead.

While we waited to check out, Jacob disappeared. When a
quick look around the cashier stands didn't produce him, Nina
began to panic. The clerk called for security. Nina produced
a picture of Jacob from her wallet and described what he
was wearing. Wal-Mart employees scattered in all directions,
searching up and down the aisles and near the front of the store,
calling out Jacob's name.

The scene set off something so primal and desperate in
me that I had to get out. I mumbled to Nina that I was going
outside to look. As I stepped through the automatic doors, the
heavy air engulfed me and I stopped by the soda machines,
scanned the front and the parking lot until I could no longer
see through my tears. My hands shook as I lit a cigarette and
inhaled hard, trying to force away the thoughts that swirled in
my head: that Jacob might really be gone, not just lost; that
he'd been taken by strangers and would never see his mother
again. In that moment, I was in the past — in the delivery
room, at the nursery window, in the judge's chambers —
without the protective wall of numbness that had kept me safe
back then.

They found Jacob in the candy section. By the time we
were on the road for home, I was so wrenched I couldn't speak.
In her relief, Nina was chatty enough that no one seemed to
notice.

That evening everyone collapsed in front of the TV, and I
decided that if we were to have any meaningful time together,
I had to get Josh, Marissa, and Naomi out of there. I looked
through the Triple-A book I'd brought along and suggested we

go to Biloxi Beach, Mississippi, only about three hours away, for the weekend.

"Can you get tomorrow off?" I asked Josh. "That way we can stay two nights. I'll pay for our hotel and food. We can kick back, go to the beach."

"They have casinos there," Josh said.

"That part won't be my treat," I said.

We arrived in Biloxi on Friday afternoon, checked into our hotel room, and spent a couple hours relaxing by the pool before heading out for the evening. After dinner, Josh and Marissa wanted to gamble. The only problem was Naomi; minors, even babies, were not allowed on the casino floor. Marissa was underage, but she had an easy time convincing the doorman that she was twenty-one and had left her identification in the hotel room. Not being much of a gambler, I offered to stay with Naomi in the upstairs snack bar while they played.

"Damn, I forgot to get a money order for our land payment," Josh said to Marissa the next morning. "Why didn't you remind me?"

When I suggested that we find a place that sold money orders, he said never mind, since he didn't have the address with him. I offered to stash the two hundred dollars for safekeeping.

"Nah, that's okay," he said. "We won't spend it all."

We started the day at the beach, where they insisted on renting a Jet Ski and left Naomi with me under an umbrella on the shore. Next they wanted to go to the water slide, and again Naomi and I watched while Daddy and Mommy whizzed past us on inner tubes. After that, it was go-carts.

I was beginning to feel like a babysitter. Determined to get what I wanted — time with Josh — I convinced them to go back to the hotel and relax before dinner.

"Tell me more about your life," I said to Josh, as we lounged in the hot tub.

"Like what?"

"Anything. I want to know it all."

"Believe me. You don't want to know." He gave Marissa a knowing look, and she nodded her agreement.

I swallowed. "Nothing you tell me could be worse than what I might imagine."

"Someday I want to write a book. I already know what I'm going to call it: *The Book of Joshua*. Pretty clever, huh? Except I can't type for shit, so I'd have to talk into a tape recorder and have someone transcribe it."

"If you're serious, I can help you. I'm a fast typist and a pretty good editor."

"Phew." Josh rolled his eyes. "There's no way I could say what I need to if I knew you were going to hear it."

"Why? What are you worried about?"

"I've done a lot of bad things," he said, staring into the water, as if something interesting was swimming below. "I'm afraid you won't want me anymore."

"That's crazy, Josh. You're my son. I love you."

In the silence that followed, I tried to picture what could be so bad, and quickly pushed the images away.

"Is there anything I could do to make you stop loving me?" he said.

"What kind of question is that?"

He didn't answer.

A shudder ran through my body. "It would have to be something really horrible. Like if you committed murder. And even then I think I'd still love you. I just might not want to see you."

"Can we change the subject?" Marissa cut in.

I listened as they talked about their hopes for the future: wanting a home in the country, Josh pursuing a cleaner, more-profitable line of work, maybe moving to California. I felt them watching my reactions, and found myself wondering what they expected: encouragement, advice, money?

"I'd love it if you moved to California," I said. "But I know that's not in the cards right now, so I'm not going to pressure you about it."

"I like hearing that you want me closer," he said. "Most of the people in my life have told me to get away. I like feeling wanted."

"Forget about it, Josh," Marissa piped up. "We can't afford to move to California. Our savings account is way down after all the expenses for the baby and all the money we've spent since we found your mom."

I bristled. "What money have you spent because of me?"

She shrugged her shoulders. "The phone bills. And Josh taking time off work."

"Well, maybe we should forgo the gambling tonight, so you guys aren't tempted to spend all that cash."

"But what if we hit big?" Josh said, spreading his arms as if to demonstrate how huge that might be. "We could go home with double or triple our money."

"What would we do instead?" Marissa whined. "This hotel doesn't even have the movie channels. I want to go to the casino across the street, the one that looks like a pirate ship."

Children weren't allowed past the front entrance, and we took turns sitting with Naomi in the outdoor patio area. It didn't take long for me to go through the twenty dollars I'd been willing to donate to the casino, so I spent the most time in the pleasant night air, with my granddaughter sleeping soundly in her stroller.

The next morning after breakfast, they insisted on returning to the casino before we hit the road.

"Just for an hour," Josh begged. "Please, Mommy, *please*."

Again, I took Naomi duty.

"Have you seen Marissa?" Josh asked when he came out an hour and a half later.

"Not since you guys went in." I said. "You wait with Naomi and I'll go round her up."

I found Marissa at the blackjack machines. She was up ten dollars and not inclined to leave, so I sat down at the machine next to her, figuring another few bucks wouldn't hurt. Once we'd both hit zero, we headed out. We heard Naomi wailing as soon as we rounded the corner, and saw Josh pacing around the stroller, red faced and scowling.

"Goddamn it, Marissa, she's been screaming like this for almost an hour!" he roared. "She wouldn't stop and people were looking at me like I'm a kidnapper or something. You're off having fun and I'm stuck here not knowing how to shut her up!"

Marissa tried to interrupt. "Josh…"

"Josh!" I said, staring at my son in disbelief.

"That's it!" Glaring, he lifted Naomi and shoved her into Marissa's arms. "From now on, you take care of her! I'm not going to do squat! I'm doing my part by working. Now you do your part and take care of our baby!"

People stared as we passed on our way to the parking valet. I lagged behind them, scared to get too close but afraid to leave them alone. Josh handed our parking ticket to the valet and continued to seethe until the Jeep appeared. Marissa and Naomi disappeared into the back seat, while Josh slammed the stroller into the folded position and stashed it in the back. His face was still flushed as he jumped behind the wheel, turned the key, and gunned the engine. I slid into the front seat next to him.

My parents did not shout at each other, even when they argued. They rarely yelled at us kids. No matter how mad they were, they made their points and doled out punishments in calm, measured tones.

Josh's father was the first man who had ever yelled at me…

We'd been on our way to visit a couple he knew who lived in married housing on base, where we would make our home after our wedding. Going around a corner, his motorcycle skidded and fell. Luckily, we weren't going very fast. I was thrown onto a patch of grass near the sidewalk and he managed to jump aside before the bike fell over.

"Damn it!" John barked. "You didn't lean into the turn!"

"Yes, I did."

"If you had, this wouldn't have happened! How many times have I told you? Now look at my bike!" He pointed to a scratch in the chrome side pipe. He didn't ask if I was okay…

I stole a glance at Josh. In the harsh light of the sun beating through the windshield, his glowering profile was an exact replica of his father's. I shivered and looked away.

As we made our way onto the highway, Marissa comforted Naomi while Josh intermittently fired off more insults. Once Naomi was asleep, Marissa began to speak in a low voice to Josh, and finally he stopped yelling. I stared out my window in silence, my eyes stinging beneath my lids.

Marissa stuck her head between the front seats. "Hey Mom, it's okay. We just fight sometimes."

I opened my mouth but the words caught in my throat and I began to sob.

"Mom?" Josh said, trying to catch my eye as he drove.

His earlier question reverberated in my head: *Is there anything I could do to make you stop loving me?* I was ashamed of him, appalled and even frightened by his behavior. It hurt to think that my son was the horrible person I had seen fuming in front of the casino. I loved him, but until that moment, it had never occurred to me that I might not *like* him.

I waved them off and we rode for the next hour in silence. Josh and Marissa began to joke with each other. I continued to stare at the passing hillsides and trees, roadside coffee shops and gas stations. I wanted nothing more than to be home. As soon as we got back to Max and Nina's, I thought, I would call the airlines and see whether I could get a flight out that night, no matter what it cost. Then I'd call Henry, pack my things, and take a cab to the airport. But by the time we reached the outskirts of Metairie, I found myself agreeing that we would order a pizza and rent a movie.

I did what I was best at. I turned off my angst and pretended everything was fine until my scheduled flight the following afternoon.

"You can just let me off at the curb," I said, desperate to be gone.

"No," Josh said. "That's not right. We'll park and go in with you."

At the gate, I hugged Josh and Marissa quickly, kissed Naomi's forehead as she slept in her stroller, and hurried onto the plane.

What kind of mother doesn't like her child?

I'd never quite believed my mother loved me, and yet, somehow, I had always thought she liked me. If I couldn't have both, I wondered, which would I choose?

Love, definitely. Love is the basis for good wishes and forgiveness, the thing that keeps mothers hopeful, and children secure.

My answer to Josh's question had been right. Nothing could make me stop loving him. "I might not want to see you," I'd told him. The possibility pierced like a knife in my side.

Chapter 11

LONG-TERM PROJECT

"I'm telling you, he was a raving lunatic!" I ranted at Henry. "He came completely unglued, and then two hours later, he acted like nothing had happened. It was like Jekyll and Hyde.

"And Marissa — what a piece of work! Hitting on me to buy them things, and then trying to make me feel responsible for their not saving any money! Hell, it's no wonder she seemed so out of it. She's seventeen, for crying out loud! All she wants is to have fun, and now she's stuck living at her mother's house, with a madman for a husband, and a baby to care for.

"I'm so worried about Naomi with those two for parents. Thank goodness Nina's there, at least for now."

Henry listened, nodding and grimacing in the appropriate places. He was my only outlet. Soon, my brother, sister, and friends would call, wanting news of my trip and Naomi, and I'd have to don my blissful grandma persona. I couldn't share what had happened during this visit, not even with my dearest friends. They had raised their kids, and their kids were okay. Mine was not.

And it seemed there was more. "Bad things," Josh had said that afternoon in the hot tub, "things you don't want to know." I wondered whether his hesitancy to tell all came from a real concern about my ability to handle the truth or shame for what he had done.

Our phone calls dwindled to once or twice a week.

"How is everything?" I would say.

"Great!" he'd say.

Work was fine. Marissa was fine. Naomi was growing like a weed.

"She misses her grandma though."

"I miss her, too. Give her a hug and kiss from me."

"I'll do it."

Even in the calm, I couldn't forget the storm. I replayed the casino scene until it became as surreal as an ancient nightmare.

"It was eerie how much Josh acted like his father," I said to Henry one evening after dinner. "Do you think it's possible that he inherited John's temper?"

"I guess it could be."

"He's so screwed up. I hate saying that about my own son, but he is. For all the good I see in him, I can feel the turmoil simmering underneath."

"He was a street kid, Deedee. Trust me, I saw plenty of them when I was growing up in New York. He doesn't know how to function in the civilized world."

"What are you saying, that he's like a kid raised by wolves?" I laughed even though nothing was funny.

"Yeah, in a way. He did whatever he had to do to survive. That's what he knows. He wants more out of life now, but I don't think he knows how to get it."

"It wasn't supposed to be this way. They said he'd be better off without me. They *promised*. I never, not for a second, doubted that he had a home and a family and a chance at a good life. They lied to me!"

"No one could have predicted how things would turn out."

"I know damn well I could have done a better job than the Goldbergs!" I said, my chin raised in indignation. "They gave up on him. I would never have done that."

"I always thought I was doing a good job with Jeff, and he still had problems."

"And Jeff's fine now. You got to lay the groundwork for who he would become. The only mark I made on Josh's life was leaving him."

"It's not your fault."

"How do you know? What if all his problems were because of the adoption? What if I *am* to blame?"

"Deedee, Deedee," he said, shaking his head. "There's no way you can know that. Some things could have been better, some might have turned out worse."

His words stopped me. What if John and I had gotten married? His temper might have escalated, and Josh would have witnessed that firsthand. What if I had managed to keep my son on my own? I would have been a working mother, struggling to make ends meet and having little time to spend with my child. Chances are I wouldn't have finished college. I might still have ended up with Don, or someone like him, and taken my baby on the road like the hippie mamas I'd seen during our travels. If I had raised him, I probably would have mimicked my mother and been too strict and rigid, as I had with Jeff. Indeed, Josh might well have been worse off for having stayed with me.

Henry put his hand on mine. "Your son is a long-term project. I know you. You see a problem and you want to jump right in and fix it. But this one is going to take some time."

I squeezed his hand and smiled. "Patience was never one of my strong points."

"But persistence is. Josh has no idea that when his mama sets her mind on something she's not about to give up easily."

I wanted someone or something to blame: society, my parents, the Goldbergs, the institution of adoption. All those years, I believed I'd had no choice, that I had been a victim of circumstance. Now I wasn't so sure.

Although Sandy had not known me as long or as well as some of my other friends, she was the one who was there during most of my pregnancy. She was the one I called.

"I can't stop thinking that maybe I could have done something to keep my baby. Do you remember? Did I have a choice?"

"You were just a child yourself," Sandy said. "You weren't ready to take care of a baby. Besides, there's no way you would have defied your parents back then."

"But did I ever say anything? About wanting to keep him?"

The anxiety in my voice must have rattled Sandy. Suddenly, she sounded nervous, almost defensive. "You acted like it was a done deal."

"I thought it was." I wanted to scream at her: *Wasn't it?* I was a kid, for God's sake! Sandy had said so herself. I'd had no choice but to trust the adults who were supposed to be looking out for me.

Sandy sounded as if she had read my mind. "If I'd known how you felt, I would have helped you. We could have worked things out, even the expenses. I thought you knew that."

Had I? I'd replayed the scenario in my head a thousand times, wondering what might have happened if I'd bucked authority and tried to raise him on my own, foregone continuing my education and gotten a job as a waitress or a sales clerk, put him in day care, and hoped to meet a man who was willing to take on a woman with baggage.

For the first time, I contemplated my own culpability in the loss of my son. I couldn't make John marry me, but I could have done *something*: stood up to my parents, traded in my airline ticket and ran away, asked my friends for help, something. I hadn't asked the Daniels or Sandy to help me. I didn't call Social Services. Instead, I had called a game show, like some loser buying lottery tickets to support his family instead of looking for a job.

Unable to accept what I had to contend with, then or now, I escaped into fantasy. I pictured myself raising Josh. I saw him doing all the right things my friends' kids had done and pondered the rewarding paths he might have taken as a result of my presence. The beautiful images I created by day crept into my dreams. I nurtured them like children, as if they might someday mature into reality and replace the unbearable truth.

I had always thought myself a rational person. Now, six months after my first conversation with Josh, I found myself caught up in the notion that I could undo the past if I believed hard enough. One minute, I was all-powerful, and the next as helpless as I had felt at nineteen.

As I floated between the dark and light of my inner and outer selves, that once-silenced young girl disturbed my sleep and sickened my appetite. Her vigilant guard refused to yield. She threw herself into her work, kept lunch dates with friends, and successfully chatted her way off uncomfortable topics.

I couldn't help but notice the parallel to my pregnancy, when I had fictionalized my letters to keep others from worry. Lying in person tested my skills, but if anyone noticed the circles under my eyes or the sag in my posture, they didn't let on.

Except Henry. His concerned looks told me that he sensed my distress. I couldn't tell him the truth. The few times I tried, my stomach lurched as if I were falling.

Whenever Josh called, I rallied my light side. I welcomed updates on Naomi, but wished he would spare me the details of his family and job problems. He hated his new boss. Marissa and her mother were at each other's throats. He was considering taking a maintenance job on an oil rig in the gulf off Galveston. It would require him being offshore for ten days at a time, and back home the next ten.

"I'm not sure it's a good idea for you to be away from home so long," I said.

"When I'm off, we'll have ten whole days together. Marissa is okay with it. Not to mention, the money is great. This way we'll be able to get our own apartment sooner."

After Josh went offshore, there was no way to reach him directly, and his calls to me were sporadic. Although talking with Marissa had become less rewarding — she seemed bored with everything, including me — I forced myself to call her regularly whenever Josh was away.

A full night's sleep was still a rarity for me. When Josh called at one-thirty in the morning, I panicked, and then fumed.

"I just got off shift and was thinking about you and didn't realize what time it was." He went on about his job and all the things that he and Marissa were able to buy since he was making better money, until I told him I was going back to bed.

"Call me when you're back home, okay? But not in the middle of the night."

When we talked a week later, he said. "I'm thinking about leaving Marissa."

The indifference in his voice was troubling. He could have been deciding what to have for dinner.

"What do you mean? Why would you leave her?"

"I keep wishing I'd found you before I met her, or that I'd never met her," he said. "If it weren't for Marissa and Naomi, I would already be moved out there and we would be together."

"You can't just leave your daughter," I said. "Naomi needs you. You have a responsibility to her."

"Max and Nina will always provide for Naomi," he said. "She'll have a lot more with them than with me."

Hadn't I used the same rationale when I let the Goldbergs take my son? It had been wrong then and it was still wrong.

"Don't you even think about deserting another child," I said, without trying to keep the irritation from my voice. "You already have two out there."

"You had to bring that up!" he said sharply.

"Josh, for crying out loud, you can't keep making babies and then leaving them."

"But I want to live closer to you!"

"Good. Great. So, let's work toward that."

"How about you moving here?"

"Henry has a job, a *career*. We can't just give up our life and move across the country."

"Why not? I'm willing to give up my life to be near you. Marissa and Naomi will be okay. I'll leave them all the money we have, minus my plane ticket."

"Don't even think about it," I said. "I'm not going along with you abandoning your family and showing up on our doorstep, expecting you can just flop here and not support her."

"What if Marissa left me? Maybe she's not happy either."

"Are you saying you're not happy? Is that the real reason you're considering leaving?"

He sighed. "We just don't seem to be clicking like we used to. You know what I mean? The magic is gone."

"The magic doesn't last forever, Josh. That's what gets people together: the chemistry, the lust. After that, if it's going to last, a deeper love takes over — respect, commitment, common goals. Marriage takes work, especially once you have kids."

"It shouldn't be *work*."

"Well, it is. You're building something together, a family, a future." I paused and then took a chance on repeating the advice I'd offered before. "Maybe this offshore job isn't such a good thing. Marissa and you need to be together right now. If your relationship is suffering, then the extra money isn't worth it."

Josh got quiet, as he always did when he didn't like my response or couldn't come up with a retort. After we hung up, I worried that I might have come on too strong. It bothered me that I had forbidden him to come at the outset, that I could not open my home to him unconditionally. But it troubled me more that he would consider walking out on another child.

The word "magic" lingered in my mind. In the beginning, our reunion had felt magical. Now it was getting real, requiring attention and hard work. I had to wonder: at forty-six years old, was I up to the task?

That night, a memory from my sixteenth summer invaded my dreams…

Leanna and I had bicycled to Makapuu Beach, where the ideal body surfing conditions and the bronze-skinned hunks it attracted were renowned. Fancying ourselves hot stuff in our new Tahitian print flower bikinis — mine bright pink and orange, hers lime green and turquoise — we spread our towels on the middle of the expansive beach, sparsely populated for a weekend. For the next two hours, we basked in the salt and suntan oil-scented breezes, until it was time to cool off, and show off, in the surf.

The waves ran high and fast that day, but crested close

enough to shore that we could stand in the waist-deep water while we waited. As each new set approached, we made quick decisions on whether to catch the wave and let it carry us in, or take a breath and duck under.

I came up from a big one and found myself on the other side, beyond where the swells began, the ocean floor well below my reach. Leanna waved to me from the shallower water and I waved back to let her know I was okay. I started to swim in. When I stopped to check my progress, I scanned the beach for my friend and spotted her on the sand, appearing much smaller than she had before. A wall of water slapped my face, forcing salt into my eyes. I shook my head, blinked and strained to focus on the shore. I drew a breath and stroked, harder this time. When I emerged again, I found Leanna farther from where we had left our towels, as she followed my path toward the jagged rocks at the south end of the beach.

My arms ached and a cramp squeezed my right calf.

Don't panic, I commanded myself. Lay back. Float.

I took a deep breath, threw my head back, and willed my torso to the surface. As soon as my arms stopped treading, my body began to sink. My heart pounded and my ears filled with the buzz of one compelling realization:

I'm going to drown.

Dozens of thoughts fired in my head. I would never finish school, never become anything, never see my family again. I wondered how my mom and dad would feel, whether they would be sad, whether they would be mad at Leanna. The thought of my friend hurting made me want to keep swimming, but I could not make my body move. Waves lapped around my head and with each breath I took in less air.

This is it. Nothing more I can do.

A warm numbness engulfed me. The pain in my arms and legs dissolved. I felt myself falling, surrendering to the relentless current below. I disconnected — from my friend, from the water, from staying alive…

I sat straight up in my bed, sweaty and gasping for breath.

"I gave up," I murmured into the dark.

Henry stirred under the covers beside me. Shivering, I slipped out of bed and tiptoed to the living room. Seated on the sofa, I played out the rest of the story of that day in the ocean...

The steady slap of arms stroking the water had snapped me out of my trance. I saw a man swimming parallel to the beach, several yards away.

"Help. Please. I can't get in." My voice was like a whisper against the roar in my ears and I was sure he would not hear.

I felt an arm clamp around my chest, and the rest was a blank. I only remembered tumbling through the surf and landing hard on the sand, and then Leanna running toward me, calling "Are you okay?" The man who saved my life was nowhere in sight...

"You gave up," I admonished myself. "You resigned yourself to dying. Just like you resigned yourself to losing your child."

Henry hadn't given up on Jeff, even when our differences about how to handle his behavior had threatened our new marriage. He had stood by his son, without lowering his expectations. He'd let go when he had to, but even then, he had never stopped believing.

Whether or not being relinquished was at the root of Josh's problems, even if I was not responsible for his troubles, I had to stand by him. As his mother, I owed him that.

Chapter 12

BABY'S FIRST CHRISTMAS

If I were to start fresh with Josh, I needed to replace the mental pictures of my August visit with new, more positive ones.

"Let's invite them for Christmas," I told Henry. "I miss Naomi. And I want you to meet Marissa and tell me what you think. Maybe Jeff can drive up from L.A. to meet Josh."

Since Josh was scheduled to work the holiday, we decided on a mid-December visit and I booked their flights. Two weeks before the trip, Josh called to tell me that he and Marissa were getting a divorce.

"She slept with my best friend while I was out on the rig."

"Oh no! How did you find out?"

"I could tell something was wrong as soon as I got home. She kept saying I was imagining things, but then she broke down and told me. She balled Joey right here in our bed, with our daughter sleeping a few feet away."

"I guess we'd better postpone your trip," I said.

"No! I don't want to."

"What do you mean? Do you still want to come? Will Marissa let you bring Naomi?"

"I mean all of us."

"Let's just hold off. I can get a credit on the tickets. Maybe you and Marissa will work things out and you can come later. If not, then you can come by yourself another time."

"Marissa will never forgive me if she finds out our trip got cancelled because I told you what's going on. She's never been to California and it means a lot to her."

"And why am I supposed to care about what Marissa wants?"

"Because you care about me."

"Josh," I said, exhaling heavily. "I can't believe you still want her to come when you're about to get divorced. It'll be awkward for everyone."

"To tell you the truth, I was hoping you could help us sort things out. I still love her and maybe talking to you will help us save our marriage."

What? One minute he was adamant about getting a divorce; the next, he wanted to work things out. "If that's what you want, then you two should see a marriage counselor," I said.

"I got my fill of counseling as a kid. It never did me one bit of good."

I told Josh I had to discuss it with Henry, and I'd let him know what we decided.

"I don't want Marissa here," I told Henry.

"Okay. Tell them not to come."

"But I've got things planned. I already sent out invitations for the open house. Everyone's looking forward to seeing Naomi."

"So cancel the party. It's not the end of the world."

"I know."

"From what you've told me, I'm not crazy about having them here at all, let alone under these conditions."

"What if they end up getting a divorce? Even with what Marissa's done, I have to stay on good terms with her so I can see my granddaughter. In any case, I might not see Naomi again for a long time."

"It's your call," he said. "Either way, we'll make the best of it."

A rumbling in my gut told me not to do it, but I decided to let our original plans stand — not because I thought I could help them save their marriage, or that I even wanted to. All I wanted was to see my son and my granddaughter.

When I called Josh to tell him, he said, "Sometimes I feel like you're holding back."

A flash of heat hit my face like an accusation. "I don't know what you mean."

"You say you love me, and I believe you. But it's like you're hesitating, like you're scared to open up."

"I think I've been very open."

"Maybe I'm not saying it right." He paused. "I hope you won't take this the wrong way, but it seems like unless things are going perfect, you can't deal with it."

No, wait, that's not me. That's my mother. She was the withholder. She's the one I could never please. Every time I failed to meet her expectations, I felt her acceptance — and her love — being pulled farther from my grasp.

"You give me a lot to deal with, Josh," I managed to croak. "I worry about you. And Naomi."

"It feels good having someone worry about me."

"Oh, thanks a lot."

"No, really, that's what mothers do. They worry, right?"

"Well, this is all new to me. I've never been anyone's mother before."

"You were Jeff's."

"Not really." I sighed. "I'm doing my best, Bub."

Long-term project, I reminded myself, and then said to Josh, "We'll figure it all out. Anyway, I can't wait to see you."

With the expense of their airfare, the party, and the sightseeing we would do, Henry and I had agreed to cut back on Christmas gifts.

The present I most wanted to get for Josh would not cost much. I wanted to give him his original birth certificate: the one with his birth name, where I was listed as his mother. Not having searched for him, I didn't know most states had laws that prevented birthparents and adoptees from obtaining any sort of documentation.

I called the State of California Vital Records Department and punched in numbers until I reached a clerk who handled birth and death records. I explained that I needed a copy of my son's birth certificate.

"His date of birth?" she asked.

"May twenty-fourth, 1970."

"Last name?"

"Janson."

"First name?"

"Erick Alan."

"I'm not finding an Erick Alan. What county?"

"Los Angeles," I said. "Maybe it's under Goldberg. Joshua. His name was changed after he was adopted."

"He was adopted?"

"Yes."

"Why didn't you mention that before? Those records are *sealed*. I can't give you any information."

"I don't need any information. I know what's in the records. I *gave birth* to him." I paused to let my deliberate sarcasm sink in. "Look, I just want a copy of his birth certificate."

"Like I said, Ma'am, those records are sealed. They can only be released by court order."

"Court order?"

"Yes, Ma'am. If there's a compelling reason, like a medical emergency, the adopted person can petition the court to open the records. Would you like me to send you the forms?"

"No. Thanks." I started to hang up. "Wait! So, can my son get a copy of his own certificate?"

"Not without a court order."

"So who can? Without a court order."

"Only the adoptive parents or legal guardian. They must appear in person, with identification that proves they are the child's parents as stated on the amended certificate."

"He's not a child. He's twenty-six."

"Doesn't matter. That's the law."

"Unbelievable," I muttered as I hung up the phone. I thought back to the day Josh had shown me his revised birth certificate. I hadn't simply been removed. I had been obliterated.

Shortly after Mother's Day, I had asked Josh for his adoptive father's address, telling him that I wanted to take a shot at getting his baby pictures. The only childhood picture he had was the one of him and Jonathan that he had sent me in his first letter.

"He won't give you anything," Josh said.

"Maybe not," I said. "But it never hurts to ask."

I couched my request in a letter of condolence for Mrs. Goldberg's passing, explaining that Josh and I had recently met, and expressing my gratitude to them for having raised him. Almost six months had gone by with no response. Any chance of surprising Josh with a baby album for Christmas was gone.

It's just as well, I thought. If I had a gift for Josh, even if its value was more sentimental than monetary, I'd have to get something for Marissa. I already had a pile of presents for Naomi, including a frilly burgundy party dress, lacy tights, and patent leather shoes for her to wear at our party. I bought three red-and-white felt Christmas stockings and used a gold glitter pen to add their names. These I would fill with small wrapped gifts so Josh and Marissa would have something to open. To prepare them, I announced that we were only buying for the kids this year.

"What do you mean?" Josh whined. "Me and Marissa are kids, too."

"Seriously, Josh. We need to cut back. You shouldn't buy us anything either."

"But we already got presents for you guys."

"Really, you shouldn't have. You should save your money."

"Too late," he said.

My anxiety mounted as I readied the house, stocked up on groceries, and bought a few presents for Josh and Marissa. What most people considered "the most wonderful time of the year" had been the most angst-ridden when I was growing up — especially once the Santa myth was dispelled, and the responsibility for delighting others and being delighted shifted to our own young shoulders.

Memories of Christmases past clicked through my head like a slideshow. I saw three little faces, waiting breathlessly through breakfast for the moment of truth, when we were allowed to unwrap our gifts and find out how good we had really been.

I saw my mother's frown when my sister opened the tie meant for my father, all because I had insisted that, at six, I could read well enough to pass out the gifts and then accidentally given the present tagged *Daddy* to *Debby*. I heard her scolding us for tossing the tinsel onto the tree instead of carefully placing each strand. I saw myself grown, refusing to let others hang the tinsel, lest the tree turn out anything short of perfect.

I held no illusions that Josh and Marissa's visit would be perfect. But since this was Naomi's first Christmas — and Josh's first, I learned, even though he hadn't practiced Judaism in years — I was determined to give it my all, in spite of my promise to Henry to keep costs down.

Once they arrived at the airport and I saw no traces of tension between Josh and Marissa, I began to relax.

"We're going to have so much fun," I gushed on the drive home from the airport. "Tomorrow we'll get a tree and decorate it. Then I'm making a turkey dinner and we'll open presents. We also have to take Naomi to the mall and get her picture with Santa."

"Don't forget," Josh said. "We need to set aside some time for you to talk to me and Marissa about our marriage."

Henry gave me a sideways glance from the driver's seat. I hadn't mentioned Josh's request that I counsel them. I shrugged and turned back around to Josh and Marissa.

"We'll have plenty of time to just hang out and talk," I said. "Jeff arrives on Saturday, and that night is the big party."

Our house was small: two bedrooms, the second barely adequate for one guest, let alone three. I'd considered offering Josh and Marissa the master bedroom, which had plenty of space for their luggage and the portable crib I had borrowed from a friend. But since Henry had to work most of the days they would be here, it didn't seem fair to inconvenience him. Given the shortage of space and the extra gear required for an infant, I'd expected some degree of chaos. What I hadn't anticipated was Josh and Marissa's sloppiness.

Clothes and towels ended up in a heap wherever they were last used, dirty dishes rarely made their way back to the kitchen, and I'd find wadded-up disposable diapers anywhere that they might have been removed from Naomi's tush. Caught between astonishment at their lack of consideration and the rules of propriety that had been drummed into me as a child, I was at a loss for how to react. The first two days, I picked up after them without a word. Next, I tried hinting.

"Henry will be home soon," I said, straightening up the living room with exaggerated motions that I hoped would produce some guilt.

"Relax, Mom," Josh said. "Don't you know it's impossible to keep a house neat with a baby around?"

"Here." I dropped a pile of Naomi's discarded clothes in his lap. "Put these in your room."

"What are we going to do tonight?" Marissa yawned and stretched out on the couch. "Can we rent a movie?"

It was tempting: put on a video and plop them down in front of the TV, like toddlers who had to be distracted so the adults could get some peace. But I didn't give in. "We've been out all day. Let's just spend a quiet evening."

Henry had no poker face when he was irritated. Even after almost fifteen years of marriage, his displeasure unnerved me, whether or not I had caused it. I knew that if Josh and Marissa's presence became intolerable to him, my resolve would falter and my ability to create an enjoyable, if not flawless, visit would be threatened. In addition to restoring order before Henry arrived home from work, I refrained from complaining and did whatever I could to mitigate his grievances.

"Today went well," I said as we got ready for bed after our first full day with the kids.

"They seemed disappointed that we didn't get them more presents," Henry said.

"You think so?" I said, even though it was an accurate statement. "Well, too bad if they are. It's not like we haven't spent plenty on them already."

I didn't tell him how miserable our trip into San Francisco had been, how they had carped at each other every minute that they weren't occupied by cable cars, bridges, and snacks. How Josh had pulled out his wallet to buy tacky souvenirs, but hadn't offered to pay for our lunch. I didn't tell him how Marissa had rolled her eyes at me when we went to exchange Naomi's party shoes for a bigger size and the store was out of black that matched her dress and I got the white ones instead of driving around town to find the perfect shoes. Even so, by day four, Henry's discomfort was palpable, and I surrendered to my own frustration.

I whispered my grievances after Josh and Marissa had gone to bed. "They are so self-centered. It's like they expect to be entertained every second. Then, they step back whenever it comes time to pay for something. Not like I didn't anticipate paying, but they never even pretend to want to pitch in, even around the house. They sit on their asses and watch me do everything." I paused to let my heart rate slow. "I'm so sorry, Hon."

"You have nothing to be sorry for."

"I know. But I'm the one who insisted on having them."

The next morning, the toilet in the guest bathroom backed up. Since we were stuck at home, waiting for the rooter service to clear the clog, Josh decided that would be a good time for the three of us to hash out their marital problems. While Naomi napped, I sat with Josh and Marissa at the dining room table, resolved to just listen.

"I still love you and I want us to hold on to our marriage," Josh began. He sat tall in the chair and looked straight into Marissa's eyes. "I'm willing to forgive and forget and move on from here."

"Okay," she said, meeting his gaze.

"I'm willing to work and pay the bills. But I want you to do your part, like pay more attention to taking care of Naomi and our home."

"A baby is a full-time job." She slouched in her chair and pouted. "I don't always have time to clean."

"But you have time to hang out with your friends," he said angrily. "Not to mention, bang my friends."

"Wait, Josh," I interrupted. "Accusations aren't productive."

"Yeah," Marissa said, leaning forward with a smug look. "I thought you were going to forgive and forget."

"Come on, you guys. Just stick with saying what you feel and what you need from each other."

"I need you to promise you'll be faithful," Josh said. "And honest with me."

Marissa frowned. "I can try, but I can't promise."

"You can't promise not to cheat on me?"

"No, I meant the honest part. You knew that when you married me. I've always been a liar. It's who I am."

Josh shook his head and looked over at me.

"Well, there you go, " I said, pushing my chair back from the table. "You've told Marissa what you need and she's given you her answer. You know what you can expect and now you have to decide whether you can live with that."

I wanted to throw her out right then, even though Josh surely would have left with her. No way their marriage will last, I thought. And despite the consequences for Naomi, I was glad.

The plumber knocked on the door and announced that he had cleared the line. "Here's the culprit," he said, pointing to a soiled tampon on the ground next to the sewer drain. I had started my period the night they arrived. I couldn't help but wonder: *If Josh lived here and I saw him regularly, would I bleed to death?*

"Just three more days," I muttered to Henry.

Jeff's arrival for the weekend created the diversion we all needed. Having his own son around lightened Henry's mood and I busied myself with preparations for the party that evening. The thought of a crowd of friends adoring my granddaughter made it easy to slip back into the host and mother I wanted to be.

The morning they were to return to New Orleans, the anger I had repressed all week broke free. The night before, Marissa had asked me to wake them in time to get showered and packed, but to do it quietly so Naomi would stay asleep for as long as possible. At six a.m., I knocked on the guest room door, opened it and softly said, "Josh, Marissa, time to get up."

They both raised their heads and looked at me.

"Are you awake?"

Josh nodded. I put on the coffee, jumped in the shower, and got dressed. By then it was six-thirty and there was no sign of them.

Suddenly I became enraged at how I had catered to them, responded to their every need, and allowed them to ignore me. I stomped down the hall to their room and flung open the door. They had fallen back to sleep.

"Hey!" I shouted.

They sat straight up in the bed, looking dazed. Naomi stirred in her crib.

"You wanted it quiet, and I gave it to you quiet. It's now six-thirty." I turned around, walked out and shut the door hard.

I spent the next forty-five minutes in our bedroom, sitting on the bed, drinking coffee and watching Henry get dressed. I heard Josh and Marissa moving in the hall. My heart began to race and my breathing quickened as if I were being pulled down.

How could I have been so careless to have let myself lose control?

I'd been angry before, with my parents, friends, boyfriends, even Henry, and yet I had always managed to hold it back. Sometimes I tried to state what was bothering me, calmly and clearly, but the feelings were so overwhelming that I'd had to retreat. If I kept going, I might not be able to stop. I might explode. I had been right to fear my rage. Now I was drowning in it.

I heard the sound of suitcases being dragged out to the living room. I waited another five minutes and then walked out to the kitchen. Josh was sitting at the table, while Marissa finished getting Naomi ready.

"I guess you Californians really aren't too good in the morning until you've had your coffee," he said in a tone that was half-teasing, half-accusing.

"I guess not," I said. Still angry, and ashamed for letting it show, I couldn't look at him. I busied myself at the sink.

No one said much during the hour-plus drive to San Francisco Airport. The mood was tense as we waited at the gate. The adults squirmed more than Naomi did, shifting our weight, avoiding each other's eyes.

"I'm glad you came," I said, which wasn't as true as the sadness I felt now that they were leaving. I kept waiting for one of them to say thank you, wishing for those two words that might have softened my rancor. But they didn't come.

"What was going on this morning?" Josh asked when he called that evening to let me know they'd made it home. "You seemed pissed off or something."

"I didn't want to get into it. "I was just tired, Josh. It was a busy week." I wished he'd say good night and hang up.

"Things seemed to be going pretty well until the last couple days. Then last night and this morning, you hardly said a word."

He'd opened the door for me to speak my mind. I hesitated, considering what to say. *No accusations,* I reminded myself. *Just say what you're feeling.*

"I did my best to make everything nice for you guys and I don't feel like you appreciated it. I even sat and listened to you and Marissa when you asked me to."

"You're my mother. I shouldn't have to *ask.*"

Without thinking, I lashed out. "Fuck you!"

A palpable silence hung in the lines. "I can't believe you said that."

"I shouldn't have. I'm sorry. Look Josh, I can't talk to you right now. I'll call in a couple days."

After we hung up, I slumped onto the edge of the bed and stared down at the floor. It was the exact spot where I'd been sitting when we had talked for the first time almost nine months before. Tonight, the first blush — the magic — of our initial connection vanished.

Chapter 13

MY MOTHER'S NAME

In the wake of Josh's departure, a childhood nightmare returned...

Dad, Mom, Debby, Bob, and I are standing in the middle of a western saloon. Ghostly figures — cowboys, gamblers, and barmaids — hover in the background, oblivious to our presence. Above us, a huge crystal chandelier starts to tremble and loosen from the high ceiling, but our feet won't move. We huddle together, helpless to do anything except stare up at the tinkling mass, which suddenly breaks free and plunges toward us...

I awoke just before it crashed, as I always had, sweat-soaked and panting.

The dream reminded me how fragile my family had seemed when I was young, and how fragile we still were — like a mobile of intricate glass figures struggling to maintain its balance. As a child, I'd had a vague sense that someone was missing. Later, that someone had become Josh. *Is there more?* I wondered. *Something I've forgotten? Or was the nightmare's reappearance simply a manifestation of my anxiety?*

Feeling stuck between my parents, who had yet to acknowledge Josh's existence, and the son I was unable to please, I did the only thing I could think of that might lift us out of the depths, something I'd never done before. I composed a newsy letter to include with our Christmas cards:

1996 was quite a year for us. I became a "new mom" and a grandmother all in the first six months. In March, I was reunited with the son I gave up for adoption in 1970. Joshua and his wife, Marissa, live outside New Orleans. I flew there to meet Josh for the first time over Easter weekend; then he came here in May to celebrate his birthday with us. I went back again in August — after my angel of a granddaughter, Naomi Ruth, was born on June thirteenth — and the three of them just left after a pre-Christmas visit, which is partly why this is so late getting to you. There is no way I can express in this short letter how much having Josh in my life means to me and to Henry as well, and how grateful I am for this second chance.

While Josh was here, Jeff came up from Los Angeles. It was just two years ago that he came back into our lives, and nineteen months ago that our first grandchild, Jordan, was born. Jordan is an adorable, curly-headed little ball of fire. He was here with Jeff for Thanksgiving, along with Henry's mom from New York, and Henry's brother Ron and his family from L.A. With the sudden expansion of our family, our lives haven't been quite the same — in lots of wonderful ways.

I sent the letter to everyone except my father's relatives. When his words replayed in my head — "it would kill your mother" — I stopped to consider whether I was excluding them out of obedience and decided I was not. But I still felt a twinge of guilt. They were my extended family and I had warm memories of visiting my grandparents' farm as a child. My grandmother, Lydia, died when I was seven, and my grandfather, Henry, passed away shortly after I graduated from high school. But I still had uncles, aunts, and cousins who were always excited to see me, no matter how much time had gone by between visits.

My mother had no family except us. She had been an only child, she'd told us, and very young when both her parents died. I thought it was odd that she didn't have a middle name — just Catherine, she said. After she married my father, she started using her maiden name as her middle. Mom didn't like answering questions, so I knew little about her life except that she was from Virginia — partly because she was so proud of it, but also because of her Southern accent.

I didn't know her parents' names until just before I married Henry. There were little family-tree diagrams for the bride and groom in my wedding memory book, right next to the places for our respective baby pictures.

"I need your mother's and father's names for my book," I said, showing her the pages as if to justify my request.

"Edward Malcolm Kendall and Sarah Agnes Utterback," she said.

I dutifully printed them across from my paternal grandparents' names, grateful that she had answered without complaint.

My next attempt to learn more about my mother — six years later — did not go as well. Mom and Dad were passing through San Francisco, as they did often on their way to and from winter escapes from Alaska. This particular time, Mom handed me two rolls of film and asked me to get them developed while they were gone. There were some of Bob and his kids, she said, if I wanted to look at them.

The day before they were to return, I picked up the photos. Among the usual shots of Becky, Eric, and Emily posing with exaggerated grins, were several pictures of a woman who looked like my mother. I thought it *was* my mother until I saw them both in the same picture, sitting side by side with matching eyes and smiles.

I couldn't wait for the next evening when Henry and I would meet my parents for dinner at their hotel. They were barely off the elevator when I began questioning her.

"I got your pictures," I said, shuffling through the prints. "Who's this woman who looks like you?"

"That's my sister," Mom said, tossing off the words as if I'd asked what city we were in.

"Wait a minute — what do you mean sister? I thought you didn't have any family."

"Well, I guess you don't know everything, do you?" She lifted her chin and pursed her lips, signaling that as far as she was concerned the discussion was over.

I looked at Dad and, finding no help, turned back to my mother.

"Did you know you had a sister? Why didn't you tell us?"

"Why don't you stop being so nosy and just mind your own business?"

My jaw dropped, but hers was set as she continued walking toward the restaurant. For a few drawn-out seconds I thought about turning around and leaving. Even by my mother's standards, this was above and beyond cold. Henry's lips tightened as if he were holding back a rush of expletives. We looked at my father in unison. He stared after my mother, his mouth twisting the way it always did when Mom behaved badly.

"The food's pretty good here," he said.

As usual, I soothed myself with the possibility that I had misunderstood, even hallucinated the whole exchange. I let Dad change the subject and we followed Mom into the dining room. Henry and I sat quietly through dinner while Mom and Dad chatted enthusiastically about their trip to Mexico.

Once Henry and I were in the car to go home, I let my rage fly. "Do you believe her? God, I wanted to just walk out! I should have!"

"I'd have been right behind you."

"I'm so sick of her crap! Why the hell would she give me that film, knowing what was on it and then act like I'm out of line for asking for an explanation?"

"We're talking about your mother. Why does she do anything?"

"Well, you know what? If she doesn't care enough to tell me what's going on, then I don't care to know."

I was still seething a few weeks later when I received a manila envelope from my brother. He wrote about meeting Aunt Mabel while she was visiting Mom and Dad. By then my mother and her sister had been corresponding for two years. Mom had kept this from all of us — even my father — until Mabel was due to arrive in Anchorage. Bob had included copies of genealogical information that our aunt had sent him since.

Oh no, you don't! I said to myself after a cursory glance at the pages. *I wasn't invited and I'm not going to play.* I put everything back into the envelope and stuffed it into the back of the file cabinet.

That same year my son had turned eighteen and I'd kept my own secret, contacting the registry in hopes of finding him and telling no one except Henry and Sandy. With Josh back in my life, I was determined to free my private ghosts, even if my mother did not.

Just before Christmas, I received a card from an address I didn't recognize — someone with the last name Kendall in Virginia. The handwriting was almost identical to my mother's: "I hardly know where to begin," Aunt Mabel wrote. Somewhere in the back of my mind, I knew that my brother and she had stayed in touch, but I hadn't dealt with my aunt's existence on any conscious level since Mom had pissed me off that night eight years before.

"Your brother dropped quite a bombshell in his last letter. He said that you were oh so happy at finding your child and grandchild. I sense a painful story here. Would you share it with me? Also, would you give me the names, dates and places of birth, and names of parents of both Joshua and Naomi? After all, they are part of you and our family tree."

She'd enclosed the documentation that she and one of my cousins had gathered on the family — pages very similar to the ones Bob had sent. I scanned them and returned to her letter.

"I am trying to complete the information on the nine children of Edward Malcolm and Sarah Agnes Kendall."

Nine? My mother had eight sisters and brothers? I had aunts and uncles, and who knows how many cousins. I had a whole other family that had been withheld from me!

"I'm afraid I may be opening a Pandora's box in writing to you, but my desire to know the family is overriding my reluctance. I know your mother would be furious with me if she knew. I don't want to be a traitor, but I feel I must make contact with living relatives. I want my children to meet, or at least know who and where their cousins are.

"The death of a father is a terrible thing. It sure destroyed this family."

What did she mean? My mother had told us that both her

parents had died, and I'd assumed at the same time, like in a fire or some other disaster, which would explain why she'd been raised by another couple.

I delved into the stack of papers. There was a genealogical chart with horizontal and vertical lines. At the top were Edward Malcolm Kendall, 1884-1929, and Sarah Agnes Utterback Kendall, 1887-1962. My grandmother hadn't died until 1962, the year I had turned twelve.

Nine lines hung vertically from Edward and Sarah's, each with a name I'd never seen before: Clifton Malcolm, Emma Roberta, John Alvin, Dorothy Lee, Thomas Flatford, Roy Jackson, Mayme Catherine, Winfred Rudacille, and Ella Mabel. On separate typed sheets, under headings that read, *First Child of Edward Malcolm and Sarah Agnes Kendall, Second Child, Third Child* and so on, were lists for each sibling, with their spouses, children and grandchildren. According to the chart, only the last four — Roy, Mayme, Winfred and Mabel — were still living. Under the seventh child, Mayme Catherine, were my father's name, and mine, Debby's, Bob's and those of his three children.

This had not been a simple omission. My mother had *lied* to me, to all of us! She had been six when her father died and a grown-up married woman by the time her mother passed away. There was no way she didn't know that she had brothers and sisters. Even her name hadn't been true. *Mayme Catherine Kendall*, the paper said. *Mayme* — the name made me snort. It was so old-fashioned and strange to me.

That evening I called my brother.

"I got a letter from Aunt Mabel today," I said. "She sent a bunch of family history stuff. There were nine of them, Bob. Mom was one of nine kids."

"Yeah, I know."

Annoyed by his nonchalance, I swallowed and pressed on. "Bob, Mom's mother didn't die until 1962. Our grandmother was around for years after we were born."

"Really? I didn't look at the papers that closely."

"Why didn't you tell me how big this was?"

"You didn't seem interested. That one time when I came to visit you, I brought it up and you stopped me. You said you didn't want to know."

He was right. I'd been so angry with my mother that I'd shut my eyes and ears to anything even remotely related to the family she had denied. But that had been a long time ago — before Josh had come back into my life. I had changed my mind.

I called Aunt Mabel.

Her voice was so like my mother's — slow and reedy — that I was immediately taken aback. But the longer we spoke, the more I sensed a willingness — that my mother did not possess — to speak and hear the truth. For an hour, I rode the ebb and flow of Mabel's drawl, delighted in her good-natured laugh, as we traded answers to each other's questions.

She explained that my grandfather had died suddenly at age forty-four, leaving my grandmother with eight children between the ages of two and seventeen, and another — Mabel herself — on the way. At some point during the next year, Sarah Agnes had scattered her children to the winds. The oldest two went out into the world to find work or marry. The younger ones were placed with whomever was willing to take them. My mother became the only child of the Nelsons, who were highly respected in the community and owned the general store. Born two months premature, Mabel had not been expected to live.

"But here I am at sixty-seven, still plugging along."

Sarah Agnes handed the sickly infant over to her twin sister, who already had eleven children of her own. At age two, she was fostered out to an older couple, who abused her physically and emotionally until she escaped by getting married at seventeen.

A few of the Kendall siblings had regular contact, most knew where to find each other, and by the 1950s everyone except my mother had reconnected. She'd left town the day after she graduated from high school, moved to Washington

D.C., and not been seen or heard from again until Mabel located her forty years later.

"Why would she do that?"

"Maybe she too had something to escape."

I didn't understand what had been so shameful or painful that she'd felt compelled to hide it from her husband and children, but it was clear that she'd done what she felt she must to survive.

Maybe there was more. What if the reason she'd disappeared so quickly had been that she was pregnant with some high school boyfriend's child? What if she too had been forced to give up a baby? And even if she hadn't, how could she — after losing her father, being abandoned by her mother, and sent to live with another family — have allowed me to relinquish mine?

But perhaps that's *why* she could.

Chapter 14

CIRCLES

As eager as I was to share the news of our expanding family circle with Josh, I couldn't bring myself to talk to him about anything important. Since he and Marissa had moved into an apartment in one of Max's investment properties, our phone calls had diminished in both frequency and substance. When he was home from the oil rig, they were hard to reach, and when we did connect, it often sounded as if I were interrupting their partying.

I tried to convince myself that Josh wasn't pulling away, that he was just busy with his work and family, or that we had finally arrived at that "normal" place we'd joked about in the beginning. But I knew the truth. He was disappointed in me. We were both disappointed.

As I pondered our early conversations and visits, it became clear to me that Josh had envisioned an instant bond, as natural and effortless as that of a mother and her newborn. Although I wished it were so, I'd had no such expectation. I'd had eight years more than he: waiting for the registry, dreaming of what might happen once we were matched, and concocting scenarios where disillusionment and rejection were as likely as satisfaction and acceptance. Given our roles at the point of separation, the difference in our perceptions began to make sense. Josh had always thought of me as a grown woman, while I still pictured him as an innocent baby. In his dreams, I was the nurturing mother, the womb where his life began — the place to which he longed to return. In mine, he was both miracle and mistake, and now a mystery.

There would be no normalcy for us. But after learning my mother's history, my mission to wipe the cobwebs of secrecy out of our family closet gained momentum.

After many more letters and conversations, I gave Aunt

Mabel the go-ahead to share the facts about my son and granddaughter with the other aunts and uncles and my cousins, warning her that my parents would not be pleased. When Dad had cautioned me against telling his relatives, he had assumed correctly that I'd had no contact with Mom's family. I knew he'd widen the safety net if he knew of my communications with the Kendalls.

Josh had said he'd always wanted a big family and I was going to give it to him. I decided to reestablish contact with my father's relatives.

Uncle Jerry and his wife Freda, their daughter Llyn, and her husband Phil, gathered at my Aunt Barbara's for an early supper on the Sunday that Henry and I visited. For the first hour, I mingled nervously, unsure of where to start. Once or twice I thought about scrapping the whole plan. Finally I noticed Uncle Jerry and Aunt Barbara standing together off to the side — my father's older brother and sister, whose eyes never failed to light up when they saw me — and I knew I'd found my chance.

Afraid if I paused I'd never get it out, I said in a rush, "I have something important to tell you. When I was nineteen, I got pregnant. I had a boy and I gave him up for adoption. Last year, we found each other and he's back in my life. His name is Joshua. I have a granddaughter, too — Naomi — she was born in June."

I waited for alarm to harden the gentle curves of their elderly features. Uncle Jerry's pale blue eyes welled. Aunt Barbara blinked in quick succession, as she often did, and the corners of her mouth lifted in an understanding smile. Our three pairs of eyes locked in a loving gaze, and I knew I had done the right thing.

"I'm glad you told us," Uncle Jerry said in his usual unruffled and soft-spoken manner. "We love you and nothing will ever change that."

"Thank you," I said and leaned in to give them each a hug.

It was strange and wonderful, hearing those words from

this man who looked so much like my father, with his deep laugh lines, full lips, and the trademark long Janson ears. My heart warmed at the compassion on my aunt's face, a woman whose late husband had been a minister at the church where she played the organ and who had followed God's laws to the letter. I relaxed, happily answered their questions, and took out the pictures I'd brought of Josh, Marissa, and Naomi. Soon my news had spread to everyone else in the room.

Aunt Barbara pushed her wire-rimmed glasses higher on the bridge of her nose. Her head of silver-blond curls bobbed as she spoke. "I want to tell you something I learned after your Uncle Milton passed away." She paused. "Don't look back. Just take things from here."

Her words reminded me of what Josh had said during our first visit, when I had broken down in the park — that we should forget the past and only look forward.

On the drive home, I told Henry how empowered I felt to have finally come clean. "I don't know why I was nervous. They were so accepting. I feel like a huge weight has been lifted."

"I think your father would have reacted the same way, if it weren't for your mom," he said. "These are his people. He's bound to feel like they do."

I reminded him of what my brother had told me after visiting Mom and Dad in Tucson. Dad had pulled him aside to ask what he thought about my reunion with Josh.

"I told him I think it's great," Bob said. "And he said, 'I do, too. But your mother believes what's buried should stay that way.'"

My first reaction had been relief at hearing Dad's true feelings. But the longer I thought about it, the madder I got, that my father couldn't tell me himself, that he let Mom's opinions dictate his response.

"He knows better," I told Henry. "He could help her instead of just going along with her bullshit."

"Maybe he's trying. You don't know that he isn't."

"Then why can't he tell me so? Why hasn't he said, 'Your mother's having a problem with this, but I support you and I'm doing my best to turn her around?' I'll tell you why. He's never sided with any of us kids over Mom. And he never will."

However I had resented my mother's past behavior, I felt as if she had an excuse. I might never know the full story — whether losing her parents had been the pivotal point of no return or if there was more to the story. One thing I was sure about: my father did not deserve the same reprieve. My anger shifted and swelled with fresh fuel to burn. But my tenuous relationship with Josh still consumed me, and I had little time to tend other fires.

After our Christmas party, where I had painted a perfect picture of our reunion, I found it increasingly difficult to talk to my friends. There was no way to answer, "How are you? How are Josh and Naomi?" when everything felt so far from "fine." I couldn't bring myself to tell them about Josh's marital problems or how unsettled their visit had left me. I was terrified of what I might see in their reactions, that behind a "Oh, I'm so sorry" look they'd be thinking, "What did you expect? You didn't keep him; you gave him to strangers." Or worse, that they would think him a "bad seed" when I was so close to believing he might be.

In the glow of early reunion, I'd loved talking about Josh, sharing every bit of news with anyone who would listen. Now I dreaded it and found myself quickly switching the topic to Jeff and Jordan, who were living a regular and reportable life, with whom we had steady contact, pictures and positive news. Listening to my friends talk about their kids' achievements and plans filled me with jealousy. They had what I wanted — children they could be proud of and excited for, instead of disappointed in and afraid for. It wasn't just for me; Josh had missed out as well. These promising young people became walking, talking reminders of what I believed should have been.

I was at an all-time emotional low in January when I

received another life-altering phone call. Jacquie and I had
known each other for several years, but mostly through
business, so we hadn't revealed much of our personal lives.
"I've been meaning to call ever since I got your Christmas
letter," she said. "Did you know that I'm adopted?"

I hadn't. She said that a few years before, she had searched
for and found her birth family. We exchanged stories and
finally I confessed to being an emotional wreck.

"I thought giving up my baby was the hardest thing I'd
ever done," I told her. "But this is even harder."

She told me about a local organization called PACER —
the Post Adoption Center for Education and Research — that
she'd found when she was searching. They offered support
groups for both adoptees and birthmothers.

"Birthmother," I repeated. I didn't realize there was a term
for women who had given up children.

"Reunion is an emotional roller coaster for everyone
involved," Jacquie said. "You need all the help you can get."

It hadn't occurred to me that there might be others out
there who understood. I had never met another birthmother. For
all I knew, I might have been the only one on the planet, except
that I had met and known of so many adoptees, there had to be
others. They were as invisible to me as I was to them, afraid to
show themselves, like humans hiding from the alien pod people
in sci-fi movies.

For years before I had found Josh, movies about adoption
and reunion had popped up on TV. They were like magnets
pulling me in, even when they were mediocre or downright
dreadful. The ones that involved birthmother-versus-adoptive-
parents custody battles were the hardest to watch. As strange
as it seemed, I often found myself rooting for the adoptive
parents, especially when they'd had the child for years. I'd
think to myself, *What is that woman doing, disrupting that
poor little girl or boy's life? She made her decision and she'll
just have to live with it.* It was as if I were lecturing myself.
Only when the woman in the movie had yet to relinquish and

was having doubts did my gut wrench and I wanted to scream at her, "Don't do it!"

"Why do you do this to yourself?" Henry asked me once while I sat riveted to the screen.

I couldn't explain my fascination. Maybe it was some bizarre sort of validation. These stories provided a rare opportunity to witness situations like mine, to see how others felt and try those feelings on for size.

Jacquie recommended a number of books. I bought the one with the title that resonated — *Birthbond* by Judith Gediman and Linda Brown — and read it cover to cover in less than two days. Even the bad news about adoption reunion was welcome. Anything to help me understand.

Hundreds of other birthmothers had reported having the same feelings and concerns during reunion. They too had felt overwhelmed by guilt for having given up their children and by the fear that they might lose them again. Grateful for a second chance, they were obsessed with doing everything "right," which made them hesitant to express themselves too openly, set boundaries, or refuse any demand their adult child might make. Women who learned that their son or daughter had a good life seemed to find greater serenity in reunion than those who made unhappy discoveries. Feeling betrayed by a system that had assured them their child would have a better life without them, they tended to take on the responsibility for "fixing" their grown child's problems.

Suddenly, I wasn't alone.

"Listen to this," I called to Henry, whenever I happened upon an interesting passage:

Female adoptees are much more likely to search than males.

The greatest number of adoptions ever recorded was in 1970, the year I gave up Josh.

It's not uncommon for adoptees to "repeat the sins of their birthparents." Mostly girls getting pregnant at the same age as their birthmother did, even when they don't know how old she was, but boys too, fathering and relinquishing children. In the post-reunion timeline, less than a year was practically nothing, and three years was still rather new. Five or six years or more, the book reported, might be required before significant turning points were reached and major problems resolved.

"What did I say about long term?" Henry said.

"And it says here that geographic distance between mother and child can slow the process."

"We are *not* moving to New Orleans." Henry folded his arms and gave me his best "don't start with me" face.

Desperate to know more, I called PACER and found a birthmother support group just thirty minutes from my home. As nervous as I was to walk into a group of strangers, I immediately felt a sense of belonging.

The group was small, just six or seven, all intelligent, competent women. Most had gotten pregnant and surrendered their babies in the same mid-sixties-early-seventies timeframe that I had. The world had changed since then, and so had adoption. Birth control, legalized abortion, and societal acceptance of single motherhood provided choices that we hadn't had. Open adoption was more the norm, giving birthmothers a chance to have some part in their children's lives, or at least know that they were happy and thriving.

What was once called "relinquishment" — voluntary termination of parental rights — was now referred to as "making an adoption plan." Those of us who had given up a baby back then didn't feel like we'd had a "plan, let alone that we'd had any choice.

I didn't share much that first night — only that I'd met my son almost a year ago, how wonderful our first few months had been, and that our relationship had become rocky since. I listened, clinging to every word from the women who shared my experience. Some were searching and some were already in reunion, with varying degrees of success. They had relinquished daughters and sons, and a few had given up more than one child. Some had gone on to have more children; others, like me, had not.

Meeting once a month wasn't nearly enough. I wished I could see the other mothers every day and touch that stone of camaraderie. I continued to read at a voracious rate. Hungry for connection and clues as to where my reunion might be headed, I highlighted passages I could relate to, savored the happy stories, and whizzed through the ones with unfortunate outcomes.

I knew there was no way to predict or fully prepare for what would come. But not being alone — having a community of kindred spirits as well as a newfound, supportive family — felt like circling the wagons around my heart.

Chapter 15

GOOD ENOUGH

Josh promised to call on our anniversary — one year since the registry had connected us — because he'd be out on the rig and I wouldn't be able to reach him. He wasn't sure what time, so I rearranged my schedule to stay home all day.

The air felt unusually warm for late March and I spent the morning out on the deck, paging through my alternately ecstatic and anguished journal entries from our early days. Still dewy from a recent rain, the azalea and rhododendron flowers sparkled against the bright green of new growth and I felt hopeful for the first time in months.

I started a new entry on the blank page following what I had written about the birthmother group a month before.

Dear Josh, No matter what happens, I will never regret finding you. It's hard sometimes, watching your life, worrying about you, and feeling like I let you down. But I'm stronger than that and I'll work through it. From what I've heard, a year in reunion is like a week in real time. We're still novices. We'll get better at this.

When I listen to the birthmothers who have yet to find their children, I realize how lucky I am. Anything is better than nothing, better than not knowing who and where you are. I love you so much and I'm in this for the long haul.

By mid-afternoon my chest began to tighten and several times I checked the phone for a dial tone.

What if he doesn't call?

That's ridiculous. This date is as important to him as it is to me. He told me he'd made our reunion date his ATM pin number. He'll call.

By dinnertime, I knew he wouldn't. The silence of the phone roared in my head.

"You mean Marissa didn't call you?" Josh said when he

phoned two days later. "I was afraid I'd get too busy, so I asked her to. Don't worry, I'll give her shit when I get home."

"No, don't," I said. "It wouldn't have made that much difference. You're the one I wanted to talk to."

We talked once during his next ten days at home.

"Hey, Bubba! How you doin'?"

"Couldn't be better," Josh answered. "On top of the world." He sounded high — not drunk, more like accelerated — and I heard loud laughter in the background.

"Did I catch you in the middle of something?"

"Nah. A few friends are here, that's all. We're celebrating Marissa's birthday. Did I tell you I got her one of those diamond tennis bracelets?"

"Aren't they really expensive?"

"Not that much. The diamonds are pretty small. Besides, she's wanted one her whole life."

All eighteen years of it, I thought. Wouldn't want to make her wait.

"How's Naomi?"

"She's great." Another round of giggles drowned out his next sentence.

"I should let you go. Call me when you have time to talk, okay?"

I was almost relieved when he returned to the oil rig without calling back. As troubling as our last conversation had been, I had an overpowering sense that something worse was on the horizon.

A week later, Josh called at six-thirty in the morning to report that Marissa had run off with a group of underage druggie friends. She'd left Naomi with a teenaged babysitter who called Nina when Marissa didn't return.

"Oh my God!" I said. "Is Naomi okay?"

"Nina picked her up and says she seems fine. The apartment is trashed, and it looks like Marissa took our truck and everything else of value, including my tools."

He called me several more times before catching the

first possible flight out of Houston to New Orleans, and again that night after he'd arrived. Marissa had emptied their bank account, he said. The apartment was a disaster, not just filthy but purposefully wrecked. There was obscene graffiti on the walls and drug paraphernalia, including a crack pipe made out of a cola bottle.

"How could she do this?" His voice broke and I could hear that he was crying.

"Josh, did you see this coming at all?"

"No," he groaned. "We were doing so well. Things were good between us. I talked to her just two days ago."

"Did you know these people she left with?"

"Some of them. They came over to party with us sometimes."

"What about the drugs? Were you guys doing them together?"

"No way!" He said he was taking Naomi to the doctor the next day to have her checked for any signs of abuse or drug exposure. "If there's anything wrong with her, I swear I'll make Marissa pay."

The next day Nina called to ask if Josh and Naomi could come to us. "He's despondent. He's worried that he can't take care of Naomi anymore, and even wanted to sign her over to me. He really needs to get away from here."

"Of course," I stammered. "I'll have to talk to Henry, but I'm sure it'll be okay."

My mind whirled with excitement and horror at the thought of my son and granddaughter living nearby. A year before that had been my greatest wish. In recent months, I'd come to appreciate the two thousand miles between us. But he needed me. Naomi needed me. I was obliged to put my reservations aside and do whatever I could to help them. *Who knows?* I thought. *Perhaps what began as a crisis might turn out to be a blessing.*

"I don't need a vacation," Josh told me after Nina approached him and offered to pay for their airfare. "I've got to think about what to do next, how to take care of my daughter."

"Josh, you've been through a huge trauma. You need a break, a chance to think things through," I said. "Besides, I want to see you."

"If you mean for a week or two, forget it," he said. "Are you saying I can move there and get a fresh start?"

"That's a possibility. Please just come and we'll see what happens. You know I'd love for you to live near me."

"But do you really think it will work out? That I could stay?"

His words took me back to the previous fall, when he had been intent on leaving Marissa and Naomi and moving to California.

"I don't know, Josh. Let's see how it goes."

Henry was willing, even though it would be a big change having another adult and a very mobile ten-month-old in our two-bedroom house. We agreed we would have to set some ground rules, but decided to wait until they had been here for a few days and Josh got his bearings.

On the way home from the airport, Josh handed me a note from Nina. In it, she detailed Naomi's schedule, her favorite foods, and tricks for getting her to sleep. At the end, she wrote, *Enjoy motherhood! It's wonderful.*

My stomach reeled. Whose mother was I expected to be? My granddaughter's? I had no experience taking care of babies. At forty-six, I couldn't give up my work, my life, to raise a child. Yet when I looked at the bald, chubby, cherub-faced Naomi, part of me was drawn to the idea. It would be like coming full circle — not having the chance to raise my son, and instead raising my granddaughter.

My abdomen cramped and then released. I shifted in my seat, and felt the familiar dampness in the crotch of my underpants. For the fifth time in a row, my period had signaled my son's presence.

Josh spent most of that evening venting about Marissa.

"I can't believe I trusted that bitch! I did everything for her and she goes and pulls this shit? Now what am I going to do? How am I going to work *and* take care of a baby by myself? I just thank God that Naomi's okay. If anything had happened to her, I would kill Marissa. I mean it, I would. I wouldn't care if I went to prison for it."

The next day Josh wanted to go shopping for a child gate to put between the living room and kitchen. That was simple enough, but once we were in the store, he insisted Naomi needed some toys since he hadn't been able to bring any. I was browsing in the toddler educational toy section when he called me over to look at a massive inflatable tent filled with plastic balls.

"We don't have room for that," I said. "It's too big."

"No, it's not. We can put it in the living room. It will help keep her contained, like a playpen."

"But it costs almost a hundred dollars. I really don't think it's necessary."

"I've got four-fifty cash," he said. "Don't worry, I won't have any trouble finding a job."

Job? After one night, he already saw himself here for good. Not being honest about my qualms was starting to backfire.

Henry was taken aback when he came home from work to find a five-foot diameter, four-foot high plastic giant tent next to the TV. Naomi had no problem crawling out of it. She hated the gate that imprisoned her in the living room. I divided the next few hours between childproofing the house and chasing her out of the kitchen cabinets, toilet, and houseplants.

Josh continued to obsess over Marissa. At least once a day, he'd say he shouldn't be here, that he should go back and try to find her. His reasons swung between wanting her arrested for endangering their child and getting to her before the authorities did so he could help her avoid going to jail. He spent hours on the phone — to Nina at least twice a day asking if she'd heard anything, to the police in New Orleans, Marissa's father in Florida, and every friend on the east coast with whom she might have gotten in touch. He told his story over and over, which seemed to fuel either his anger at being victimized or his worry for Marissa, depending on his mood.

In many ways, Josh proved to be far more demanding of my time and attention than Naomi. He didn't like being left alone with her and clearly preferred that I tend to her needs. Since by then I was working from home, I was able to accommodate him, but I still had to spend at least a few hours a day in my office, which was in a little utility building we'd converted. Sometimes I went out there just to escape, which rarely lasted more than thirty or forty minutes.

"Whatcha doin'?" Josh would say when he appeared in the doorway — without Naomi if he could get her to nap, but often with her in tow, which would send me into a frenzy of keeping her out of the computer cords.

"Working. Just give me another half-hour or so."

"What are we supposed to do?"

"You could take Naomi to the park. It's only a few blocks away."

"I don't want to go alone. We'll wait for you."

He spent a lot of time scanning the classifieds and Yellow Pages, looking up auto shops where he might apply for a job and calling daycare centers to inquire about prices. I began to feel anxious that we had yet to talk about house rules or make a plan. On the fifth day, he announced he'd made an appointment at a low-cost divorce service and asked if I would drive him there.

"You know, Josh, there will be plenty of time to take care of this later," I said. "What if you file for divorce here and don't end up staying in California?"

"I want to get things settled as soon as possible," he said. "I need to make sure I get custody of Naomi and that Marissa never sees her again."

I couldn't sit silently in the paralegal's office and listen to Josh rage about Marissa in between answering questions about the length of their marriage, property owned together, his job history and income. When she asked about Marissa's income, Josh laughed.

"None, unless you count turning tricks."

"Josh," I interrupted. "Don't say things like that."

"How do you know she hasn't? Or what she's doing for money now?"

He sounded like he knew something I didn't. I stood up and said I was going to walk Naomi around a nearby shopping center. The paralegal said they'd be finished in about an hour.

I clung to my expectation that Henry and I could help Josh and Naomi and still maintain the life we were used to leading. Weeks before Josh's arrival, we'd made a date to meet our friends, Rich and Mary, for dinner and a few games of electronic trivia at a nearby restaurant. I left it up to Josh whether to come along, assuring him that the place was casual enough to bring a toddler. He wanted to come.

"So how long are you going to be here?" Rich asked Josh as we sat down at the restaurant.

"I'm staying," Josh said. "Didn't my mom tell you?"

"Uh, we're still working on that," I said.

Naomi enchanted everyone — except maybe whoever was going to have to clean up the ring of crackers and cheese on the carpet around her chair. For the next two hours, we took turns holding her whenever she fussed and following her when she wanted to wander. Josh seemed to be having a good time.

Once our dinner arrived, I realized that I hadn't seen him or Naomi for fifteen or twenty minutes. I found them in front of the restaurant — Naomi wailing, Josh red-faced and glaring at me.

"What's wrong with you? Don't you realize that you can't keep a baby out this late?" he sputtered.

I held out my arms to take her, but he spun away from me. My chest hitched and my vision blurred. For a moment, I feared I might faint.

"Just come back in," I said, catching my breath. "Eat your dinner. Then we'll go." Back at the table, I explained that we'd have to leave soon. Josh finally came in and sat down, pouting and refusing to eat. Rich and Mary each offered to take Naomi, but he scowled and shook his head.

"I'm sorry, you guys," I said.

"Don't be silly," Mary said. "She's just a baby."

I was too embarrassed to say that I'd meant to apologize for Josh's behavior.

When we arrived home, Josh carried Naomi straight to their bedroom and didn't come back out. Henry and I sat in the living room, talking quietly about what had happened.

I couldn't help but remember the scene outside the casino the summer before. Perhaps Josh was uncomfortable with cranky babies. I felt a little helpless around them myself.

The next morning, I woke to the sound of Naomi crying, but didn't hear Josh. When I opened their bedroom door, I saw that he was still sleeping and my granddaughter was standing in her crib. Her big eyes brightened and a grateful string of drool slid down her chin. I tiptoed in and lifted her out. I was feeding her cereal when Josh appeared a half-hour later.

"Morning," Henry said brusquely.

"Morning," Josh grunted back.

"Morning," I muttered.

No one said a word about the night before, or much of anything else.

After breakfast, Henry went outside to do some yard work and Josh followed. I decided to take Naomi along on my shopping errands. I kept her out too long and had a hard time getting her to nap. She cried every time I tried to put her down, so I sat in the recliner in the living room and held her. She would start to drift, then wriggle and murmur, force herself awake and look up at me with her big sleepy eyes. Around four-thirty, she settled down.

"I finally got her to sleep," I said, when Josh walked through the room.

"Oh great," he said. "Now she'll be up until midnight."

When he left the room, I pulled my granddaughter's limp

body closer and kissed the top of her fuzzy head. I was doing my best but it wasn't enough — just like with Josh's father. John's last words to me boomed in my head...

He'd been ecstatic when I told him I was pregnant and promised we'd get married at city hall right away. We bought wedding bands. He put in a request for family housing on the base. My girlfriends threw me a surprise bridal shower. I tried not to worry when John kept postponing our appointment for the blood tests that were required before we could get a marriage license. I couldn't help but be concerned when he called one morning and said we needed to talk.

We met in a park near the Marine base. As John approached, the harsh intention in his eyes sent a dizzying jolt through my body.

"I can't marry you," he said once we were seated on a bench. He spoke slowly and firmly, as if lecturing a child.

"What do you mean?" I gasped.

"You're not what I want in a wife. You can't cook. You don't even try to make yourself pretty. You don't fix your hair."

Stunned, I opened my mouth to tell him I'd try harder.

"I'm sorry," he said. "You're just not good enough."

His words punctured my gut, left me bloody and raw. Believing them kept the wound alive inside long after my skin had healed over.

Chapter 16

STRANGERS

In the early months of our reunion, Josh had showered me with little gifts — the sorts of things that a young boy would have chosen: *I Love You Mom* magnets, stuffed animals, and flowery knickknacks. The same was true of the greeting cards he sent. They were the kind that would have melted me if he were seven or ten. Even though it had seemed a bit odd, I had enjoyed his regression.

I was struck by how the stages of our relationship paralleled those of a normal mother and son, and how quickly he had evolved from an adoring little boy into the defiant teenager who was living under my roof.

We had several more run-ins over the next week. If he were on the phone when I put dinner on the table, he'd wave me off and keep on talking. He said Naomi could eat the same foods we ate and then got furious with me when she got a bad case of gas after I fed her broccoli. As long as she was happy, Josh was happy. The minute she started to whimper, he'd fly into a rage.

"Shut up, Naomi! I *don't know* what you want!"

"She's a baby, Josh. Don't yell at her."

"I don't know how to make her stop crying."

"Just give her some attention. That's probably all she needs."

"If she could talk, if she could tell me what she wants, I'd give it to her. I can't relate to kids until they can talk. Mothers are supposed to do that. You're a mother. Can't you do something?"

I felt as if I were sinking, pulled down by the riptide of my son's unrelenting needs. Everything about Josh screamed, *I'm here, deal with me.* And as the days went on, I felt less inclined to try.

The night of my monthly birthmothers meeting, I left Henry, Josh and Naomi to fend for themselves. It was only my third meeting, and the first where I spoke at length, regaling the women with the details of Josh's behavior since his arrival.

"I can't do this," I said. "I thought I could. I wanted him here. But not like this. I'm thinking about telling him he has to go."

"He's your *son*," one of mothers interjected. "Can't you find a way to work things out? Imagine how he'll feel being sent away a second time. And what about your granddaughter?"

"What about *me*?" I glared at her. "Do I have to put up with whatever he dishes out?"

The facilitator raised a hand to halt the debate. "Ground rules, ladies. That's why we have them. Our purpose is to provide a safe place where we can express our feelings without having to defend them or contend with unsolicited advice."

"I'm sorry," the woman said. "I was out of line." Her face told me that she meant what she'd said before and had apologized only because of the rules.

"It's okay." I covered my eyes with my hand and took a breath. "I've had the same thoughts. I hate that I'm acting like my own mother. Not loving him unconditionally. Sending him away because he has problems that I don't know how to deal with."

In the quiet that followed, I remembered Josh accusing me of that very thing. *Was he right after all?*

"Are you open to feedback?" the facilitator said.

"Yes."

"Loving someone unconditionally doesn't mean that you're always going to like his behavior," she said. "I can be furious with my sixteen-year-old daughter for staying out past her curfew, and still love her. I wonder if you would consider being honest with Josh, as you have been here and I applaud you for that. Can you tell him the truth? How upset you are with his behavior and what you need from him if this arrangement is to work?"

The thought sent a shiver down my spine, the same sensation I'd had when I envisioned telling my parents how I felt about their denial of my reunion.

"I don't know. It scares me."

"What scares you?"

"That he'll get mad, that he'll stop loving me. That I might never see him again."

Another birthmother spoke up. "Our relationships with the children we let go seem so fragile. We're afraid to make a move. Afraid we might lose them again."

"Maybe it's time to stop living in fear," the facilitator said. "We aren't in control of their feelings and reactions. If we keep walking on eggshells around them, how will they ever realize the impact their behavior has on us?"

During the drive home, my body trembled as I pictured telling Josh the truth. I could not risk having to face his wrath, the rage that his father had used to make me feel wrong and worthless.

I let my fantasies take over. If only Josh would decide to return to New Orleans of his own accord. Or Henry would get fed up and tell him to leave. Maybe a neighbor would need a house sitter for a month or so, and he and Naomi could stay there while I got my bearings.

There was no such rescue on the horizon, no easy solution to the situation. But I was completely out of my depth — and out was what I needed.

"I don't think I can do this," I told Henry that night. "Josh is beyond control. All the ranting and pouting — it's like having a stranger in my house."

"You *are* strangers. It would be stressful having anyone live here with us — Jeff, your sister, even Leanna, and you know them. You and Josh have had what? Maybe a month of days together total?"

"Exactly. So now what?"

Henry shrugged. "It's your call. He's your son."

"Yeah, but it's our home, *our life*."

"I can see the toll this is taking on you and that's my main concern. Not like it's been a picnic for me, but you're the one who has to contend with Josh, whether he stays or doesn't."

"Maybe if his problems weren't so huge. Or if it weren't so twenty-four/seven. Maybe if he were nice to me. I mean, taken individually, he hasn't done anything all that horrible — inconsiderate and rude at most."

"I've said all along, you're not going to see big changes overnight."

"And what about Naomi? She's already lost so much."

"If you want to try, we'll do our best to work things out."

I tossed and turned that night, pondering my options. I still hoped that we could avoid a confrontation and end his visit on good terms. For that to happen, I couldn't make his behavior the issue. What if he promised to try harder if we let him stay? How could I say no? In truth, I wanted my life back. I wanted Josh in it, but not in my face. Most of all, after what had happened with Marissa, I didn't want Josh to feel worse than he already did.

Yes, I decided, I would take the fall.

I told Josh we needed to talk, and as soon as Naomi went down for her nap, he, Henry and I went out to the deck.

"I've got to be honest," I said. "I just can't handle this right now. I feel totally overwhelmed. Even though you're my son, we're like complete strangers."

Josh looked confused, but for the first time since his arrival he remained calm. "You're my mother. How can we be strangers?"

How could we not be strangers? He really doesn't get it, I realized. He honestly thinks that because I gave birth to him that everything will simply fall into place. Hadn't that been my expectation, long before we'd found each other? I scrambled to restore my composure.

"Because I didn't raise you. Twenty-six years of history is missing."

"Think about it, Josh," Henry spoke up. "How much time

have you and your mom actually spent together in the last year? You wouldn't move in with or marry someone you barely know."

Henry realized the irony of his example at the same time I did, and we exchanged a furtive glance. Josh didn't seem to notice.

"That shouldn't matter," he said.

"Maybe it shouldn't," I said. "But it does. Don't you see that? It's nobody's fault. Okay, let's say it's mine — that I'm not ready for the realities of motherhood. This is all so new for both of us. Maybe it's just too soon."

His eyes blazed, but his voice was subdued. "I thought this was what we both wanted, to be together."

"I thought so too," I said. "But it's not working out."

"So, what are you saying? You want me to leave?"

I averted my eyes, suddenly ashamed when he uttered the words that I couldn't bring myself to say. "Yes. I'm sorry. But that's how it has to be, at least for now."

Josh stared at the ground. After a few minutes of silence, Henry got up and went into the house.

"I really am sorry, Bub," I said. "This wasn't what I had in mind."

"Don't worry," he said. "I'm used to it."

What do you mean? I started to ask. But I knew. This wasn't the first time he'd been sent away, not the second or even the third. I couldn't look at Josh without wanting to take it all back. I had to fight the urge to grab him and try to make him understand how little it would have taken for things to be different. Instead I shook off the pangs and settled into making the next few days with him and Naomi as pleasant as possible.

Josh called Nina, who arranged for him to fly back the next week.

"She said, 'You must feel awful,'" he seemed compelled to report. "'Like you're being rejected all over again.'"

Her comment galled me, but I realized that was what everyone was going to think unless I revealed every awful thing Josh had said and done. As much as I would have liked to clear the air, I still felt the need to shield my son. I would take whatever heat came as a result of my actions.

The next day, after more than two weeks missing, Marissa surfaced in New York and contacted her father, who sent her a bus ticket to come to him in Pensacola. Once she'd arrived, Josh and Marissa talked on the phone, and he began to sound as though he wanted to get back with her.

"She pawned the tennis bracelet and her engagement and wedding rings," he said. "I guess I'll have to buy her new ones — at least a wedding ring."

I urged him to think twice about going back to her, for his sake and Naomi's.

"I don't have a choice," he said. "You won't let me stay here and I have nowhere else to go."

My eyes narrowed. Was he really trying to make me responsible for his return to his devious skank of a wife? How could he be so clueless one minute — unable to see that his behavior had led to his eviction — in the next minute, be shrewd enough to prepare an alibi?

"You have lots of options, Josh," I said. "As many as you would have here. Let Marissa stay at her father's. I'm sure Nina and Max will help you get back on your feet. Trust me, this is for the best."

Something about those words — "for the best" — left an ugly taste in my mouth, and I turned to exit the room.

"Can I leave Naomi here?" Josh called after me.

"What?" I whirled back to face him.

"Would you keep her for me until I figure things out?"

I stared at him, stunned by his request and my reaction. My mind fluttered around the possibility of having my granddaughter with me and then crash-landed on one thought: *He isn't coming back.* If I let him leave her, he would replicate his past.

"I'm sorry, Josh, but I can't do it. Naomi has experienced way too much loss. She needs you, now more than ever."

At the airport when I looked into Naomi's sweet face, I questioned the wisdom of my decisions. Josh would not meet my gaze, and suddenly I saw John — just as I had in the first pictures Josh had sent.

I'd seen John once more after that day in the park...

Once my parents arrived in town, Dad demanded that I get John on the phone. My father had been an officer in the Navy and I suspected that this straight-laced Marine was exactly what he'd envisioned for a son-in-law. Listening from the hall, I kept waiting for Dad to take him down for getting me pregnant or insist that he marry me.

Instead, he calmly told John that he expected him to share the financial burden of sending me to a home for unwed mothers. They agreed on an amount and Dad suggested — "for your own protection," I heard him say — that John visit the Marine Base attorney and have an agreement drawn up, stipulating that with this payment, he would have no further responsibility.

A few days later, my father and I went to the base. John sat poker-faced in the corner while the attorney did the talking. He handed my father a cashier's check for a fraction of the amount they had agreed upon.

"Well then, I guess we don't have a deal," Dad barked, standing and motioning for me to follow. "We'll see you in court."

But when the attorney spoke, we sank back into our seats.

"I suggest you take the money because if you pursue this, you'll end up with nothing. My client is prepared to testify that your daughter was not a virgin when he met her. He has friends who will swear that they slept with her."

"But that's not true!" I cried, looking at John in disbelief. He would not meet my gaze.

"He will also testify that your daughter was using drugs, which will go a long way toward proving she's an unfit mother should she try to get child support."

My heart sank into my stomach. I couldn't look at my

father. After a minute of silence, he took the check and the attorney slid the contract across his desk. I signed, renouncing the right to any further claims against John, and we left.

"I don't think I could possibly be more disappointed in you," Dad said once we were in the car.

As if it weren't enough to desert me and our child, John had betrayed me in the worst possible way. He had turned my father against me. I took a deep breath. "It's true," I told him. "I took some drugs. But only marijuana," I lied. "And it's true that I wasn't a virgin when I met John, but I didn't sleep around."

I couldn't tell whether Dad believed me, not that it mattered. Any possibility of support from my parents was gone...

John would never know the outcome of my pregnancy — whether I'd had a boy or a girl, whether I'd kept the baby or given it up. I relished Sandy's prediction that someday he would regret what he had done and end up alone and pitiful. I had loved him, even if for all the wrong reasons and without really knowing him, but by the time I'd given birth, resentment was all that remained. Regardless of what the attorney said, John knew that the baby was his. Chances were he'd found someone who met his needs, gotten married and had a family, made a life and never thought about us. As the years passed, the child I'd had and lost became mine alone, as surely as if by Immaculate Conception.

John had become irrelevant, until our son returned to my life. Josh hadn't mentioned his father since our afternoon in the French Quarter.

Three days after he and Naomi left, Nina called.

"I talked to Marissa. She said Josh was in on everything. He was also doing drugs and he knew she was having sex for extra money. I discovered that some of my jewelry was missing, and Marissa said Josh was also in on that."

She and Max had confronted Josh when he arrived. He admitted that he had been doing drugs, but denied knowing about the stolen jewelry or Marissa turning tricks. They told him he could not stay, drove him and Naomi to Pensacola the next morning, and left them with Marissa and her dad.

"You were right not to let him stay there," she said. "Those two are nothing but trouble. They deserve each other."

I didn't feel any more right than when I'd sent him out into the world as a helpless infant. But for the first time I felt outright resentment toward Josh for lying, manipulating, and taking advantage of me. And for not being the sweet, innocent child I'd left behind.

Chapter 17

THE BIG HURT

Josh's reconciliation with Marissa lasted less than two months. She put up a half-hearted fight to keep Naomi — by then one year old — but Josh insisted on taking her and found a rental house nearby. He contacted the California legal service where he had started divorce proceedings, sent his final payment, and told them to file. Shortly thereafter, Marissa disappeared again.

Since Josh didn't have a phone, our contact dwindled. He called collect from work or from a payphone.

"Good news," he said. "I've rekindled an old flame."

"Who?"

"Angel."

He seemed to have forgotten that he'd told me about his relationship with Angel, the woman he had left for Marissa, and how their attraction had been based solely on sex and drugs.

"How did you know where to find her?" I asked.

"I have my ways."

I squirmed as he explained that Angel stayed with Naomi during the day while he worked at an auto shop, and he was home nights when she worked as an exotic dancer. He said he hoped to convince her to quit and be a full-time mother to Naomi, maybe even stay with her while he went back to working on the oil rig.

"What makes you think things are going to be better for you two this time?" I said.

"I don't know that they will, but I hope so. She loves Naomi. She's a good mother to her, better than Marissa ever was. And there's still a spark between us."

I took a deep breath and swallowed hard against the criticisms that pushed up in my throat. "Josh, I'm really proud of you for keeping Naomi. But after everything that's happened, I think the best thing you can do is focus on her and give your love life a rest."

"I don't like being alone," he moaned.

"I know you don't, but you've got to start putting your own needs aside for your daughter's sake."

"Seems to me all I've been doing lately is putting my needs aside. Don't you realize how hard it is, taking care of a child with no help? Oh, that's right, you *don't* know."

Ouch.

"You just don't get it," he said. "Why can't you just accept me as I am?"

It was a fair question, and while I struggled with the answer, I heard Josh sigh.

"Look," he said. "I'm just doing what I have to. If I had my way, I'd still be with Marissa or living there with you. I've been getting the short end of the stick my whole life. I know I've made some mistakes, but now I'm really trying to pull things together, and no matter how hard I try, nothing goes right."

"Not everything that happens to you is somebody else's fault, Josh. It's time to stop making excuses and grow up."

"Why should I? Seems to me this grown-up shit isn't all it's cracked up to be."

"Because you're a father now, that's why. Naomi is depending on you. I'm sorry if I came down too hard. I'm just worried. About both of you."

From then on, we kept our conversations brief and light. I knew Josh would do whatever he wanted — whatever he felt he "had to do," as he put it — and I would just have to wait it out.

While my connection with Josh waned, my relationship with my mother's family grew. Aunt Mabel and I continued to talk on the phone and write each other long letters. Although everyone in the family referred to her as Mabel, I started calling her "Auntie Em," for Ella Mabel. The idea of having an

Auntie Em — like Dorothy's aunt in *The Wizard of Oz* — made me smile.

At her urging, I made contact with Uncle Winfred's children: my cousins David, Brenda, and Pam. Their similarities to my mom were eerie — the handwriting, voices, and the expressions they used — even though they had never met her and their parents hadn't grown up together. Could these things be genetic? I grabbed onto every little coincidence, as I had when I'd first found Josh.

The story of my unwed pregnancy and relinquishment left my cousins unfazed. "It could have happened to any of us," Brenda said.

Pam, who had a nine-year-old adopted son, told me how grateful she and her husband were to Ben's birthmother for the "gift" she had given them. "He knows he was a chosen child," she said.

I didn't have the heart to tell her that, from what I'd read about adoptees, they know that being chosen means someone before had not chosen to keep them.

David, the most conservative of my cousins, praised me for having done "the right thing." As uncomfortable as that sentiment made me, I took no issue. I was relieved to have told the truth and still been accepted.

Em also encouraged me to write to my cousin Tom, the self-appointed family genealogist. She said he hoped I would provide some details about our branch of the family.

Tom wrote back: I must say I am in a mild state of shock. Your pictures fell out when I opened your letter and I could not believe what I saw. You are definitely part of this family. You, Mabel, and my youngest sister look like triplets.

Tom was clearly proud of his Kendall roots.

Originally from Northern England, our ancestors came to America in the 1500s. Abraham Kendall was a shipmaster for the Sir Francis Drake expedition, and John Kendall was among the first of our ancestors in New England. In the Virginia settlement, George Kendall was shot while leading the first known act of rebellion against the Council of Jamestown in 1607.

We have nothing to be ashamed of in our branch of the tree. Our ancestors were good, decent, hard-working people who lived through several difficult time periods that greatly affected Virginia's Northern Neck.

The *big hurt,* as he referred to it, was that our grandmother hadn't done whatever was necessary to keep the family intact.

Most of our aunts and uncles don't like to talk about it, but the bitterness runs deep. It seems that most of them were abused one way or another in their foster families — some mentally, some physically, some both. The boys often ran away and the girls married early to escape their new homes. I can't help but wonder: if their mother didn't want them, why didn't the older children join forces and hold the family together?

Who was this woman, Sarah Agnes Utterback, my grandmother? What kind of mother had she been before she'd lost her husband and abandoned her children? Anyone old enough to remember her in the early years was gone. I pulled the photo of her from the stack of pictures that Tom had sent and stared into its sepia tones, looking for answers.

By then, Sarah Agnes was already middle-aged. Decked out in a short-sleeved striped dress with contrasting dark buttons and belt, two-toned pumps and a wide-brimmed hat tilted just so. *She was stylish just like my mother,* I noted.

My mother had inherited her mother's shape as well: padded shoulders held erect above a full bosom, making her seem taller than her average height; the way her slender arms hung straight at her sides; one knee bent, as if she were about to take a step. I had dozens of pictures of Mom in that pose.

I strained to make out her features, and even with the bright sun casting the shadow of her hat, I could see that they too were my mother's: a round face punctuated by high cheekbones and a straight European nose. Her thin lips were drawn tight, neither smiling nor frowning. I'd heard that smiling for pictures was not fashionable in those days, and that film speeds were so slow that the subject had to stay very still, making a smile difficult to hold. But it may also have been that she didn't have much to smile about. By the time this picture was taken, she had probably given birth to eight babies — one every year or two since she was twenty-four. Maybe she was already pregnant with her ninth.

I saw hardness in her face. Despite how cruel life must have been in rural Virginia during the Depression, I did not mistake this for strength. I saw a proud, self-righteous woman, who was willing to sacrifice her family for her own needs, but stubborn enough not to break down and let her weakness show. Even if she had felt lost and frightened after her husband died, she would have kept up appearances and gone off to church, praised Jesus and never risked burning in hell by cursing Him for her fate. And she would be damned if she'd let anyone see her cry.

According to Tom, Sarah Agnes stayed in town after scattering her children, found work as a housekeeper, attended the same church, and frequented the dance hall at Sinclair's Corner. She simply went about her business, as straight-faced and determined as my own mother had been when she sent me off alone to wait out my pregnancy and give up my baby. I imagined my mother was the brightest of Sarah Agnes' pupils. Whatever had not been passed down genetically, she must have learned by age six: how to pose for pictures, how to keep her feelings in check and the neighbor's judgments at bay; how to mask her discontent; how to let go.

As I poured over the other photos, I realized how Josh must have felt, seeing people who looked like him for the first time. Although I'd been told I favored my mother, I had identified with my father's family for so long that my resemblance to anyone else was a revelation. I was disappointed when I couldn't find the remarkable likeness to my aunt that Tom had mentioned. But our emotional bond surpassed the physical.

Sharing our mutual frustrations with my mother fed our

camaraderie. Apparently Em and Mom had clashed over some combination of politics and religion and had not spoken during the past few years. The stories I told Em about my childhood, my pregnancy and Josh's relinquishment fanned the fire she already had burning against my mother. And I didn't care.

My communications with Mom and Dad were still sporadic and superficial. They didn't mention Josh or Naomi, and I evened the score by not disclosing my contact with the Kendalls. Any news about my mother's interactions with her family came by way of my cousins, which was how I learned that she had finally agreed to talk on the phone with her younger brother, Winfred, after several years of contact with Mabel.

This breakthrough prompted my cousins Brenda and Pam to plan a full-blown family reunion in Virginia over the Fourth of July weekend, the first in more than twenty years. Invitations went out and Brenda reported that Kendall relations would be coming from all over the country. Apparently, the potential presence of the mysterious and beloved Mayme Catherine was the big draw.

Bob, Debby, and I had booked our travel, but according to Brenda, who was spearheading the event, my parents had yet to commit to attending.

"Do you think they'll come?" she asked me. "My dad and mom will be so disappointed if they don't."

"It's hard to say. My mom's probably a little nervous about seeing everyone after so long."

Later I told Em, "They'll come. They have to, now that their kids will be there. For damage control, if nothing else."

When Dad called, I knew what he wanted to talk about, even though he made idle chat for the first ten minutes.

"Well, my goodness, seems there's a big reunion coming up," he said.

"Yeah, isn't it great? We're looking forward to it."

"Have you been in touch with the folks back there for long?"

"A while. Aunt Mabel at first, and then the cousins."

"I was surprised that you kids are going, especially Debby, since she probably had trouble getting time off from work."

"Actually, she was the first one to book her flight. We're all eager to meet Mom's family." I paused, waiting for some acknowledgment that my mother hadn't had a family for forty years, but none came. "Mom must be excited too."

"Yes," he hesitated. "Although we haven't decided whether or not we'll go. Your mom isn't sure she's up to it."

"Is she okay?"

"It's her back again. She's in a lot of pain. Sitting on a plane for several hours might be too hard on her."

"I'm sorry to hear that. This is a big deal for her brothers. For all the Kendalls."

"I know. I think we should go, and I'm working on convincing her."

I didn't reply, anticipating his next question.

"I hope you haven't told any of them."

"Told them what?" I wanted him to sweat.

"About Josh. You know what it would do to your mother if they knew," he said.

Don't say it! Not again! But I knew he would.

"It would kill her."

"Some of them know."

"Oh, Lord."

"They don't care, Dad. They really don't. Mom's got to quit caring. Like it or not, Josh is my son. He's family."

After a pause, he sighed loudly. "Well, what's done is done. I'll figure out some way to handle it."

I was agitated as I boarded the plane for Virginia. For the second time in just over a year, I was on my way cross-country to a blind date with blood relatives, people I should have known my whole life.

Buckled into my seat, I remembered my last e-mail exchange with Tom. He was preparing a genealogical booklet for the reunion — listing the original siblings, their children, grandchildren and great grandchildren — and planned to make copies for everyone who attended.

A few days before I was scheduled to fly east, he had written, I thought I should check with you. Do you want Josh and Naomi included in the family tree? I have them in there, but if it's going to cause problems for you, I can remove them for now.

At first I'd been outraged that he would suggest leaving them off. Then I realized that this had been my doing. Every time I'd told a family member about Josh, I'd made it clear that Mom and Dad didn't want them to know. I pictured my mother having a heart attack in front of the entire clan and everyone blaming me.

I started typing my response: *I guess it would be best if you took them off.* And then I burst into tears. For twenty minutes, I sat with my face in my hands, sobbing.

What are you doing? It sickened me that I had considered erasing my son and my granddaughter, as easily as my mother had edited her family out of her life, and my grandmother had disposed of her children.

I wiped my eyes and wrote back to Tom: *Leave them on. I'll deal with it.*

As the plane took off, I wished the oxygen masks would drop from overhead so I could catch my breath. A tinkling sounded in my head, and before I could shake it off, an image flashed: a crystal chandelier falling. This time, unlike in my dream, I saw it crash to the floor and shatter, and I felt my family breaking into a million pieces.

Chapter 18

VIRGINIA

I'd seen plenty of pictures of Auntie Em, but coming off the plane to find a woman who looked so much like my mother was disconcerting.

She was taller and thinner, her face rounder and her cheekbones more prominent. She'd let her hair go natural, wavy and gray, unlike my mother, who in recent years had hers colored blond and tightly permed. But with her clear blue eyes, soft rounded chin, and large hands, even the style of glasses she wore, she and Mom could have been twins.

Their physical resemblance was the least of it. Her voice was even more like Mom's than I'd heard on the phone. The inflections in her speech, the way she cleared her throat and repeated certain words were eerily familiar.

My eyes and ears were riveted as we made our way through the airport, collected my bags, and drove to her condo in Leesburg. That evening as we chatted and looked at pictures, I could sense my aunt's edginess, and wondered whether she was as overwhelmed by my presence as I was being there.

"This is strange, isn't it?" I said.

Em sighed. "Yes," drawing out the word longer than her drawl required.

"We should have known each other before… always."

"Yes, we should have, and it makes me… just so… *mad.*" She looked exactly like my mom when she was disgusted: nose scrunched, lips pursed. "*Damn mad.*"

"Me, too."

"But I'm just so glad you're here now." Her face relaxed as her gaze met mine. "So *very* glad."

"Me, too," I said.

The next day was the only one we would have alone together before all the relatives descended and the festivities began. We drove to Fauquier County, where my ancestors had settled, my mother and her siblings had been born, and my grandmother had left her family behind. We visited downtown Marshall, the Baptist Church, and the school that most of the Kendall children had attended. We found my grandparents' gravesite in Hume, two of the houses where they had lived as a family, the Nelson house where my mother was raised, and the house across the street where their general store had once stood.

As we made the rounds, I tried to visualize Mayme Catherine on those streets and in those buildings. Until then, the only images I could conjure were the ones of her as my mother. She had no one, no siblings, she'd told us, and no photographs from her childhood. The night before, Auntie Em had showed me a picture of my mom taken when she was six.

"Where did you get this?" I gasped, studying the photo of a blond girl who looked a lot like I had.

"Your mother gave it to me."

She was standing on a ragged wooden porch, in a pose almost identical to Sarah Agnes' except that she was smiling broadly, which made her eyes crinkle up like mine.

Em also showed me Mom's senior picture, taken from her Marshall High School yearbook in which she was listed as Mayme Nelson. She was brunette and voluptuous, with a mischievous glint in her eye that bordered on brazen. I thought about what Auntie Em told me about growing up female back then, how the girls had been warned repeatedly not to get pregnant. It was the foremost rule, the greatest shame.

"Catherine left town the day after she graduated from high school," Em told me. "No one in Virginia ever heard from her again."

Why so quickly? I wondered. *And so furtively?* It was the first time I contemplated that Mom might also have had some scandal in her past. Clearly, she had been embarrassed by her mother's desertion or she wouldn't have kept this fact from her husband and children. I was surprised to learn that she had also been ashamed that the Nelsons hadn't legally adopted her.

"She begged me not to tell your father," Auntie Em said. "I don't know why she was so concerned. The Spencers didn't adopt me. I had to wonder if your father is so uppity that it would bother him."

"No," I said, "he isn't. I can't fathom why she wouldn't want him to know."

Was there more? If she had gone to such lengths to keep something so innocuous concealed, what would she have done if she'd had something truly shocking to hide — something as bad as her daughter's illegitimate pregnancy?

Mayme Catherine moved to Washington, D.C., where she lived with Nelson family friends, enrolled in secretarial college, and landed a responsible job with the U.S. government. She reinvented herself: ditched her first name, took back her original surname, and became Catherine Kendall, until she married my father seven years later. In my youth, my parents' wedding portrait was the earliest photo of her that I'd seen. She was a beautiful bride, slender and graceful in white lace, looking radiant beside my father, his Nordic fairness contrasting with her dark curls. She liked to tell me that her waist size was just seventeen inches then, the same as Scarlett O'Hara's in *Gone With The Wind*. She also told me, on the eve of my own wedding, that she did not love Dad when she married him.

"But I knew he was a good man and in time I came to love him." She was certain Henry was a good man too, because he had a high forehead, "like your father," she said.

Miss Kendall comes from a fine old family, read the yellowed wedding announcement that Auntie Em gave me. Although the ceremony had taken place in Washington, D.C., the notice had appeared in her hometown newspaper, and most of her siblings had seen it. *One of her bridal accessories was a copy of the Kendall Coat of Arms.* At that point, her fine old mother and her eight fine siblings were still alive, but it would be more than forty years before the rest of us knew they existed.

I'd spent most of my adult life trying not to become my mother. I had her eyes and cheekbones, her sense of style and flair for throwing parties, but not her flawless skin, small waist and thick ankles. I'd fought hard to avoid taking on her harsh view of the world, her icy judgments and cruel admonitions. Sometimes I heard her words in my head and had to stop myself before they came out of my mouth.

Do as I say, not as I do.

If you don't stop crying, I'll give you something to cry about."

"You've made your bed, now lie in it.

Recalling my amazement at the traits Mom shared with the relatives she had not grown up with, I wondered whether secrecy could be inherited.

I had dreaded the moments when new friends or strangers would ask, "Do you have children?" Not because I didn't know what to say, but because of how the answer made me feel. Each time I said no, I avoided their eyes. There were times I sat in a group of women who were comparing their pregnancies and children's births, listening silently to their stories, resisting the impulse to chime in that I'd had a baby too, that I'd gained forty pounds and labored for almost twenty-four hours. But the truth always seemed too dangerous. These women had kept their babies. Whether they were married or had raised their children alone, they were better than me.

Hadn't I also kept the truth from my best friends? Not confiding in them that I was searching for my son? Leaving out embarrassing details about Josh's life, both past and present? Holding them at arm's length when they might have helped me get through the worst times of my reunion with him?

As I walked the streets of Mayme Catherine Kendall Nelson Kendall Janson's hometown, fear seeped into my bones that despite her efforts, she had been unable to escape her mother's legacy, and no matter how hard I tried, I might never escape mine.

Em's sister-in-law loaned us her country home outside of

Marshall, which would serve as our headquarters for the next several days. The place was ideal — near the main road, but surrounded by acres of fields and trees, with enough bedrooms to accommodate multiple guests and a screened-in porch where we could enjoy the warm night air without fighting the summer bugs.

My one-on-one time with Auntie came to a halt once my sister arrived. While Bob and I had grown accustomed to the ins and outs of "black sheep" status, Debby had been stuck in gray her whole life. She was bright and hardworking, but rough enough around the edges that she was usually underemployed. She was generous to the point of selflessness, but insecure and defensive after years of being harangued by Mom about her weight and carelessness toward her appearance.

I had been worried about Debby — whether she would feel comfortable and how she would fit in. She was immediately at ease with Auntie Em. Unlike my initial reaction, being in the presence of a woman who looked so much like our mother and yet was warm and accepting seemed to have a soothing effect on my sister.

By the end of the evening, we were joking about showing up at the reunion wearing overalls, with blacked-out teeth and chewing on grass stems. Or not showing up at all.

"Our own private protest," Auntie said.

"As in 'hell no, we won't go?'" I said, which brought hearty laughs from Debby and Em. "There's no point. They won't get it. Besides, we'd miss all the fun."

"What fun?" Debby said. "Mom calling me fat?"

"She'll behave," I said. "She always behaves in public."

Em's daughter Kendall arrived the next morning, and the four of us set out for the valley.

This is it, I thought. I'd be meeting the people who worshipped my mother for no good reason, and seeing my parents for the first time since I'd reunited with Josh. Despite the breathtaking drive through the Shenandoah Mountains, I couldn't help but feel like I was leaving my safe haven and entering the valley of doom.

Our first stop was Uncle Winfred's house in Bridgewater. My uncle looked even more like Mom than like Em, even though he was thin and angular with Kendall features more delicate than his sisters'. Still, there was something — maybe the shape of his smile — that was undeniably Mayme. His wife, Ann, was as warm and soft as she looked, her farm-girl roundness providing the perfect contrast to her husband's slight frame. My brother Bob, his wife, Amy, and his teenaged daughter Emily were already there.

"We've been praying for this day to come," Aunt Ann said. "When Catherine would return to us and we would meet our wonderful nephew and nieces."

"Amen," Win added.

Later that afternoon, we all headed over to cousin Pam's for dinner. I was excited about meeting the cousins I had been e-mailing for months. Brenda was petite but athletic, with short, reddish hair, her mother's big smile and an easy laugh. Her sister Pam looked more like Win, tall and skinny as a rail, with glasses and long brown hair pulled back into a braid. She was nervous and giggly, as she scurried around offering soft drinks and preparing supper.

My parents were scheduled to arrive at their hotel in town that day and were expected to join us. Just after we sat down to eat, the phone rang.

"It's Catherine," Pam called out when she answered. "They're here!"

"Tell them to come on over," Ann said.

After Pam hung up, she reported that they wouldn't be joining us that night. Mom said her clothes were wrinkled from being in the suitcase and she had to do some ironing. Besides, they were tired and wanted to turn in early.

"She wanted to know if her children were here," Pam reported with a chuckle. "She said, 'I can't believe they're imposing on y'all like that. I hope they're behaving themselves.'"

Everyone laughed it off and went on eating and talking.

I finished my meal quickly and excused myself to go outside for a cigarette. Sitting on the back steps, I could feel my tears surfacing. I was angry again, for the first time since I'd gotten off the plane, and frightened — of what I wasn't sure. I wished it were over. I wished I could disappear.

The evening took a pleasant turn after Cousin Tom arrived. A charming and well-spoken man, he awed everyone with genealogical tidbits and stories about the early Kendalls. As the sun set behind the trees and the light dimmed on the huge wooden deck, we all seemed to get braver, expressing more opinions and asking more questions.

"It just doesn't make any sense," I wondered out loud. "Why would my mother feel the need to hide her family from us?"

"There were those who thought the Kendalls were trash," Tom said softly. "I'm afraid the Nelsons were among them. They discouraged your mother from having contact with her sisters and brothers."

"But she *lied* to us," I said. "She said there was no one."

"It's not the same as a lie," Bob piped up. "She was just trying to protect her kids."

"Protect us from what? These people?" I bellowed, motioning around the deck.

"Come on, Denise," Bob said, rolling his eyes. "I'm sure she was just doing what she thought was best for us."

Everything got quiet until Tom conveniently brought the subject back to our grandfather, Edward Malcolm.

"I can't help but think that Malcolm's parents' decision to leave the Shenandoah Valley and return to Fauquier County was a mistake, literally a fatal error," he said. "The story is that Edward Malcolm's father, John, was killed by his own brother — our Great Uncle Buck. Buck was rumored to have killed a few men, but he had the sheriff buffaloed and never spent a day in jail."

It was Buck's daughter Corrie who had organized the Kendall reunions that brought some of the siblings back together in the fifties and sixties.

"Why wasn't my mother invited?"

"No one knew where she was," Tom said.

"But her wedding announcement ran in the Marshall paper. You knew her married name. You could have found her."

Tom looked away. "I located her fairly early on in my research, but my father forbade me to contact her. He never forgave her for cutting off ties with the family. After he died, I wrote her a letter, but she didn't write back. Not until Mabel wrote to her several years later."

If only… If only Edward Malcolm's parents had stayed put. If only he hadn't died young and Sarah Agnes hadn't left their children. If only Mom had answered Tom's letter.

I was still keyed up when the time came to turn in. Upstairs in one of Pam's guest rooms, I tried to relax, but at two a.m. I was no closer to sleep. I had a bad feeling about the next day. The scared little girl rose inside me, as close to the surface as she had come in years.

In the months prior to the reunion I had looked forward to showing pictures and boasting about my son and granddaughter. But by then Josh's life was in shambles. I was embarrassed — which reminded me of my mother, who had been ashamed of her kids regularly — and that made me feel even worse. It was just easier not to say anything.

The reunion was held at the community center in Bridgewater. Debby and I rode with Pam and even though we arrived almost an hour ahead of time to help set up, Mom and Dad were already there.

"Here goes nothing," I said under my breath as we walked in and surveyed the small group of early birds. Uncle Win glowed in the presence of his long-lost older sister, guiding her around the room and introducing her as more people arrived. I hadn't seen my parents in two years, the longest we had gone between visits since I'd been married to Henry. They looked the same, young and fit for being in their early seventies, and I wondered what I had been expecting. Mom reveled in the attention: her face aglow, her smile especially warm, and her

Southern drawl slower and thicker than usual. Dad beamed like a proud father as he watched her. Debby and I approached them for the obligatory hellos and hugs.

"Hey, Mom," I said, a little too exuberantly in an attempt to disguise my nervousness. "You made it! Isn't this great?"

"Hello, Denny." She smiled, but her face didn't move, and her eyes reflected the apprehension I felt.

"Hi," Debby said in Mom's general direction.

"Debby," Mom said coolly. "Where are you two staying?"

"With Mabel," I said. "At her sister-in-law's house outside of Marshall."

Mom's lips pinched. "I see."

Eventually there were about fifty of us, and everywhere I looked I saw people who looked like my mother or me or each other. We all wore paper badges on our chests, with our names and relationship to the Kendall siblings. I wondered whether it bothered my mom that each of us, even Dad, had used her real name on our badges: *Mayme Catherine's... husband, daughter, son.* I was certain that she had no idea how much I knew about her past.

Just before lunch, Uncle Win took the microphone to say grace. He went on for more than five minutes, his voice rising and falling like a Southern preacher. When at last he released us, everyone helped themselves to an extensive buffet of chicken, potatoes, and salads. I sat next to Em, across and down the table from my parents. Bob and Amy sat beside them. Debby had positioned herself as far away as possible, at the other end of one of the long banquet tables.

After lunch, Tom passed out the family tree booklets and explained some of what was in them. Panic gripped me as I sped through the pages looking for Josh and Naomi's names. I glanced over at Mom and Dad, watching for a reaction, waiting for them to see. They were still on page one.

Next Tom announced the special awards. Bob received one for having traveled the greatest distance, and Pam and Brenda for their extraordinary efforts in organizing the reunion. Then I heard my name being called: Youngest Grandmother. I didn't look at Mom and Dad as I walked to the front to receive my certificate. Pam did. Later she told me their faces were buried in the booklet, as if far too engrossed to notice.

"Did you see what Denise did?" my mother said, as everyone finished eating and began circulating around the room. My father moved in closer, looking down at the open booklet she was holding. She pointed at the page. "I told you this would happen."

I was standing no more than fifteen feet away at another table where we could look at the family photo the photographer had taken earlier and order prints. Didn't they realize I was right there? Did they think I couldn't hear them?

Did you see what Denise did?

She sounded as if she were talking about a ten-year-old, like I had just spilled grape juice on the sofa, which never would have happened because I would have thrown my body in front of the tumbling glass or whatever else it took to prevent her wrath. I pretended to scan that side of the room, sneaking a look at them, but I couldn't see their faces.

I turned away and stared at the floor, dizzy with having disobeyed them, wishing I had the guts to walk up to them and say, "That's right. I told them about my son. He's not a secret anymore. And if you don't like it, you can kiss my ass." I wished I'd had the courage to say that a year ago, twenty-six years ago.

I made my way through the crowd to the front door, walked out into the heavy July heat, and lit a cigarette. I knew I'd be safe there. No one who didn't absolutely have to would brave the muggy Virginia air, and I'd already met the two or three others who smoked.

For the next two hours, I waited for my parents to confront me while making it difficult for them by surrounding myself with others. When we said our goodbyes, Dad looked vaguely like he wanted to say something, but didn't. Mom acted as if nothing had happened.

They stayed in the area for the next two days to visit with Win and Ann and do some sightseeing. Auntie Em, Kendall, Debby, and I returned to the house near Marshall, and the next afternoon Bob, Amy and Emily, and Em's son Rob and his wife joined us there for dinner.

The reunion had left me exhausted and emotionally raw, and I found myself on the verge of tears several times that day. I was surrounded by people who reminded me of my parents — Em, with Mom's features and mannerisms; Bob, modeling Dad's condescending peacemaker style; and Debby, a constant reminder of our family's dysfunction. I'd had enough and all I wanted was to go home.

Auntie Em started to cry after we hugged goodbye and I turned to board my plane. The image of tears on that face, a reflection of the woman I'd grown up with, compelled me to rush back to hug her again.

"I love you, Niecy," she said.

The words I needed, coming from that familiar voice.

"I love you, Auntie."

On the flight home, I realized that having so many relatives would make my life more complicated. In just over a year, I'd gone from having a small, manageable family — a husband, stepson and grandson, parents and siblings who didn't live close enough to see often, and a handful of aunts, uncles, cousins, nieces and nephews I saw even less often — to having a son and granddaughter of my own, and an enormous extended family, all with enormous expectations.

"I believe we really touched Catherine," Aunt Ann had said after the reunion. "I think we got to her heart."

I couldn't bring myself to hope. More than a month after I returned home from Virginia I still had no word from my parents. More than ever, I felt like a motherless child, still needing something I could not get from a woman I did not really know.

I wondered whether Josh might be thinking the same thing.

Chapter 19

MOTHERLY ADVICE

"So, how'd it go?" Josh called shortly after my return home from Virginia.

"Good," I said, pleasantly surprised by his interest since he had sounded almost indifferent when I'd shared the news of reconnecting with my mother's family. "Auntie Em is wonderful. They're all really nice people. I got the Youngest Grandmother Award."

"Cool. Did your parents say anything? About me?"

"No, but the cat's out of the bag. You're not a secret anymore."

"That's *it*?" His voice was shrill with disappointment.

"It's something, Josh. Once they see that no one cares about the circumstances of your birth, they'll come around." I winced at the words, hoping he wouldn't see through my feigned optimism.

"Yeah, right."

I couldn't fault his doubt. We'd both been waiting a long time. I offered to send pictures, addresses, and more information about his great aunts and uncles and cousins, but it was only a matter of days before his attention to anything not directly related to his own needs vanished.

He and Angel were still together, although Josh sounded less enthusiastic about their relationship than he had the month before.

"Are you doing drugs?" I felt driven to ask.

"No. At least, I'm not. I don't know what she does when she's at the club." He added that Angel had been complaining about wanting a commitment from him and a child of her own. "Things probably aren't going to work out with us."

Their potential break-up cheered me until I realized that the next girlfriend might be worse. For the next week, I stewed, imagining my granddaughter put in risky situations at Josh's whim.

My desire to speak out mounted like a hurricane, gathering strength from the unspoken grievances of past months. I reminded myself that my purpose was to make a difference in my son's life. All he needed was a little motherly guidance. Hadn't he complained that I had been holding back? Because my previous attempts to express myself in person or on the phone had been futile, I decided to write him a letter. I worked on the wording for days until I was certain that I'd struck the right combination of compassion and reason.

Our last conversation left me upset, but rather than fire off a letter in the heat of the moment, I tried to give it some thought. I love you very much and I want to be a positive influence in your life.

The longer we know each other, the clearer it is to me that you expected when we found each other that your life would just magically get better. I wish that were so. We are not so different, as you say. With the exception of your quick temper (which I realize is just like your father's), we are actually a lot alike.

I've never been disappointed in anything about you, except your refusal to be honest with yourself and accept the consequences of your actions. No matter what happens, all I ever hear is how it's someone else's fault: Marissa's, Max and Nina's, your boss', or mine. I've never once heard you say, "I screwed up and it's mine to fix." You're a grown man, and you can't go on saying your life is what it is because of anyone else or because you got a rotten deal. At some point, you've got to take charge, and that means taking responsibility. You make your own choices now, whether to marry someone or change jobs or what to spend your money on. And whatever you choose, you must also live with the outcome, good or bad.

It's time to get over this "I don't want to grow up" crap. Yes, you missed most of your childhood and being with your real family. But we can't do it over. All we have left is from

now on, and we have a choice what to do with that. Once
you conceived and committed to having a child, you gave up
the option to continue being a child yourself. Naomi needs a
parent, not a playmate. That doesn't mean the fun has to stop,
but it does mean you have to bite the bullet and make decisions
for her benefit. It means you don't jump into relationships
simply to meet your own needs or because you need help
caring for your daughter.

You complain that I don't accept you as you are, but you
seem to have a hard time accepting others. You keep making
choices that require the women to change. It would make a
whole lot more sense to get clear on your own vision and find
someone who fits into it, someone who shares your needs and
goals, even if it takes some time. If you give yourself half a
chance instead of going for the easy out, you'll find the right
woman to share your life with.

I'm sure this isn't what you want from me. Maybe you
would prefer a mother who agreed with everything you said
and did, who felt sorry for you, and who would defend your
position no matter what. Well, I can't do that. Not because
I don't love you, because I do — more than you know. I'm
determined to do right by you. I didn't when you were born,
and that's the biggest regret of my life. But I will now, even if
you don't like it or appreciate it.

Someday, you'll be on the other end of a reunion with
Sammy and Judah. Maybe then this will all be clearer. There
are two sides and neither is easy. I'm trying my best to work on
my issues, things that only surfaced after you and I reunited. I
believe we can make this relationship work.

And then I threw down the gauntlet.

If it's going to work, I need you to deal with me honestly
from now on, even if you think I won't like the truth. I
expect that you will never (EVER) again take drugs, even
recreationally; that you will never again put Naomi in a
dangerous situation; and that you will start looking at your
own accountability for what happens, and stop automatically
placing blame elsewhere.

It's okay if you can't do all of this right now. But I refuse to stop believing in you or let you down by expecting less. I know you can do better.

This is a two-way street, and I invite you to be honest about what you expect from me.

Once I'd mailed the letter, I revisited what I had written and grew nervous about what Josh's reaction might be. Even though I played out every scenario, I wasn't prepared for the lashing I received two weeks later.

Dear Mother.

He had never called me "Mother" — only Mom.

I wish we could discuss this in person or on the phone, but we can't because you're so breakable. I want a guarantee that you won't throw one of your fits and walk away or tell me fuck you. If we're gonna dance, then we're gonna dance until our feet break or until we're complete. I read your letter thoroughly and I feel encouraged enough to answer. Now I'm going to tell you what I think, so put on your big girl pants, because the truth hurts.

You don't have a clue what I expect. I want a fulltime mother. I don't care how old I am. I'm either going to get you fulltime (close to me) or I just won't be "emotionally ready for it." Isn't that the way it goes? I'm not having a long-distance relationship with someone who means so much to me.

I'm angry and resentful about so much. I get set off easily but really, if I didn't care I wouldn't get set off because it wouldn't bother me, right? I'm so confused. I don't know what's right or wrong anymore. I have intentions to do the right thing, but sometimes it just doesn't turn out that way. As far as taking responsibility for your own actions, you have no room to talk, and until you start taking responsibility for something you did a long time ago, we won't even discuss responsibility.

You're right, I'm trying to relive something I've missed and I'll never get it back. I'm not giving up and it's not going to be long distance. I'm not getting hurt again. You're going to have to move here. I was willing to move there and try, but I got shot down, so it's your turn. That's the only way it can be. I know you have your own life in California with Henry and I respect that, but if you want to be a part of my life, come on down and live in reality for awhile, not a week, and let's be a family. Are you willing to make a sacrifice for me? Or are you too comfortable?

Oh Miss Hippie, don't you EVER use drugs. Right! Hypocrite!!! I made a mistake doing drugs with Marissa, but I thought it would change something in our relationship. You don't know how much I loved her. I would have done anything to make it work. I tried and was wrong, but don't you dare tell me about drugs! EVER!

I want to be closer to you than anyone. I want to tell you things that no one knows, but just because you fucked up twenty-seven years ago doesn't mean I have to pay for it now. I know your simple mind is going to think everything I'm writing is to make you feel guilty, but it's not. I want you, I love you, but I've been let down before. I didn't give you up, you did me, and I can forget and forgive, but you need to make a sacrifice to be closer to me. I tried and was pushed away because this "stranger" was going to get in the way of your cushy lifestyle.

When the day comes with Sammy and Judah, I don't care if I've got millions or if I'm living in a cardboard box. I'm going to be there for them one-hundred percent because they didn't do anything wrong, I did, and I'm going to tell them that. I can't make up for it, but I sure can start from that day on.

You don't know anything about me. I cried out for you the day I was born and the day we found each other and all I got was pushed away. Fuck that! You could start being a real mother and I can be a real son. It's just how bad we want it. I know I have and still do. Now you decide.

Your son, Joshua (Erick Janson) Goldberg. It doesn't fucking matter what name!

I was too stunned to cry on my first read, but the second time, I broke down in sobs, and again as I watched Henry read it.

"This is some serious shit," he said. "For saying he isn't trying to make you feel guilty, he sure as hell did a good job."

"Now what?" I moaned through my tears. "How do I answer that?"

"Maybe you shouldn't. Let him sit for a while and think about what he said."

But I felt compelled to defend myself. Much of what he'd written was flat-out wrong: I wasn't a hypocrite for telling him not to use drugs, he hadn't been the one making a sacrifice by coming to California, and my lifestyle was hardly cushy. Obviously, he didn't really respect my life with Henry to make such an unreasonable demand that I move to Pensacola.

"You don't deserve this," my birthmother friends agreed when I shared his letter at the next support group meeting.

"He said he wasn't angry," I said. "That he didn't blame me. Now I feel like I can't trust him."

"Lots of adoptees experience rage," one woman said. "Even when they've had good lives in their adoptive homes. It doesn't always surface right away."

"He's testing you," another chimed in. "He wants to see if you'll stay this time."

"But what if he means it?" I whined. "What if I never see him again?"

"That's not likely to happen," said a birthmother who had been going back and forth with her daughter for years. "He might pull away for a while. In any case, you have no control over his reactions, so it's best not to get caught up in the worst that could happen. Just let it play out."

"And don't give up," another birthmother said.

I clung to their words for a day or two before my guilt resurfaced. Underneath the venom, Josh sounded like a baby screaming for his mommy. I wished I could soothe him, as if he were the sweet infant I'd seen in the nursery bassinet. I longed to save him, like the wounded birds I'd tried to rescue when I was a child. Every time I'd found one below the trees in our backyard, I gathered them up, nested them in a shoebox with grass and leaves, provided water and seed, watched over them. And yet, they died, too damaged to heal. I buried them in the yard, marked their tiny graves, and mourned their passing. My parents assured me that it was not my fault, that I had done my best. It was simply nature taking its course.

Now I wondered, What if I had hurt the bird, even if by accident? What if I had frightened a young one out of its nest before it was ready to fly, or thrown a ball and knocked it out of the sky? What if I had brought it harm and then failed to save its life?

These thoughts led to the memory of my first real job, at sixteen, in a dog kennel where Dobermans were bred and raised for show. One day, I had hefted too many wriggling puppies at once and dropped them. One of the pup's legs appeared to have broken in the fall. I went home in tears and continued to cry even after my employer called to say that the break was minor and the puppy would be all right.

As hard as I fought the images of my son as a wounded bird, a puppy dropped by someone he had trusted, I could not shake the thought that I had let him fall. His wings, his leg, his psyche had been damaged, and I might not be able to save him.

The sting of Josh's reproach faded when I considered that his letter was more honest than anything he had communicated before. Despite the harsh words, he had revealed his true feelings. As much as he had hurt me, I understood what he wanted. It was what I'd wanted from my parents: acceptance and unconditional love.

The juxtaposition was confounding — finding myself caught between the parents I felt had let me down and the son who felt so let down by me, with no idea what to do about either.

Chapter 20

BEST LIGHT

A week later, I wrote Josh back. I refuted his accusations and explained my position, while making it clear that it would be his choice, not mine, if he cut me off. I said that moving to Florida was not an option, but that didn't mean I was abandoning him. Again, I told him that I loved him and believed in him.

After a month of silence, he started calling again, as if our exchange had never occurred. Despite the lack of resolution, being back in regular contact assuaged my fear of losing him.

Josh had a new girlfriend. Her name was Holly and they'd met when she'd brought her ailing car into the mechanic shop where he worked. From the things he said and the noises I heard in the background when we were on the phone, I suspected they were already living together. It took him almost a month to tell me that she had moved in a few days after he'd repaired her car.

"Don't worry," he said. "I can't get married until my divorce comes through and that's at least four more months."

"Oh Josh." I heaved an obvious sigh.

"I'm just kidding," he said, but I was pretty sure he wasn't. "Holly and I get along great. She's a much better mother than Marissa. Or Angel."

"You just met her, Josh. Please don't jump into another marriage right away."

"So, tell me this. How long do you think two people should know each other before they get married?"

"I'd like to see you give it a year."

"A *year*?"

I knew I was on shaky ground. Henry and I had only known each other for five months when we got engaged, and a little over eight months by the wedding. If I'd told Josh, he must have forgotten. He certainly wasn't above calling me on giving advice that didn't match my actions.

"You're already living together," I said. "What's the big hurry?"

"Yeah, but you know, since we live together, we see each other more than people who are just dating. So you got to figure each month is more like three or four months, right? By January, it'll be like we've been together a year."

"It sounds like you're going to do whatever you want. Why are you asking my opinion?

"Because I want you in it with me. I want you to approve."

"Let's just see how it goes, okay?"

Holly had grown up in Pensacola and had a close-knit family. She was twenty-two, married once, and had a nine-month-old boy named Christopher. When she'd met Josh, she was living with her parents almost an hour north of town. Josh raved about her mom and dad, and told me that he, Holly, and the kids spent every Sunday at their house. In November, Josh and Holly had a professional family portrait taken, each holding the other's child on their lap, and sent prints in their Christmas cards. She was a beautiful girl, with long brown hair, bright eyes, and a sweet smile. I talked to her on the phone a couple times and she sounded nice, even called me "Ma'am" in her Southern accent. Naomi was already calling her "Mama."

Josh gave Holly an engagement ring for Christmas, and in early January he called to tell me that he'd received his final divorce decree and they had decided to get married on March twenty-ninth at her parents' home.

"You and Henry will come, right?"

"I don't know, Josh. We'll have to see if we can take time away from work and if we have the money."

"But I want you to be there. You missed my first two weddings. You've missed out on so much of my life."

"Let me think about it, okay? I'll let you know."

Almost immediately after hanging up, I regretted my reluctance. Jumping into relationships quickly seemed to be a pattern with Josh, and here he was doing it again. But he was going ahead, regardless of how I thought. What had he said? "I want you in." I decided to put my reservations aside.

"He's happy," I told Henry. "I should be happy for him."

The next day I called Josh and told him I'd be there, even if Henry couldn't come.

After months of withholding from my family any details about Josh, I treated his upcoming wedding like good news and wrote to my parents, brother and sister, aunts, uncles, and cousins. I was thrilled when most of them — including Mom and Dad — responded by sending cards and gifts.

I arrived in Pensacola three days before the wedding. Coming through the airport gate, I spotted Josh squatting next to Naomi.

"Go to Grandma." He gave her a little push and she toddled into my arms.

"Hey, my sweet girl!" I said, crouching to embrace her. "I've missed you so much." How could I have let a whole year go by without seeing her?

Naomi grinned and I caressed her soft curly tresses.

"She's got some hair," I called to Josh.

"Yes, she does." He laughed and moved forward to embrace both of us.

I saw Holly sitting off to the side with baby Christopher. When Josh didn't make a move to introduce us, I stepped toward her.

"Holly. Hi, I'm Denise. It's good to finally meet you."

"I'm glad to meet you, too," she said, setting her boy down and standing to greet me.

I gave her a hug, and then leaned down to greet Christopher, who burst into tears and grabbed his mother's leg.

"Sorry," she said. "He's a little shy."

"Don't worry. We'll be great friends in no time."

Just a few months short of turning two, Naomi thrived on the extra attention of my presence. She loved dancing to "Bananas in Pajamas" and being read to, and followed me everywhere, even into the bathroom where she would sit on her training potty right next to the real toilet until I was finished. Even though we hadn't seen each other for more than a year, she seemed to remember me. Josh thought she probably recognized my voice from talking on the phone.

I liked Holly. She made the kids a priority. Unlike Marissa, she seemed interested in what I had to say and attentive to my comfort. I especially appreciated the way she stood up to Josh when he got out of hand and her ability to joke him out of his moods.

Still, judgments crowded my head. I hated where they were living — a tiny sty of a trailer in a rundown mobile home park, making me glad I'd declined Josh's offer to stay with them and taken a hotel room nearby. It bothered me that they ate fast food or at all-you-can-eat-for-two-ninety-nine buffets instead of cooking regular meals. Then, there were Holly's tattoos, which hadn't been visible in any of the pictures they'd sent. Like Josh's, they were large and elaborate, designed by her last boyfriend who was a tattoo artist. Remembering how I'd felt after Dad's harsh reaction to Josh's tattoos, I scolded myself for focusing on the negative.

When I met Holly's parents, I watched them closely, looking for some indication of disapproval of Josh, the imminent wedding, or even their own daughter and found none. They had married young and raised three children. Holly's dad told me how he had driven for two days straight to bring her and her infant home after she'd called to say that her husband had become abusive. I caught myself comparing their unconditional dedication to their children with my attitude toward Josh, as well as what I thought my own parents might do in a similar situation.

Josh wanted me to see where he worked and meet his boss, Peter, who would be his best man. Holly and I stopped by after our shopping, during which I bought her wedding shoes and Josh's wedding tie.

"Cool," I said dutifully, as I followed Josh through the

shop where he pointed out a big hunk of equipment and an array of greasy tools.

"You said you want me to be honest with you, right?" he said when he dropped me at my hotel that night.

"Yes. Of course, I do." *What now?* I thought.

"Something's bothering me. You didn't get very excited about the shop."

"I probably don't appreciate the ins and outs of it, but I thought it was very nice. It was... really something." *Damn it,* I thought. *I sound like my father reacting to the news of my reunion.*

"I guess I thought you'd be more impressed."

"I *am* impressed," I said, at a loss for more specific words.

"Because it's what I do and I want you to be proud of me." He looked deflated, like a little boy whose mother had been less than enthusiastic about a drawing he'd brought home from school.

"Oh, Josh, I am proud of you. The shop is great. You're obviously a wonderful mechanic."

"Okay... well, I just thought I should tell you. That I was a little disappointed."

"I'm sorry, Sweetie. I'm glad you told me. I promise to pay more attention from now on."

Once I settled into my room for the night, I wrote in my journal. This is a positive step. At last, Josh told me straight up what he needs, and it's something I can do. If we can be honest with each other and about how we're feeling, I feel sure we'll make great strides in our relationship.

Josh was off work Friday, and the five of us spent the day together running last-minute errands before Holly and Christopher would leave to spend the night with her parents.

"Does it worry you that Josh has been married twice before?" I asked her while Josh ran into the dry cleaners to pick up his suit.

"Twice?" Holly spun around to face me, her eyes narrowed.

"Oh God."

"He said he'd only been married to Marissa."

"He didn't tell you about his sons?"

"He told me about Sammy and Judah. But he never said he'd been married to their mother."

"Well, he was. At least that's what he told me. Shit, Holly, I'm sorry."

"It's not your fault."

Josh opened the back door and hung his suit on the hook next to me, then jumped into the driver's seat.

"Hold on a minute there, Bubba," I said before he could start the car. "You got some 'splainin' to do."

"What'd I do now?"

"You didn't tell Holly this is your third marriage."

"What?" he said sheepishly.

Holly glared at him. "You were married to Rebecca?"

"Yeah… didn't I say so?"

"No, you did not."

"I thought I did."

"Whatever." She socked him in arm. "You're just lucky I'm too much in love with you to call off the wedding."

That night, when I took Josh and Naomi to dinner, I confronted him. "What the hell were you thinking, not telling Holly the truth?"

"I don't know. I guess I was trying to present myself in the best light. I didn't want her to think I was a two-time loser."

"And you thought it would be better if she found out after you're married?"

"Sure." He grinned. "Because then she'll be stuck with me."

We drove out to Holly's parents' house early the next morning to help with the preparations. I had worried in advance that they, or someone else at the wedding, would misunderstand our relationship and ask me questions I couldn't answer, like what Josh was like as a boy. But he assured me that they knew and nothing embarrassing would happen. He was right. They were warm and welcoming, and I relaxed into my role as mother of the groom.

Josh and Holly's dad set up the gazebo and chairs in the back yard, while Holly, her mother, and I finished the reception food. When the time came for everyone to get dressed for the ceremony, I was put in charge of Naomi.

I had just lifted her out of the bathtub and was on my knees wrapping a towel around her. All of a sudden, she threw her tiny arms around my shoulders, buried her head in my chest, then pulled back and looked hard into my face. I felt her eyes boring into my soul.

I'm not sure how long we sat on the bathroom floor, hugging and staring, little Naomi silently begging me to meet her eyes and her touch, making that primal connection. In that instant, without fear or practical thought, I committed to her.

"Naomi, my darling," I said. "I promise to stay in your life and love you always, no matter what, even when I can't be with you."

The way she looked at me, I knew she heard. I knew she believed.

I missed most of the wedding. In addition to Josh's boss as best man and Holly's sister as matron of honor, Naomi and Christopher were included in the wedding party. After the procession, Christopher turned and bolted into his grandmother's arms. Naomi took off running into the empty field behind the gazebo. I ran after her, stumbling through the dirt ruts in my heels, and by the time I caught up with her and coaxed her back, the ceremony was over.

It was a good visit, "our best so far," Josh said the next day before we left for the airport. I had to agree. For the first time in more than a year, we'd both spoken our feelings openly, without fear of conflict or reprisal. In spite of my initial doubts, I felt hopeful.

I hadn't decided whether Josh was predictable or I was psychic. One or the other had to be true, because within two months of the wedding I was struck by an overwhelming sense of dread. Josh's effusive pronouncements — "Everything's wonderful" and "I've never been happier" — brought me more alarm than comfort, as I recalled the light and prosperous days when he and Marissa were setting up housekeeping not long before she'd left. Holly, however, did not sound so lighthearted when we talked. She confided that Josh had been increasingly moody, sulking over the smallest upsets and sometimes raging in front of the children to the point that she often took them and left. When she would return a few hours later, he always acted as if nothing had happened. I braced myself for another disappointment.

They separated in September, five months after they had married.

Chapter 21

INTO THE FOLD

On New Year's Eve — almost three years into our reunion and four months after leaving Holly — Josh met my family.

In November, he called to tell me that his boss had decided to relocate his auto repair business to Tucson, Arizona, and wanted Josh to move with him.

"I'm giving it serious consideration," he said. "I wouldn't have any problem finding another job in Pensacola, but I like working with Peter, and maybe this would give me and Naomi a fresh start. Plus, I'd be a lot closer to California."

My body buzzed with the familiar mix of exhilaration and fear. Josh gave no indication of remembering that my parents lived near Tucson. He had no way of knowing that my brother's daughter Becky, a student at the University of Arizona, would be getting married there on New Year's Day. Bob and Amy, my sister Debby, Becky's mother, stepfather and sister — and of course my parents — would be attending. Henry and I had made plans to go, and I'd offered to take the wedding pictures and create an album as a gift.

"What do you think?" Josh asked.

"About your going with Peter?" I stalled for time, trying to decide whether to reveal the full implications of his move.

"Yeah. I'm nervous about moving to a state where I don't know anybody."

Was he really unaware that he had family in Arizona? Or was he baiting me?

"I'd be totally on my own with Naomi," he said, as if thinking out loud. "I'll have to find another job while Peter gets things set up, and an apartment and day care."

If I tell him, he'll go, I thought. He would have expectations — *reasonable* expectations — that I could not trust my family to meet. Although my current relationship with

Josh was far from ideal, at least we had one. *What if my parents refused to meet him? Or worse, if they met and then rejected him? What if Josh flew into another rage?* Too many things could go wrong. I would have to do whatever I could to prevent him from coming.

"And what if the job doesn't work out or I don't like it there?" Josh continued. "I guess I can always move back."

On the other hand, maybe this was meant to be. Why else would Peter be moving his shop to Tucson, of all places, and why now? Withholding information from Josh would be wrong, a manipulative attempt to obstruct the course of fate. Despite my qualms, I would have to step aside and let the scenario play out.

"You know," I said cautiously, "my mom and dad live there."

"Really? Did I know that? Maybe I forgot." He sounded genuinely surprised, and I let go of my earlier suspicions.

"And this is really weird," I said. "My niece — Bob's daughter, Becky, who lives in Tucson — is getting married on January first. We're going to be there. The whole family will be."

"Wow, you're kidding! That *is* weird. The timing, I mean. Because Peter's plan is to close down the week before Christmas, when business is slow anyway. Then we'll load everything up and be on our way by the twentieth."

The impact of what was happening didn't hit me until Josh called the next day to say he'd told Peter yes. They would each drive a rental truck, loaded with the shop equipment, their personal belongings, and Josh's car. Peter's wife and two children would drive in their car, and Naomi in the truck with Josh. They expected the trip to take no more than three days.

"So I'll get to see you when you come down for the wedding," he said.

"Yeah, and everyone else too," I said, my mind whirling with how I would break this news to my parents. Brother Bob had told his kids about Josh and reported that they were excited about having a cousin on his side, although none had made contact with Josh. I wondered whether Becky would invite Josh and Naomi to the wedding. I offered to give her a call.

"Do you think she would be okay with me calling her before I get there? Maybe she can give me some leads on apartments for rent."

I said I would feel her out and call him back. When I talked to Becky, she was her usual laid-back self. "Of course, Josh and Naomi should come to the wedding," she said, and that it was fine if he wanted to call her. After that, she and Josh talked a few times, and he told her he would get in touch once he arrived.

His excitement heightened as the move date approached. Once my initial anxiety subsided, I got excited too. Whatever had happened between us, I was grateful for any opportunity to see my son and granddaughter. Maybe a major change was what Josh needed to turn his life around. Most of all, I felt certain that the timing was right for him to meet my family — *his family* — the people who should have welcomed him into the fold long ago.

This was what I had wanted from the beginning of our reunion, like any new mother expects her parents, siblings, and extended family to rejoice in the arrival of her child. I realized that when my parents failed me, I had divided myself between the roles of mother and daughter, just as I split into the grieving girl and the courageous woman after losing Josh. Perhaps it was time to start integrating all of these pieces into one.

If not now, when?

"Josh and Naomi are moving to Tucson," I told Dad over the phone. Before he could respond, I launched into an explanation of how his decision to relocate had transpired, emphasizing how valuable Josh must be to his boss that he wanted him to come along. "They'll be there by Christmas."

"I see."

"He and Becky have already been in contact, and he's coming to the wedding. You're finally going to meet him."

"This is unexpected." It had been a long time since I'd heard Dad sound so rattled. "I'll have to think about how to handle it with your mother."

"Do you want me to tell her?"

"No, I'll take care of it." He cleared his throat. "On second thought, maybe you should tell her."

"Okay."

"But I don't want her to know we already talked. Call back in about ten minutes. I'll make sure she answers the phone."

Shit, I thought, as I hung up and glanced at the clock. Dad had always let me off the hook when it came to delivering difficult news to Mom, like when I was pregnant, when I'd found Josh, and even as recently as telling them that Josh and Holly had separated. My chest pounded as I contemplated her most likely reaction. She would not be glad. Certainly, she would object; she might even yell at me.

You're a forty-eight-year-old woman, I scolded myself. Why are you still acting like a scared little girl?

"Hi Mom, it's me."

"Well, Denny, what a surprise."

"How are you?"

I was sorry I hadn't forged ahead, once she launched into a monologue about the weather and all of her latest aches and pains. My stomach started to churn and I knew if I didn't get it done quickly I would lose my nerve.

"I have some news. Josh and Naomi are moving to Tucson later this month."

"Why?"

"Because the company he works for is moving there. Anyway, they're coming to Becky's wedding, so you'll finally get to meet them."

"You know, Denise, a lot of people don't want small children at their weddings," she said matter-of-factly. "They can get fidgety and misbehave."

"Becky's okay with it, Mom. She invited them."

"How old is the girl?"

The girl? "Two. Actually, two-and-a-half."

"Does Josh realize that Tucson is a terrible place for a child? The crime rate here is very high. We're always hearing on the news about children being abducted."

I stifled a groan. My mother was very skilled at steering any discussion away from the real issues. "That can happen anywhere, Mom. I'm sure there are lots of families living safely in Tucson."

"I'm telling you, it's really bad."

"I'll tell Josh to be careful."

"What's he going to do for a living?"

"The same thing he's always done. Auto mechanics. His boss in Florida is moving his shop there."

"But where will he live?"

"He'll find an apartment."

We bantered for another fifteen minutes with no further mention of the wedding or meeting Josh. As I hung up the phone, I shook my head, chiding myself for having expected anything more than smoke and mirrors from my mother. But I had delivered the bomb. Dad would have to deal with the fall-out.

Josh's enthusiasm lasted cross-country and for the first couple days in Tucson. By Christmas Eve, he'd left Becky a few messages and received one back, but they still hadn't connected. My heart sank, learning that he and Naomi would be alone on Christmas. Recognizing that my parents wouldn't make the effort, I regretted that I hadn't done more on his behalf with my niece.

"I'm sure she's really busy right now," I said. "Besides the holidays and wedding plans, I know she had finals."

"I'll tell you this, if I heard from a cousin I'd never met, I'd be there in a minute," he said, his voice prickling. "Nothing could keep me away."

"I'm sure you'll hear from her soon."

"Well, it might be too late, because I'm about ready to turn around and go back to Florida!"

"Josh, just hang on. Things will work out. I understand it's hard being in a new place, but you were going to move there before you even knew you had a cousin and grandparents there."

"Yeah, my grandparents — where are they? They know I'm here, right?"

"I told them you were moving, but I didn't say exactly when. They know they'll meet you at the wedding."

"Well, I've about had it. All I ever wanted was to be part of a family, and here I am, two, almost three years down the road, and they're still holding me off."

"Josh, please…"

"I don't know why I put myself through this. Fuck you and your whole fucking family!"

He hung up. That horrible sinking feeling was back, the same nauseous, light-headed helplessness I'd felt when Josh had raved in Biloxi and outside the restaurant here and in the letter he had written me a year-and-a-half before. Or when John had yelled at me for tipping over the motorcycle: feeling wrong when I wasn't, and at the mercy of someone I loved.

Josh was right. *Where the hell were my parents: three years ago, twenty-eight years ago, and especially now?* I could hardly condemn his anger at them. But how could he possibly blame me for their behavior? I'd told him what they were like. Why couldn't he just accept them for who they were, and work around it, as I had?

No, I thought. *This is too much. How dare he take out his frustrations on me?* I'd given him an opportunity and he was crapping all over it simply because everything wasn't going the way he envisioned. I couldn't trust my son any more than I could trust my parents, and that realization chilled me to the bone.

By the time I related our conversation to Henry, I was already thinking about how we could get out of going to the wedding. Henry listened while I paced and ranted myself into a decision.

"I don't want to see Josh," I said. "I don't want anyone to meet him, not like this. What an asshole! Like it's my fault that my family hasn't stepped up to the plate. I should never have gotten Becky involved. What if he unleashes on her? Do you think he might be dangerous? Maybe I should call and warn her, tell her not to talk to him. What the hell was I thinking, letting this psychopath into our lives? Anyway, we're not going. Let Josh fend for himself. Let them all. I just don't care anymore."

I stopped for a breath and slumped into the dining room chair across from Henry. He looked like he was about to respond when I jumped to my feet.

"Shit! I promised Becky I'd take her pictures. I can't disappoint her. I have to be there! Maybe Josh will go back to Florida. But what if he doesn't?"

I sat down again and sought my husband's compassionate gaze.

"He'll be there," I said. "I can feel it. And I can't do that to him. I can't let him face my family alone." I took a deep breath. "So here's what we'll do. We'll go, but I'll change our flights so instead of three nights, we'll only be there for one. We'll go the night before the wedding and leave right after the reception."

"Fine with me," Henry said, once I let him get a word in. "Unlike Josh, I say the less time with your family the better."

I laughed. "Shut up!"

Two days before we were scheduled to fly out, Josh left a message on our answering machine.

"Hey, it's me. I just wondered when you're coming in." His voice was soft, almost timid. "I got together with Becky and Marcus, and we really hit it off. Naomi is going to be the flower girl. So, there's a dinner the night before and I guess I'll see you there?" He added that he'd found an apartment and just had a phone installed. "Here's the number if you want to call back."

I didn't call. Even in my relief that he had been appeased

and we might get through the event without incident, I was still too upset. A nagging thought surfaced — how, like my mother, I was avoiding an important issue simply because it might be difficult — and I pushed it away.

Our flight was delayed, making us late for the family dinner and leaving me with more time to wonder what would happen. By the time we arrived at the Mexican restaurant, everyone was already there. I inhaled and scanned the private room — Mom and Dad, Debby, Bob and Amy, Becky and Marcus, Becky's sister Emily, and Josh and Naomi — munching on chips and salsa, sipping margaritas or sodas, and chatting happily around the long table. I let out a long breath.

"We made it!" I called out to no one in particular.

In the midst of greetings from around the room, Josh stood and came over to hug me. My heart leapt as if I were seeing him for the first time all over again, and as if somewhere behind the gentle glow in his eyes he meant me harm.

"Your hair's gotten so long since I last saw you," I said, assessing his mood and demeanor.

"Yours, too," he said.

"I guess it *has* been a while." *Almost a year, since his wedding in Pensacola,* I thought. "So, you've met everyone?"

"Yeah."

Naomi stood up in her chair and I realized it had been too long. I scooped her up and gave her a big squeeze.

"And *you*! You're so big!"

She turned and held her arms out to Henry, and I heard Mom say, "Naomi knows Henry?" After he took her, I made my way around the table to greet each person and check their faces for any evidence of discomfort. Even Mom passed the test.

"Hi, Denny," she said, gazing into my eyes and grasping my hand. "We were wondering when you'd get here."

"I was wondering the same thing. Our flight left late."

"Do you want a margarita?"

"Do I ever!"

After a jovial two-hour dinner, Mom and Dad went home for the night and the rest of us went to the hotel where most of the out-of-towners were staying. Sitting around the fireplace in the lobby bar, we could have been any normal family coming together for a special occasion.

Josh showed me the little Mexican cotton and lace dress he'd bought for Naomi to wear in the wedding, white with colorful flowers embroidered around the bottom, and asked me to choose between two pairs of sandals to go with it. He said he had some leads on mechanic jobs and hoped to be working soon. He had already made some friends in his apartment building, including a woman who also had a little girl and was willing to baby-sit Naomi. I watched his face for some sign of remorse or recognition of what had happened the week before, and saw none.

Damn, he's not going to say a word. He's going to pretend nothing happened and let things slide back into the status quo. I was tempted to do the same, under the influence of tequila and gratitude for a positive outcome. But the sting of our last conversation was still there and I longed for resolution.

"So can we talk privately?"

"Okay." He followed me to a row of empty barstools at the other end of the room.

"I was pretty upset by the things you said. We almost didn't come because of it."

"I was freaked out, being in a strange place with a two-year-old child, trying to take care of her with no help."

"I know, but it wasn't fair to blast me like that. I don't have any control over Becky or anyone else."

"I was just letting off steam."

"Letting off steam is one thing. You said 'fuck you and your family.' And I'm not supposed to be hurt by that? I'm supposed to be excited about seeing you and having you meet everyone?"

"I shouldn't have said it." He looked down. "But you said the same thing to me."

"And I apologized." I waited for the words "I'm sorry," but they didn't come.

"You shouldn't run away from me because of it," he said. "I can't believe you thought about not coming. You should be willing to face me and fight it out."

"I'm here, aren't I?"

"For one night."

I wanted to tell him, You have no idea what it took for me to come here. How helpless I felt, how afraid I was, after waiting for this moment when you would meet my family — yes, my fucking family — that something, anything, everything, could go wrong and you would be back to nothing. I would be back to nothing. That deep, dark hole where I've lived for too long.

"I don't want to fight with you," was what I said.

I didn't like fighting with anyone, least of all Josh, and not just because he didn't fight fair. With him I was too vulnerable. Every conflict felt like life and death, rife with the possibility of losing him for good. It was easier to call a truce and give things time to smooth over.

Josh was taking Marcus out for an impromptu "bachelor party," so I offered to let Naomi stay in the hotel with us. She and Henry fell asleep before midnight — the first New Year's Eve Henry and I had missed since we'd met — and the longer I lay between them in the bed, the wider awake I became. I slipped into my sweats and snuck down to the lobby, where I remembered seeing a sign that the front desk had splits of champagne for sale. Back upstairs, I sequestered myself in the bathroom, drinking bubbly out of a plastic cup and scribbling frenzied thoughts onto hotel stationery to the sound of my two loved ones snoring softly on the other side of the wall.

Becky's wedding was lovely. Naomi performed her flower girl duties with a minimum of coaxing. The photography went off without a hitch despite my tired eyes. When the time came for a family shot, I set up the camera on a tripod and got one of the guests to release the shutter. For the first time, my son and granddaughter stood with the Jansons. My heart skipped and my eyes welled as I savored this scene that I'd come to expect would never happen.

I watched Josh taking in the faces of his blood relations and witnessed his joy as he found himself mirrored in the family he had not known — much like I had at the Kendall reunion.

"Becky and I have the same face," he said, beaming at me. "If I were a girl, that's exactly what I'd look like."

I laughed and stepped in to hug him, letting the warmth of the moment melt any residual resentment. "This is a great day," I said. "Oh Bubba, I do love you."

"I love you too, Mama."

During the reception in Marcus' mother's back yard, I sat back and watched Josh interact with his grandparents, aunts, uncle, and cousins. I began to regret having to leave so soon, but figured it was best to get out while things were going well. Josh walked Henry and me out to our rental car.

"It went pretty well, don't you think?" I said.

"Yeah, it really did," Josh said. "Your dad — I mean, Grandpa — asked for my phone number."

"Good," I said. "I hope they'll call you. I have a feeling my dad means to and I bet my mom will go along."

"Now that Naomi and I are here, you'll have another reason to visit."

Had he been oblivious to my estrangement from my parents? I didn't see any point in telling him that I'd never been to Tucson before, that I hadn't visited my parents in the three years they'd lived there. *No matter,* I thought. *Perhaps, at long last, those days are over.*

Chapter 22

A FRESH START

"It was good," Josh reported after he and Naomi had dinner at my parents' house a few weeks later. "Except their house is like a museum. I was afraid to let Naomi touch anything. Your mom seemed kind of nervous. She's probably not used to having kids around. But I think she really loved Naomi."

"How could she not? She's a sweetheart."

"She asked me when Naomi's birthday is and wrote it down. I don't think she likes being called Grandma. But your dad smiled every time I called him Grandpa."

I'd been thrilled to learn that my mom and dad had made an effort to see Josh. "Are you going to stay in touch with them?"

"I guess. They acted like they wanted to have us over again. I didn't tell them about Jennifer. There's no way we can go over there with all three kids."

Josh told me about his latest girlfriend. The neighbor who had been babysitting Naomi had introduced them a few weeks before. Jenn had two children: Katie, nine, and Nick, four. He didn't tell me when they'd already moved in together. Not like he had to. I knew as soon as he announced that he was moving into a bigger place. Then, during one of our phone calls, I heard someone pick up the extension, and he said sternly, "Hang up, Katie. I'm on the phone."

"So the kids are there," I said. "Are you and Jenn living together?"

"Yeah," he said sheepishly.

"Why won't you tell me what's going on, instead of making me guess?"

"I don't know. Probably because I didn't want you to try to talk me out of it."

As the weeks went by, Josh sounded more content and settled than he had since we'd met.

"Things are finally coming together for me," he said. "I can't wait for you to meet Jenn." Peter had yet to open the new shop, but Josh found a mechanic job that he liked. He continued to see Becky and Marcus. My parents were making an effort to call and visit. When Josh invited me to come in June for Naomi's third birthday, I accepted without hesitation.

Coming off the plane, I spotted Josh and Jennifer and my granddaughter standing in front of them, holding a single red rose. As I approached, Josh bent down and I heard him say, "There's Grandma, Naomi! Go give her the flower."

She hesitated, looking at me with uncertainty, and then back up at her father.

I stopped several feet away, knelt down and held out my arms. "Hey, Sweetpea!"

Naomi smiled, tottered toward me, and threw herself into my hug.

"Thank you, honey." I said, taking the flower from her fist and kissing her cheek. "Look at how you've grown, and what a beautiful girl you are!"

Unlike my first meetings with Marissa and Holly, I hadn't seen a picture of Jennifer, so I had no preconceived impression. In sharp contrast to the others — with their statuesque frames, soulful eyes and somber beauty — Jenn was a tiny ball of energy, barely five feet tall. She talked nonstop, found humor in everything, and had a big, unrestrained laugh. She and Josh seemed well matched in both size and temperament. I sensed a spark between them that had been lacking with the women who had come before.

Her daughter was the quintessential preteen — giggly, self-possessed, and endearing. She was a beanpole, and with the height she'd inherited from her six-foot-five father, there was no doubt that eventually she would tower over her mother. Nick was an angel and devil wrapped into one irresistible package — one minute sweet and cuddly, the next unruly and rough.

Although it was love at first sight with Jenn's kids, Naomi was the one who had me by the heartstrings. Every time I called her my "sweetie" or "punkin," she came back with "you're *my* sweetie" or "you're *my* punkin." She clung to me possessively and reminded the other kids, "This is *my* grandma." Her pale hair had grown into wavy wisps and her big blue eyes still had the power to reach my soul.

Once I'd had a chance to visit with the kids, Jenn took them over to her mom's where we would have dinner that night, giving Josh and me some time alone. We were cautious at first, avoiding any troublesome topics. But soon we were chatting and laughing with the ease of our early days.

"So do you like Jenn?"

"I do," I said. "She's great."

"Because I have a confession to make."

No! Not another one!

"We got married in April. I was afraid to tell you."

I was stunned. Had Josh learned nothing after three marriages? Holly had been a rebound after Marissa, but another one, less than a year later? More importantly, how could I have not suspected?

Because you didn't want to, I answered my own question. *You wanted to believe that he had gained some wisdom from his mistake.* Another thought flew into my head: my doubts that I would ever have found a husband with a child already in tow, and how Josh had so willingly taken on women "with baggage" twice, maybe three times, depending on the definition.

"Josh, I hate when you keep things from me. I'm not an ogre! All I want is for you to be happy."

He looked me straight in the eye, as if swearing a solemn oath. "I am."

"But why so fast? Is Jenn pregnant?" Even though it had been a decade since people cared about getting married before the baby arrived, it was still the only explanation I could fathom for a hasty wedding.

"No, of course not. She didn't have medical insurance and

Katie is diabetic. Now, they're all covered through my work."

"What about Katie and Nick's father? Why isn't he taking care of them?"

"Fathers," Josh corrected me. "Katie's dad is an artist. He isn't working. Nick's dad is a jerk. They were never married, so Jenn has full custody."

Jesus, I said to myself, unable to hold back the judgment. What is up with these young people? Is there a family on the planet with kids from the same mother and father?

"Where did you get married?"

"City Hall. Jenn's mom and Katie came with us, and a friend from my work stood up for me."

"And you didn't want me there?"

"Would you have come?"

"Probably not," I admitted with a self-conscious smile.

"See how you are?" Josh said with a laugh. "Look, Mom, we were going to get married eventually. There was no reason to wait."

I shook my head, at a loss for how to respond.

"Don't worry, okay? This time things are going to be different."

"I hope so. Believe me, nothing would please me more."

Our discussion turned to Marissa. No one had heard from her in months, not even her mother, who had resumed contact with Josh after her daughter's most recent disappearance.

"I'm going to do everything I can to keep her away from Naomi," Josh said. He'd kept his home phone and address from Nina, telling her she could reach him at work. He worried that Marissa might have a change of heart and decide to fight him for custody, and with Nina and Max and their money on her side, she might win.

Whatever I thought of Marissa, which wasn't much, I remained adamant that Josh must not keep Naomi from her.

"Regardless of what she's done, she's still Naomi's mother," I said. "Nothing's ever going to change that, even if she doesn't grow up with her."

"Jenn is her mother now and she's a better one. Naomi doesn't even remember Marissa."

"I can't believe you're saying that, Josh, given our situation. You had a mother growing up, but you still wanted to know me. I don't mean that you should let Marissa visit no matter what. She definitely has to clean up her act. But someday Naomi's going to want to see her biological mother and she has every right to."

I didn't push the point, or any other. My son was happy, his wife liked me, I liked her, and I was in grandma heaven, with each of the kids demanding my time to play with them, read to them, and sit in my lap. Mom and Dad came to Naomi's birthday party and seemed as delighted with their great-granddaughter as I was.

"You are just the sweetest thing," Mom said when Naomi came over to give a thank-you hug after opening the clothes they had brought for her.

I went home feeling so renewed and encouraged that I told Henry I wanted to start visiting them regularly. Eager to let go of what had happened before, I began sharing stories with family and friends again. Having grandchildren — whether by blood or marriage — felt like a gift.

When I returned in August, Josh seemed different. His moods shifted from light to dark without warning, hanging over us like the late summer monsoon. I felt a storm mounting even before Josh blew up at Jenn for spending more than the agreed-upon amount for groceries.

"Enjoy your time with the kids," he said to me, as he stomped out the door, jangling his keys. "I'm out of here."

"Josh. Wait." I caught up with him as he reached his truck.

"I just can't take it anymore. This happens all the time. We agree how much she has to spend, and she still goes over."

"I was with Jenn at the store. She didn't buy anything frivolous. She's very price-conscious."

"That doesn't matter if we don't have enough money to cover it."

"All right. But don't leave. Stay and work things out." The words rang in my head.

"I can't," Josh insisted. "We'll just end up fighting."

"So go ahead and fight. Or don't speak to each other. Whatever. Just stay, please."

"You've got Naomi. You don't need me around ruining your visit."

"I do need you, Josh. I love Naomi. I adore all the kids. But you're the one I come to see."

"Me?"

"Yes, you. The only thing that could ruin my visit is you not being here."

Josh stayed. I could hear him and Jenn arguing in hushed voices when I tucked the little ones into bed and disappeared into my room. In the morning, they had returned to behaving civilly.

"So, did you guys make up, or is this for my benefit?" I asked when Jenn was out of the room.

"For you... mostly. I don't know what's going to happen, Mom. There's a chance that Jenn and I won't make it after all."

After four months, I thought. A new record.

That weekend we had tickets to a comedy club. When it was time to leave and Katie's father hadn't showed up to babysit, Josh went to the car and sat fuming in the driver's seat. Once Steve got there, twenty minutes late, Josh started the car and gunned the engine until Jenn and I were in our seats.

"The show doesn't start until eight, Josh," she said, as he squealed out of the driveway and around the corner. "We'll be there in plenty of time."

"That son of a bitch doesn't care about anyone but himself!" Josh sputtered. "Look at this traffic! You know I hate being late. Fuckin' asshole. He's worthless!"

When we reached the club parking lot, he jumped out of the car, leaving Jenn and me to make our own way through the crowd of cars and people. None of us spoke while we waited in line. I noticed the red in his face fading, and once we were seated inside, he was relaxed and goofing with the waitress.

"I'm worried," I told Jenn the next day when Josh wasn't around. "I've seen Josh's temper before, and his outbursts seem to be escalating."

"Trust me, Josh is fine. Every couple fights now and then."

"This isn't fighting. It's rage, triggered by minor things that aren't the real issue. I don't know how much you know about adoption issues, but a lot of adoptees harbor real anger over being relinquished. Sometimes it takes a while to surface, and once it does, they don't always know how to express it, so it comes out in other ways."

"Not everything is about adoption."

"I know that. But I'm pretty sure this is."

After attending the birthmother support group for two years, I'd started facilitating a triad group for PACER. Hearing from adoptees and adoptive parents as well as other birthparents had added to my understanding. In my letters to Josh, I'd mentioned some of what I'd learned and asked carefully phrased questions concerning his feelings about being relinquished and adopted. He didn't bring up the topic, and when I did he always said, "I'm fine. I don't need to talk about that stuff."

I told Jenn that I thought Josh could benefit from a support group and offered to find one nearby. "He needs a place where he can talk openly with people who understand. He needs to hear from other adoptees, so he'll know what he's going through isn't abnormal, that he's not alone."

She bristled. "He's not alone. He has me."

"That's great, but it's not the same as getting support from people who share his experience."

"Josh is a good man."

"I know that."

"He has some problems. We all do. But I can help him."

I had already noticed Jenn's tendency to talk faster and louder when she disagreed. This didn't bother me when we were talking food, books, or politics. But this was important.

We were talking about my son.

"Help him or fix him? You can't *fix* him, Jenn. No one can fix anyone else, only ourselves."

"He just needs someone to love him and stick by him, no matter what, and that's what I intend to do."

"Okay. That's good."

"I've seen big changes in Josh since we've been together. Believe me, I'm the best chance he's ever had."

"God, I hope you're right," I said. Then, I couldn't help but add, "Just be careful."

"Mom," she said, putting her hand on my arm. "We're fine. I've got it under control."

When I got home, I searched the Internet and found a counseling center in Tucson that offered low-cost support groups for adoptees. I printed out the information and sent it to Josh, along with a copy of Nancy Verrier's *The Primal Wound*. Like many birthmothers, I'd found it one of the most challenging adoption books to get through, since it dealt with the trauma infants experienced when they were separated prematurely from their biological mothers; the impact of abandonment and loss on adoptees' development; and their difficulties with trust, intimacy, and maintaining relationships. I'd sent a copy to Auntie Em, and she said she had related so fully to its pages that she had cried while she read it. Although Josh wasn't much of a reader, I hoped he'd be curious enough to give the book a chance.

"I told you, I've tried therapy," Josh said, after he'd received the package. "It doesn't work for me."

"This isn't therapy. It's a group, with people just like you, who were adopted and are searching for or reunited with their birth families."

"No one's like me."

"No, not exactly. But it's a place where you can talk freely about your feelings and learn from others' experiences. I've told you how much my birthmother group has helped me."

"Maybe that shit works for you, but I don't get off on

sitting around talking about my problems to strangers. And I sure don't want to hear theirs."

"Will you at least read the book?"

"You know I don't like to read. Besides, what does somebody else's book have to do with us? Write your own book. That I'll read."

Jenn, her mother, and Katie had just returned from a weekend family reunion in Texas when I called to discuss my plans to visit in November for Katie's birthday.

"When I got home yesterday, Josh announced that he'd been doing a lot of thinking while we were away," Jenn said. "He said he isn't happy and wants to split up."

"Jesus, Jenn."

"I know. Like I need this. But we've been down this road before. We'll talk it out. We always do."

What she didn't know was that Josh had already rented an apartment. Two days later, while she was out running errands, he packed up, took Naomi, and left. Jenn was hysterical when she called me. She had since discovered that he had been seeing another woman for at least a few months, possibly even before my last visit.

"I didn't see this coming," Jenn sobbed into the phone. "What the hell am I going to do now? Josh insisted I quit work to stay home with the kids. Even if I was working, I can't afford the rent on this house on my own."

"Does he have a new number? I want to talk to him."

"He said he doesn't want to talk to you right now."

"Of course he doesn't. He knows what I'll say."

I was furious at Josh for treating Jenn so horribly, for uprooting Naomi again, and for inflicting trauma on Katie and Nick. In the week it took him to call me, I'd decided he was despicable beyond all redemption, not worthy of my efforts or hopes. I was done getting in the middle of his problems and giving him advice he would not heed.

Josh launched into a muddled justification — why it wasn't working out with Jenn, how he was much happier being on his own with Naomi.

"You're right, Josh," I said flatly. "You're better off without Jenn. You'll meet someone else, and she'll be a lot better."

"I know what you're trying to do," he said. "You can't use reverse psychology on me."

"No, I mean it. Besides, after what you've done, Jenn won't take you back."

"Wanna bet?"

Without meaning to, I had challenged him. I could tell by the sneer in his voice that he meant to prove me wrong. The next time I talked to Jenn, he had already approached her about getting back together and she was considering it. I urged her to be careful and suggested that they take it slow, perhaps go to counseling for a while before she made a decision. She promised she would. Two weeks later, Josh and Naomi moved back in.

"I know you're worried," Jenn said. "But I have to agree with Josh that he and I can't work things out from a distance. We need to be together and fight our way through this."

I remembered Josh's words, the night before Becky's wedding: "You should be willing to face me and fight it out." Hadn't I said the same thing to Josh in August, when I insisted he stay and resolve his problems with Jenn?

I'd never done battle for anything in my entire life. I hadn't fought to keep my son when he was born. I hadn't searched for him. That was how I lived. Even when I wanted something, either it happened or it didn't, and I lived with the consequences.

Chapter 23

DIVINE REVELATION

I held no illusions that their marriage would last, after witnessing what had happened with Marissa and Holly. Even when Jenn told me she had convinced Josh to go with her to counseling, I still had serious doubts. Every time the phone rang, I braced myself for the next crisis. But because my worries intensified if too much time passed between calls, I felt compelled to keep in close touch. I figured that as long as I confined my questions to how the kids were doing and didn't overreact to Josh's latest plans or theories, I could maintain our connection with some semblance of safety.

"I hate my job," he would say. "I'm thinking about quitting."

"Do you have a lead on a new one?"

"No, but I'm sure I'll find something better."

"Of course you will. You always do."

"Besides, we're going to need more money if Jenn and I have a baby."

"Are you trying to have one?"

"We're not doing anything to prevent it. A child is a gift from God and if it's His will, then so be it."

What about the gifts He gave you and Rebecca? I wanted to say. Where are they? What about the upheaval Naomi has endured? Instead I said, "Sounds like more money would definitely come in handy then."

In December, Jenn's father bought them their first computer and even though Josh hadn't written me a letter since the early days of our reunion, he insisted that e-mail would help him keep in better touch. He was anxious to reconnect with Sandy, who he still referred to as his "godmother." I gave him her e-mail address and they began corresponding.

I think Josh is feeling a little abandoned because you're

backing off, she reported in a message to me. He wants me to tell him all about you when you were a teenager, so he can get to know you better. He also said he wishes you would just accept him the way he is. Not an easy task when you see your kid messing up, especially when the kid isn't a kid anymore. I believe what he really wants is for you to be more involved. He wants to be closer to you and feels that if he knows about your younger years, he'll be better able to understand you.

I had no problem with Josh reaching out to Sandy, although I was suspicious of his motives. He'd never asked me about my childhood. I couldn't fathom why he had chosen Sandy instead of Leanna or any of my other friends who had known me before I was nineteen. I considered intervening and suggesting that he ask me whatever he wanted to know. Yet I was pleased that he was seeking insight into our relationship. Sandy was willing to answer his questions, and I knew she would be honest and fair. I told her to feel free to share anything she liked.

A few days later, Sandy wrote again: Josh is a real chain jerker. You really have to read between the lines to figure out what he's trying to say, as he contradicts himself so much. One thing I know for sure is that he is a very bitter young man. She said she was still pondering how to reply to his last message.

Her next e-mail to me was even more disturbing. I am really worried about him and must tell you that he seems to be laying all his troubles on you. He desperately needs help. I truly believe that there is nothing you can do for him right now, other than let him know that you're there for him. Live your own life, be happy and pray that someday Josh gets it together. Love him, but be careful. You really don't need this shit.

She offered to forward me Josh's e-mails, *so you can see for yourself what you're dealing with.* Although part of me wanted to know, I told her not to. In addition to the trust issues that might surface if he came to doubt the confidentiality of their communication, I wasn't up for more of my son's wrath.

A few days later, I received a message from Josh. The subject was *I've had a divine revelation.*

I woke up this morning and had all the answers to our problems, he began.

Answers? I wasn't aware that we'd come up with the appropriate questions.

I haven't forgiven you for the crimes committed against me and now passed on to my daughter.

Now I was a criminal. I continued to read.

These are all my trapped feelings that you need to know about before this relationship can go anywhere. I can remember as far back as maybe five or six years old, asking my father where my real parents were and when they were coming back to get me. So there's no doubt that children have a bond with their mothers from birth. But that still does not mean that they can see eye to eye in real life.

I love you for bringing me into the world and not aborting me, but I hate you for sending me out into the world to figure it all out on my own. You tell me that I had choices in my life, and that's true, I could have done things differently. But I chose the wrong path and so have you. We've already established that we cannot rewrite history and we cannot go back twenty years to when I was just a baby. But you also can't blow it off like it never happened, like you have been.

Blow it off? For almost four years, I'd focused on little else.

Yes, I know you live in your own personal hell for what happened, but where does that leave me? You made the bad choice just as I have in the past, so where's my restitution for the crime you committed against me? All I want is to get to know my mother and try to make up for as much lost time as possible, but you're too wrapped up in your own guilt and sorrow to see that. I know that we're far apart and it's hard to see each other face to face and we can't go to therapy together, but that's not my problem. I've created my own messes in my life that I'll deal with later, but this one's on you to fix.

You know, spending time with your mother has helped me a lot. I see a lot of her in you. When there's an uncomfortable topic, you both run from it and get all wrapped up in yourselves instead of dealing with the problem.

He knew enough about my relationship with my mom to know this comment would hit a nerve. Even though he was wrong, the accusation was a low blow.

I'm still hurt over the time you asked me and Naomi to come to your house and start a new life when Marissa left, and then because the situation got a little sticky, you turned your back on us both.

There it was, the mistake I'd known would come back to haunt me.

You remember when I told you that if you didn't move closer to me, I didn't want anything more to do with you? Do you really think I meant that? That was my roundabout way of saying I loved you and missed you and wanted to be closer with you, but obviously I can't be roundabout. I just need to say what I feel and what I want. Just like before Becky's wedding, when I told you that our relationship sucked and you ran away and cut your trip short because you couldn't handle it. Well, too bad. This is about what was done to me, so just shut up and listen, and let's do whatever we have to do to make this relationship the best no matter what the price!

Yes, I am laying this one on you. If you want me to do something better, tell me and I'll do it. But this is your fuck-up, not mine. I was only a baby. I didn't have much say about anything. I know I probably would not have been the perfect child, just as I'm not the perfect son or husband, but like now that I have my wife back, I would have had you and nothing else would have mattered.

Whatever guilt you're carrying, let it go, because it doesn't help now at all.

On its face, this was the most sensible thing he'd written. Except I knew that everything else he'd said was aimed at making me feel more guilt — more than I'd taken on my own.

Look, I just want my mother back and for you to be a part of my life in every way, through good and bad, no matter what. Just tell me how I can help and what I can do to make it happen. I'm not asking for much.

He closed by saying the ball was in my court and that he hoped to hear from me before Christmas, but if he didn't, then he would know this was too much for me to handle and he would leave me alone. Again, he used the Joshua/Erick sign-off.

Nothing in my experience had prepared me for Josh's style of fighting. For all of my family's shortcomings, we would never have resorted to attacking each other so cruelly. I was angry, but more than that, exhausted from slogging back through old, rank ground. *The same old shit,* I thought. And now, thanks to e-mail, flung further and faster. I fought the urge to slam him back.

"I refuse to lower myself to his level," I told Henry. "Someone has to be the adult in this relationship."

"I have a thing or two to say," he said, his eyes blazing. "Let me take a crack at the little bastard."

As much as I would have relished someone coming to my defense, I knew it would be wrong. Everyone in the PACER support groups had talked about the importance of getting in touch with our feelings and expressing them honestly. Lorraine, an adoptee who attended my group and had become a close friend, scoffed when some adoptees claimed that they held no anger toward their birthmothers, that they'd had good lives in their adoptive families and needed nothing more.

"Either they're clueless or they're not being honest with themselves," Lorraine said. "I love my adoptive parents, I had a wonderful childhood, and I still needed to meet my mother and know where I came from. And it still hurts."

"No," I told Henry. "What Josh needs is maturity and compassion, and the way I feel right now, it might take me some time to get there. Besides, maybe it will do Josh some good to stew for a while."

A week later, Josh wrote again, asking why I hadn't responded.

"Is it because you want to ruin my Christmas, or is it because you think it'll go away if you ignore it? If you knew what it was like, how horrible it is to have waited all this time to meet your mother, and then have the kind of relationship that we do. It's just not right. I almost wonder if I'd be better off not knowing you at all."

Ignore it and it will go away. Hadn't I said the same thing about my mother? Had I become her?

No, I thought. *Josh is wrong.* My mother had never given me the consideration I had given him. And I had never given her the trouble he had given me. I wrote him back.

"I'm not trying to ruin your Christmas and I'm not ignoring you. It's not my style to fire off the first thing that comes into my head. I need some more time and promise to write a longer letter soon.

"In the meantime, I will say that I'm glad (as hard as it is on both of us) that you're finally acknowledging the deep feelings of anger and sadness that you've no doubt had all along. That is the first step to healing. I've spent the last few years working on my issues and I'm still not done, so I know it's a long process. I support you in this, one hundred percent, and encourage you to stay with it even though it isn't easy. It will be worth it.

"I also hope you can come to see that solid, loving relationships can only come through kindness, understanding, and respect, not through anger, blame, and threats. The appropriate place for you to vent your anger and frustration is in therapy (to someone who's uninvolved and qualified to guide you) or on paper (not to be sent) — not on me. I want you to tell me what you're feeling, but I'm not going to let you blast me. And I give you my promise, never to verbally abuse you."

Josh wrote back the next day.

"You've missed the point on everything I said. I've given this a lot of thought and you're probably going to misunderstand this too. But here goes nothing. I do have a lot of anger toward you for giving me up the first time, but everyone makes mistakes and I can forgive and accept that.

"To desert me the way you did when you invited
Naomi and me to come and start a new life with you, that is
unacceptable and probably unforgivable in my book. Despite
all that, I feel you owe me twenty-five years of not being with
me and giving all your time to Henry and Jeff when you could
be giving it to me.

"I'm going to give you the biggest and best gift of all. I've
been holding you hostage and I'm going to set you free. We've
tortured each other long enough. Keep your life, keep your
family. To me you are no longer anything, not a mother, not a
friend. Don't write, don't call and if you decide to come visit,
make sure Jenn knows in advance so I won't be here. I do hope
you understand that no matter how bad my life was without
you, it couldn't be worse than having a mother that I can't get
to really know.

"I want you to remember one thing though. When you're
old and in a nursing home somewhere and no one comes to see
you, just know that you had a son who wanted to be there for
you and would have done anything for you, but you chose the
wrong way."

My hands shook as I fired back.

"I think I DO get it. Do you really want me to explain
my view of what happened when you came here with Naomi?
If you do, then you'd better brace yourself. If you've been
harboring resentment over this for the past two years — in
spite of the efforts I've made since to be at your wedding to
Holly and visiting twice since you've been with Jenn — where
does that leave us?

"What time with Jeff are you talking about? I saw Jeff
twice that year and you twice that year. Looks equal to me.
And why am I explaining this to you? Do you want to see gift
receipts too? As for Henry, the man has been a saint, putting
up with your bullshit and my preoccupation with it for the past
four years. If I were you, I'd rethink that one.

"I love my husband, I love my stepson, and I love you.

I'm not giving up one for the other. Why are you leaning on the only person who really cares? Why are you seeking out the weakest kid on the playground to beat up? Hey, here's an idea: Why don't you search for your father, the one who was most responsible for your not growing up with me, and give him a piece of this action?

"I'm sure you'd love it if I said, 'that's it, we're finished.' Then you could spend the rest of your life telling everyone that your mother deserted you — not once, but twice — and blame everything bad that happens on that. You've been trying to get me to leave you again ever since we met. Well, I'm not buying into your victim mentality. I know you want to work this out, and I'll wait until you're ready. Even if you shut me out now. Please stop ranting at me and work on your issues. It's the only way."

Three days before Christmas, Jenn stepped in. I'd been wondering if she'd been aware of what was going on.

"I know that Josh has been writing you some pretty ugly stuff, she wrote. I know he's said that he doesn't want a relationship with you if he can't have it the way he wants it. I want you to know that we have talked to our therapist about this and she has encouraged Josh to let you know how he feels, but she also said he should avoid being abusive. I don't think he realizes how abusive the things he says are. He is hurting so much and, as we both know, he tends to respond to pain with anger. Not to make excuses for his behavior. Josh loves you and wants to be a part of your life, but he is very confused right now, and I think he can only cause you pain.

"For now, I think the two of you need to retreat to your corners and give this situation some space."

And so began our first "time out."

Chapter 24

TIME OUT

"Are we ever going to get back to normal?" Henry asked, as we lingered at the table after dinner.

Four years of Josh had taken its toll. As understanding as Henry had been in the beginning, the disruption and tensions had worn his patience to bare threads.

"I hope so," I said. "I know this has been hard on you. I'm sorry."

"You don't owe me an apology. He's your son and that's important."

"I mean I'm sorry things have gotten so out of whack."

"I'm not happy with Josh's behavior, but what concerns me more is what this is doing to us. All we talk about anymore is Josh — what he's done, what he's said, what you think you should be doing about it."

"That's not true. It was before, but I'm trying really hard not to talk so much about it."

"I can see it in your face even if you don't say anything." His eyes shone with kindness and a gravity that had previously been reserved for our most serious moments. "Even when he isn't here, he's here. And you aren't."

I looked away, feeling as busted as I had on New Year's Eve in Tucson. I hadn't consulted Henry before offering to keep Naomi with us, and by the time he expressed his displeasure with the arrangement it was too late. After all the drama over Josh and my family the week before, he'd looked forward to a few romantic hours with me. The hurt in his eyes had pierced my heart as deeply as my granddaughter's gaze, and the pages I'd written into the wee hours were filled with despair over my failure to please the people I loved most.

"You don't have any control over Josh," Henry said, pulling me back into the present. "I'm not saying you should give up on him. But I'm afraid if things keep going the way they are, he's going to drag you, and our marriage, down with him."

"You're right…" I choked on my response and began to cry.

"I don't mean to pile more on you," he said, reaching for my hand. "I just want my wife back."

Henry wanted his wife back. Josh wanted his mother back. I might have wanted myself back, if I'd had any idea who she was after so many years of pretense.

As she promised, Jenn kept in touch by e-mail. She insisted I should feel free to call, but the one time I did — in the middle of the day when Josh wouldn't normally have been home — he answered. I panicked and hung up. After that, I dug deeper into the safe bunker of e-mail. In addition to answering Jenn's messages, I wrote to Josh each month, telling him that I loved him and was open to hearing from him whenever he was ready.

In March, Jenn wrote to tell me that she was pregnant.

I wanted to wait to tell you, but Josh has already told your parents and Debby, and I didn't want you to hear it from them instead of us. I wasn't thrilled at first, but I'm warming up to the idea. Of course, Josh is ecstatic, seeing this as a second chance. I am hopeful that he's right and that our marriage will become stronger. I know it will be difficult for you to be overjoyed, but I know you will wish us well.

There must be no worse feeling for a grandmother than to be more worried than excited at the prospect of another grandchild. I cursed myself for my inability to meet this news with the same joy I'd felt when Naomi was on the way. In a carefully worded response, I congratulated them and said how glad I was to hear that things were going well.

The realization that my mom and dad knew more than I did about my son and grandchildren's lives was maddening. After all my efforts to bring them together and all my worries over what would happen if I succeeded, they were on the inside and I was shut out.

It's not fair. Even in my jealousy, I knew it would be wrong to jeopardize their connection. I couldn't tell them what was going on between Josh and me. Although I wasn't accustomed to them rallying to my defense, I worried that, so early in their relationship with Josh, they might pull away from him if they knew about our rift.

"When will you come down for a visit again?" Mom asked.

She sounded as if she missed me, and for a moment I considered that the years when we hadn't seen each other or talked regularly might have been equally hard on her.

"I'm not sure, Mom."

"I guess you'll wait until after the baby comes."

"Yeah," I said, welcoming the deferment. "That makes more sense."

"Jenn's due in late September," Mom said. "Maybe you'll come for Thanksgiving."

Every time Josh's life went astray or our relationship faltered, I found myself wanting to hide from the rest of the world. Again, I struggled with what to tell my friends when they asked, "How are Josh and the kids?" Usually I reverted to the stock answer: "They're fine." It wasn't a lie; as far as I knew, they were. Knowing how it would look if I withheld that another grandchild was on the way, I forced a smile onto my face and began sharing the news.

Other than Henry and my therapist, Barbara, only a handful of people — Jeff, Auntie Em, Leanna — knew that Josh and I were not speaking. And that was all they knew. Whenever I tried to say more, my body grew dizzy with panic. Even in my support groups, I shared as little as possible.

That left Barbara to coax me through my weekly monotone reports. We'd met at an adoption conference shortly before Josh's move to Tucson. She too was a birthmother and specialized in adoption issues in her marriage-and-family-therapy practice. After my clash with Josh that December, I decided I needed more help than monthly support groups could provide.

"We've been at this for a year already," I complained to her during one of our weekly sessions. "Why do I still feel at the mercy of Josh and my parents for my well-being?"

"This isn't new stuff," she said. "You've been feeling that way for a long time. That can't be undone overnight."

"Isn't there a pill I can take? Can't I get brain surgery or something?"

Barbara laughed. "I'm afraid not. If that were true, I'd be out of business, along with millions of other therapists."

Jenn's next e-mail announced that Josh wanted to get out of auto mechanics and was taking a truck driver course. The training required him to go on the road for several days at a time, but they both hoped that once he graduated, he could get a local driving job so he wouldn't have to be away from her and the kids, especially during her pregnancy.

My response — wishing them good luck — bounced back, marked undeliverable. On a hunch, I dialed their number and found it disconnected. For the next two weeks, I fought off the notion that they meant to hide from me, that Josh was cutting me off permanently. When Jenn called, my relief came out in a gush.

"Jenn, thank goodness! I've been trying to e-mail you and then your phone was disconnected. I was a little worried. Did you move?"

"I'm sorry I didn't get a chance to tell you. It happened pretty fast. We found a great deal on a nice place and went for it." The anxiety in her voice told me her call had nothing to do with giving me their new address and phone number.

"What's going on?"

"Josh is gone again."

"What do you mean, gone?"

"He got his truck driver's license and was offered a long-distance trucking job, which we decided he wouldn't take. He was supposed to look for a job in town. But apparently he took the long-distance job without telling me. He left yesterday while I was in the shower."

"So he's not really gone. He's working and he'll be home eventually, right?"

"I don't know."

When she swore she'd had enough and would never take him back, I didn't blame her. Two weeks later, she e-mailed me that she had.

"He's a goddamned sociopath!" I sputtered at Barbara. "And she's a goddamned masochist."

Barbara refused to corroborate my amateur diagnosis, but agreed that Josh and Jenn could both benefit from therapy. I was fairly certain they hadn't gone back since the few sessions after their first split. I told Barbara that as painful as it might be if I were out of his life, I had begun to wonder whether I wanted back in if things stayed as they were.

"I'm thinking seriously that if Josh contacts me, and there's no evidence of meaningful change, I might tell him it wasn't enough and not to call until he's worked on his issues."

"You could do that," she said. "But I don't think he'll respond well to an ultimatum, even though he feels free to hand them out to others. You can't make him go to therapy or behave differently. What you can do is be a positive influence by demonstrating good behavior and setting boundaries that make it clear what you won't put up with. If you change, he'll have to if he wants a relationship with you."

"A moot point — right now anyway."

"Josh will get in touch with you. I'm sure of it. But even if he doesn't, you'll have to accept that. You need to let go of the outcome."

Barbara's words reminded me of what Auntie Em had written when I told her what had happened.

Just what can you do for Josh? Do you have any control? Do you know what will bring him about-face or change his behavior? After all, he has a background to overcome and there is no magic. It may take him a lifetime. Not a cheerful thought, but realistic. This is where I have to say 'offer it up.' That ain't easy. But think about it. We have to have faith that something is being accomplished beyond us or what we can understand.

She was coming from a more spiritual approach than I was used to, and still her advice was essentially the same as Barbara's. I would have to learn to let go.

I felt like I'd been letting go my whole life: taking whatever I got, pretending to be okay with it, and burying my discontent. Why did I have to do all the work? I was the one who had been cheated. It was beyond unfair.

Josh caught me unaware when he e-mailed on Mother's Day.

I just want you to know that I'm thinking of you. I'm unsure about what to say simply because every time we talk I hurt you more and more and that is not my intention. I hate that our relationship has come to us not being able to communicate without me hurting you.

You know I really do love you and the stuff that I say is just because I want to be with you and can't stand that I can't just walk over to your house and chat, or bring you your grandchildren, or have a barbeque on weekends. Don't get me wrong. I loved it when you visited, but it just doesn't seem fair that after a few days you have to leave and go back to your life. I feel like we've spent enough time apart.

This whole silence thing sucks, but I will leave it up to you, since it's been me who has tormented you over and over. So if you wish to break the silence, just remember that I will be crabby every now and then because of the way I feel for you. Please don't ever stop loving me even if we don't talk.

Happy Mother's Day and I love you very much.

It wasn't what I'd hoped for: an apology for his behavior, an admission of his mistakes, and a pledge to do better in the future. Still, it was something. I answered right away to thank him for writing, and called him two weeks later, on his birthday.

"I miss you," he said.

"I miss you too."

"The kids are asking when you're coming back."

"Please don't pressure me, Josh. I need to know that things are okay first."

"Everything's fine. Jenn and I are stronger than ever."

"Yeah, but for how long?"

"Why would you say that?"

"Right. Like you haven't left her twice in the last year."

"See, that's the problem. You don't believe in me. Jenn does. I would think my own mother would."

"I want to believe, more than anything. I guess it takes me longer to recover."

"You're still holding back. That's okay. I know you'll come after the baby is born."

Once we were back to talking, the e-mails stopped. I was surprised at how exposed I felt, knowing that any time the phone rang it might be Josh. When I felt strong, I picked up. More often, I listened to the answering machine to see who it was, and if I heard his voice, I'd gauge my ability to carry on a light conversation or cope with anything more. I kept the calls short, as if my endurance might run out.

The distance between us was palpable. We were speaking, but saying nothing, much like my mother and I had — wanting more, but stepping gingerly around each other, lest a clash leave us with even less. *How strange and sad,* I thought, *that my relationship with my son had become so like mine with my mom.* It was all the more sad that I didn't know what to do about either one.

Josh didn't call when Gabriel was born. Instead he called my sister and asked her to let me know. It was so unlike Naomi's birth four years before, when he had included me in every part. I couldn't help but feel deprived, even though my detachment from this child's arrival had been largely my own doing.

For months, I had spared Henry all but the late-breaking headlines. "Jenn's pregnant." "Josh is driving trucks." "They moved and didn't tell me." "He left her." "He's back." Every now and then, he would ask if I'd heard from Josh. Gabe's arrival broke the silence.

"Are you thinking of going to see your grandson?" Henry asked.

"I think about it all the time. Josh hasn't said anything, and I'm sure he's waiting for me to make the first move. My mom asked again. But I can't right now. Who knows what I'd be walking into?"

I was too vulnerable and, as much as I hated admitting it, I no longer trusted my son. My head filled with pictures of Josh opening emotional fire on me in person. This business of setting boundaries and letting go was still new. I was nowhere near ready.

I thought I was safe, until that fall when I found out from my sister that Josh had been blasting me from afar.

"I wasn't going to tell you this, but I think you should know," Debby said. "Josh is saying things about you. Bad things."

I shook my head. Apparently I had underestimated his ability to get to me if I laid low. "What? Just tell me."

"Like that you didn't really have to give him up."

"Oh, for Chrissake!"

"He says you blame Mom and Dad, but that you could have stood up to them. He said you could have gotten welfare."

"And what did you say?"

"Nothing. I told him I didn't know anything about it. I didn't even know you were pregnant until you found him." She hung her head.

"I'm sorry, Deb. This isn't your problem. This is between me and Josh. He shouldn't have laid this on you."

"He thinks you aren't doing enough for him. And he asked me why Henry doesn't come with you to visit."

"Henry doesn't like going anywhere."

"That's what I told him."

"We can't afford for both of us to fly every time. I've spent a bloody fortune on that little asshole! What does he think? That we're made of money?"

She recoiled at my outburst. "I know."

"I'm sorry. I didn't mean to yell."

"I just thought you should know. Also, I don't think it's just me. I think he's been saying the same things to Becky. Please don't tell him I'm the one who told you."

Henry got an earful after Debby left. Barbara got one too. Once I'd finished ranting, I thought I could let Josh's transgression go. But his words continued to plague me, and I felt myself getting angrier as the weeks went by.

"The whole time I've known Josh, I've been so afraid of losing him again that I've let him roll over me," I told Barbara. "This is never going to stop unless I draw the line."

"I agree. You should tell him how you feel. That this behavior hurts you and your relationship."

"God, I hate this!"

"I know you do. But this is an important step and you can only grow from it. I'll help you figure out what to say."

"Do I have to do it on the phone?"

"That would be best. Or in person."

"No way."

"Okay, on the phone then."

"I'll never be able to pull it off. I'll be too nervous and forget what I want to say." I could already feel my stomach rolling.

"We'll make a script."

"He'll interrupt me or yell at me." I could hear Josh's voice in my head. The nerve endings in my fingers and toes vibrated.

I convinced Barbara there was no point in trying to talk to Josh, and the next week I brought a draft of my letter to show her:

I know that you've been talking to others about things that only concern us — what you think I could have done differently when you were born, what you expect of me now, and what you believe Henry's involvement should be. I understand that you're still hurt and angry about being given up. But there's nothing I can do about the past and dwelling on it gets us nowhere. You're going to have to work through your feelings and I will do whatever I can to support you in that. It's not okay for you to attack me in the process, whether directly or to others.

I've been holding onto my feelings about this, just as I have about so many things, and I fear that's affecting my communications with you. That's why I want to get it out in the open now. I want to come there and see you, Jenn and the kids, and meet Gabriel. I want us to work on improving our relationship. For that to happen, this kind of behavior needs to stop. It hurts us both and keeps us apart.

I'm not perfect, but I'm a good person and I've tried very hard to hang in with you no matter what's happening between us or in each other's lives. You're a good person too, and I will always do my best for you, if you let me.

Just the thought of mailing the letter made me squirm. Barbara walked me through responses for every possible outcome — questions, manipulations, yelling — should he call after he received it.

I heard the bile in Josh's voice as soon as he said hello. I took a breath and reminded myself: *No matter what happens, at least you will have spoken your piece.*

"I have every right to be angry," he said. "But I can't talk to you. Who am I supposed to talk to?"

"You *can* talk to me. I've told you that. You just can't attack me."

"Every time I try, you get upset."

"Of course I get upset when you slam me." My voice began to quiver. "I'm willing to listen if you can express yourself without yelling."

"Sometimes I just need to yell," he said hotly. "I have all this shit inside me and I have to get it out."

"I know. But if getting it out is what you're after, I hope you'll find a more appropriate way to vent, like in therapy."

"Therapy doesn't work for me. I told you that. I want to talk to you, not some stupid therapist."

"I want us to talk. It's the yelling and accusing that isn't working."

"How else am I supposed to let you know how I feel?"

"Just tell me. But try using 'I statements.' I learned that in my support groups. Instead of saying something like "you make me angry,' say 'I'm angry.'" The words sounded awkward in my head, and I thought that I probably sounded like a stupid therapist to Josh.

"Fine," he said. "I'm angry."

Okay, I thought, *maybe we really can do this.* I launched into my well-rehearsed reply. "I understand that you're angry."

"How the hell does that help me?"

"By expressing your feelings and having them acknowledged."

"So now what? I'm still angry."

"We keep talking. You're angry because…?"

"Because I didn't get to grow up with you."

"I know. I'm angry about that too."

"What do you have to be angry about? It's your fault!"

"Wait, Josh. Now you're attacking me…" My breathing quickened.

"See, I can't talk to you."

"Yes, you can. Say what you're feeling but try to stick with 'I statements.'"

"I feel like it's your fault."

"I understand why you feel that way. I deserve much of the responsibility and I've told you I'm sorry. But there were a lot of other factors, which I've already tried to explain to you. I didn't feel like I had a choice." My heart started to pound, and the notes in front of me blurred.

"Okay, if you're not to blame, then who? Your parents?" he hissed. "Somebody has to pay."

"*Pay?* Jesus, Josh! No one was out to get you. You were supposed to have a good life, with two parents who wanted and loved you. So you didn't, and now you're trying to make that everybody else's fault. You keep trying to make yourself the victim."

"I *am* a victim! Why can't you see that? Look at my life! I'm a total fuck-up, and I can't help but think things would have turned out better if you hadn't given me away."

"And I'm in such great shape, after growing up in my own family? Trust me, it was no picnic." My raised voice echoed in my ears. "Okay, wait. We're getting off track."

"We're never going to get on track until you come here and face me."

"I can't talk to you when you're yelling. Maybe we should stop for now, calm down and continue this later."

"I refuse to do this on the phone!"

"The phone is all we have. I'm not going to come there until we agree on some ground rules so we can talk to each other like adults."

"Yeah, sure. Keep hiding! Stay home, all safe and sound!"

"Look, we have a lot to work out." *Stay calm; get back to the point.* I let the chant roll in my head, willing my breathing to slow. "For now, I need you to understand that it's not okay to talk to other family members about our problems."

"You can't tell me who to talk to."

"I'm asking you to keep our problems between us."

"Who told you what I said?"

If he has to ask who told, I thought, *then Debby was right. She wasn't the only one.* "It doesn't matter. I find it interesting that you chose people you knew would tell and that what you said would get back to me."

"Of course I did. I wanted it to."

When he began to yell again, I followed my plan and told him if he didn't stop, I would have to hang up. He persisted. I stalled, trying once more to explain that we had to find ways to communicate without assaulting each other.

"I've had it with you and this whole family!"

"I mean it, Josh. Stop now, or I'm hanging up.

"You hang up and it's over!"

His words struck my gut like a sucker punch. What if he meant it? What if I never heard from or saw him again?

"I don't want it to be over, Josh. Let's cool down and talk again tomorrow."

By then he was screaming at me. I don't remember what he was saying. I set the receiver gently into its cradle.

Chapter 25

NINE MONTHS

Despite accolades from Barbara and Henry, I found little satisfaction in standing my ground with Josh. I kept hearing his voice: "You hang up and it's over." His words ricocheted in my head and shook me like an earthquake.

In more lucid moments, I realized that I had been alternating between caving to his needs while sidestepping any confrontation in defense of my own. An altercation was overdue. Perhaps that was why it had gone so badly.

My mom had always been clear about what she expected. In my quest for her love and out of fear that I would lose her, I had complied to the best of my ability. I had not been clear with Josh. How then could I expect his compliance? I worried that I would lose him as I had in the past, a fear that was at the root of my yielding and dodging.

For the second year in a row, the holidays came and went with no contact. A week after New Year's I received an e-mail from Jenn, thanking me for the kids' Christmas gifts.

Josh asked me to get the specifics on his father, she also wrote. *I'd appreciate it if you would send whatever you have.*

The timing of his request felt like a provocation, an "I'll show you, I'll find my father" jab at my buttons. From the outset, I'd made it clear that I would gladly provide what information I had, but until then Josh had shown no interest. I'd suspected his hesitancy had come from the realization that his father would be riskier to approach. My presence in the registry had been a green light, an assurance that I wanted a reunion. With John, there was none of that, and no clue of what Josh might find.

I e-mailed back, *Not a problem.* I included everything I remembered: John's first and last name, but no middle initial; that he was from Delaware and had been twenty-two when I had known him, but no date of birth; and that he had been in the Marines, served in Vietnam, and then at Kaneohe Air Base.

Go ahead, find the jerk. See how far that gets you. But within minutes of pressing the send key, I began to fret. What if John rejected Josh? I couldn't bear the thought of that man hurting our son the way he had hurt me. Then again, they were so alike. What if they met, everything clicked, and Josh chose his father over me?

In the shadow of Josh's silence, all I could do was wait, as I had so many times before: wait for John to change his mind, wait for my baby to be born, and wait for the pain of relinquishment to subside. I had waited more than two decades for my son's return. I was still waiting for my mother to love me. Why not a little longer?

In the meantime, I would refocus on the life I'd put on hold. I went back to asking Henry about his day and listening intently as he told me. I threw myself into my work, cleaned my office, and caught up on my filing. I made lunch dates, barraging my friends and business associates with questions about their lives to keep them from inquiring about mine. I stopped writing in my journal. Other than my monthly support groups, I refused to talk or even think about adoption.

For the next several weeks I set myself on cruise control, gliding through each day on a tightly synchronized track. As long as I was in motion, I was safe from feeling more than a dull ache in the pit of my stomach. But whenever I became too still — in the car, watching television, or trying to sleep — something deeper surfaced, rumbling like hunger. Eating only nourished the pain. But alcohol restored the welcome numbness.

The evenings when I stretched happy hour out until bedtime, I worried that Henry would notice. He would disapprove, but I didn't care. *He has no idea,* I thought. *No one does. I'm lucky I can walk, after what I've been through.*

One particularly indulgent night, I went into the kitchen to fix another rum and Coke. A handful of ice cubes slipped from my grip on the way to the glass and clattered onto the hardwood floor. When I bent down to retrieve them, my legs buckled under a burden heavier than my own weight. I sank to the floor and burst into tears.

Henry rushed in, his face flushed with alarm. "What happened? Are you okay?"

"No," I wailed, pulling myself to my feet and slumping over the counter. "It hurts."

"Where? What hurts?"

"Everything."

He led me back to the living room, turned off the television, and held me in his arms while I sobbed.

"If only I hadn't found Josh," I whimpered. "I would have been fine. I could have kept pretending. Do the la-de-da thing with my mom and dad, with everyone. If he hadn't come back, I could have made it. I could have lived out my entire life and… never had to…." I gulped for air.

"Had to what?"

"*Feel*," I wailed.

Only after the well-honed automatic control system that had protected me failed did I recognize how shutdown I had been — and still was. In any given moment, I had no clue what I was feeling, and even when I did, I was hesitant to show it. I had become an emotional pickpocket, taking cues on how I should feel from others, and turning in convincing performances of strong or happy or suitably saddened. As a result, I'd lost touch with who I had been before my pregnancy.

That night, my high school friend Shelley appeared in my dreams. We were nineteen again, posing for the picture taken in 1969 in front of her house after our first year away at college. Blond and tan in our mini-dresses, we leaned casually against the hood of her parents' Chevy sedan, with the deep green of the Hawaiian foliage and the brilliant blue sky in the background. Although neither of us knew it at the time, we were both pregnant.

Among our tight-knit group of six, three got pregnant

that summer. Marcy married her boyfriend in a white-dress Catholic ceremony not long after I'd been whisked out of town. They had a son and later two daughters, and had been happily married for more than thirty-five years. Shelley's parents sent her to Japan for an abortion. Over the next few years she would have two more.

A few years before Josh's reappearance in my life, Shelley and I had traveled together to Hawaii for our twenty-fifth high school reunion. Sitting in the same Shakey's Pizza Parlor we'd frequented as confused but hopeful teenagers, we assessed our lives and the paths we'd chosen that had left us both childless.

"Rick and I have been trying for almost ten years," she said. Her long, now dirty-blond hair veiled her face as she looked down at the table. "We've been through all the tests and the doctors say there's no reason that we can't get pregnant."

"I never even tried," I said, turning to stare out the window into the night. "By the time I met Henry, I felt like it was too late. Or that it just wasn't meant to be."

She didn't mention the abortions. I didn't tell her that I had been so afraid of an unplanned pregnancy that I'd had a tubal ligation a few years after Henry and I got married. However unintentionally, each of us in her own way had extinguished her prospects for motherhood.

Shelley was the only one of my high school friends who hadn't acknowledged the news of my reunion with Josh. After that, I heard from her less often, and eventually our communications dwindled to Christmas card one-liners.

Just before her fiftieth birthday, Shelley took her own life with over-the-counter sleep aids. There were no warning signs, her husband said when he called. The handwritten note she left provided no explanation, only her belief that she was *going to a better place.*

In my dream, she looked like an angel: young again, her golden hair shining around her smiling face. I had so many questions. How despondent had she been? Did she plan her exit for a long time or lose her way suddenly? Was her pain more agonizing than mine? Was she finally at peace? But when I opened my mouth to speak, she vanished.

The next morning, I pulled out the photograph from that long-ago day. Even a full year after her death, the fact that Shelley was gone touched me in new and unexpected ways — beyond the loss of a dear friend, or that I could have done something to help her if only I had known. I, too, had wrestled with thoughts of surrender, although I had no idea what that might mean. Renouncing my parents? Giving up on Josh? Ending my life?

As I looked into my friend's face — not the desperate woman she must have become, but the girl she had been and a reminder of the girl I had once been — I knew what to do. I would not give up; I would finish what I had started.

"Okay, let's do it," I told Barbara at our next therapy session. "I don't want to live like this anymore."

When I stepped into that dark hole, my intention was to repair my relationship with Josh. Anything else was irrelevant.

"What if this is a big waste of time? What if Josh carries out his threat and I never see him again? Then I will have done all this work for nothing."

"You're not doing this for Josh. You're doing it for yourself."

"But finding him is where it began. I was fine before. Honestly, I was."

"It's not uncommon, after a traumatic experience, to shut off painful feelings," Barbara said.

"I can't seem to feel anything, good or bad."

"And how long would you say that's been going on? Only after you relinquished Josh? Or could it be something you learned much earlier, in childhood perhaps?"

"Are you kidding? Feelings weren't allowed in my family."

"That's not surprising," Barbara said. "Tell me about it."

"Wait. I shouldn't have said that," I said, shaking my head. "My parents weren't ogres. They took good care of us."

"No one's saying they weren't responsible parents."

The image of our family portrait taken when I was seven flashed into my head. Two attractive parents, three bright, shiny kids with their knees crossed and hands folded neatly in their laps. We were the essence of civilized. There was no yelling in our home, no crying, and no hysterical laughter. We never got too high or too low.

"What's going on?" Barbara broke into my reverie.

"I was just thinking."

"About?"

"My mom used to say that when I was little I would get upset every time my dad went to sea with the Navy or on a business trip. But I wouldn't cry until after he left. It was always something else that would set off my tears. I'd stub my toe or spill my milk or get into a fight with my sister."

"Did your mother ever acknowledge your feelings about your dad being gone? Tell you she knew the real reason you were sad?"

"No," I whispered.

"What are you feeling right now?"

"I don't know. Sad?" I looked up tentatively, like a student waiting for the teacher's nod. "All right, fine. I'm sad."

"Anything else?"

I squirmed in my chair and closed my eyes. Admitting sadness brought some relief. Anger had always been too threatening, a hideous ride I might not survive. Whenever angry thoughts crept into my consciousness, I ended up feeling guilty, despondent, and furious with myself.

"Are you feeling angry?" Barbara said.

"I don't get angry. It's just not worth it."

"When was it not worth it?"

I flashed back to my eighth year, when I'd made a Thanksgiving shadow box for a school project...

Starting with a shoebox, I created a dining room scene with a little table and chairs cut out of cardboard. I painted a tablecloth and tiny place settings, and placed an in-shell peanut in the center to represent the turkey. A hole cut into the top of the box provided light into the scene, and I made another hole at one end for viewing.

"Do you want to see my Thanksgiving scene?" I said to Mom proudly. I held it up and showed her where to look.

"Very nice," she said, with her eye up against the viewing hole. "Oh look, a peanut." She stuck her fingers through the top hole, snatched the nut from the table, and cracked open the shell.

"What are you doing?" I screamed. "That's my turkey!"

"I thought I was supposed to take it," she said. "I thought that's why the hole was there."

"No," I moaned, red-faced and teetering on the verge of tears. "You ruined it!"

"I'm sorry!" Mom snapped. "Don't be such a baby. Just calm down and go get another peanut."

My angry words hung in the air and I felt ashamed for yelling. I had hurt my mother...

Anger is bad, I learned that day. It was bad enough when someone I loved was mad at me, but even worse when the anger was mine. Like the morning of Josh and Marissa's departure when I had shrieked at them, or that night on the phone when I had lashed out at Josh. Those episodes had convinced me that the rage I'd felt toward my parents over the years was far too dangerous to express. Anger was a monster that must be kept in its cage, a disease that, left untreated, would eat your insides.

"Never," I said to Barbara. "Never worth it." I recounted the story of the shadow box.

"It was careless of your mother to take the peanut without asking."

"Yes, but I overreacted."

"You were eight years old, Denise. That little girl needs some compassion, some understanding."

I stared down at my hands twisting in my lap.

"How do you feel now?"

"Worse. Sick to my stomach. Depressed."

"You know, they say that depression is anger turned inward," Barbara said gently.

"Fine. Let's say I'm angry. I have plenty to be angry about. What am I supposed to do about it?"

"Awareness of what you're feeling is an important first step. It might help to talk about times when you were mad at someone — relive it so to speak — and express those feelings here. Once they're out in the open, it's easier to let them go."

When my other stories failed to elicit an outpouring of emotion, Barbara suggested that I try to express my wrath symbolically: yelling at pictures of those who had wronged me or smashing something. I told her I'd think about it.

When I got home, I eyed the gold plastic clock that Josh had given me for our first Christmas. It was gaudy and noisy, something that I ordinarily would have already turned into a white elephant gift or donated to charity if it hadn't been a gift from my son. It would do, I decided; perhaps I could vent my frustrations toward my son and my mom at the same time.

I got a hammer from the garage and took the clock out to the deck. *This is going to make a huge mess,* I thought, and went back inside to get a paper grocery bag. I put the clock in the bag and took a few tentative swings. The sound of the plastic crackling was nowhere near dramatic, and I felt more foolish than angry, more feeble than liberated. Still, I kept hammering until the shards tore through the bag, and then gathered up the remains and tossed it into the garbage.

"Well, I failed Anger 101," I reported to Barbara the next week. "Pretty pathetic, huh?"

"No, it's not pathetic. Everybody experiences these kinds of exercises differently."

She reminded me how, in our early days of therapy, I had dismissed any need to address my feelings about my mother.

"There's no point in going there," I'd protested. "She can't live forever, and once she's gone, it'll be over. I'll be free."

"Nice try," Barbara had said. "Chances are you'll feel

worse if you don't deal with this while she's alive, because the opportunity to repair your relationship will be gone."

"And she'll haunt me forever."

"Something like that. Whatever feelings we have about people don't die when they do."

"Like my grandmother," I said.

I hadn't thought about Sarah Agnes in a while, and suddenly I felt hot with rage. She was the one who had set our family on its disastrous course. Whatever her reasons, she had rendered my mother emotionally incapable of parenting and left me essentially motherless. Because my mother had lost her own, I would never know what it meant to have one or how to be one, and I would lose my own son and grandchildren as well.

Maybe I couldn't break things, scream into pillows, or talk to photographs. But I could write. Screw the "I statements," I told myself. I would spit poison onto the page until there was no more. I would begin that very night with Sarah Agnes. She'd been dead for forty years, which made her the perfect target. I began.

I hate you for taking the coward's way out, for abandoning your children and leaving them in the hands of strangers. I will never forgive you for the abuse my Auntie Em suffered, or for turning my mother into an emotional zombie. They say you were a nasty, mean-spirited woman, and I believe them. They say you died alone, babbling in a mental hospital. I hope you suffered. I hope what you did to your children drove you mad. I wish you were alive to see the pain you inflicted on generations of good people.

One by one, I damned them: John for leaving so ruthlessly and sending me away feeling damaged. The Goldbergs for turning their backs on the child I had entrusted to them. My hand shook as I raged at my father for indulging my mother to the detriment of his children. I bashed Josh for expecting more than I could give and then punishing me for my inabilities, for demanding that I accept him as he was, and yet refusing to accept me. And most of all, for holding his love hostage as a means of getting his own way.

Dizzy with guilt, I stopped after every paragraph to read my words, resisting the impulse to tear up the pages or edit out the harshness. Every nerve in my body rebelled. Blood rushed through my veins and pounded in my skull. The only person left to write about was my mother. It would be several more weeks before I could go there.

"She's too big," I told Barbara. "There's too much."

"Okay, so break it down into little pieces. Tell me one thing she did that hurt you."

"She was ashamed of me."

"How do you know that?"

"She sent me into hiding when I was pregnant. She wouldn't let me see a doctor after I got home."

"Anything before that?"

I pondered all the things I'd kept from Mom out of self-protection — my innermost thoughts and dreams, my poetry where I revealed the secrets of my heart, my social failures. The night Leanna and I weren't asked to dance, the parties I wasn't invited to, every boy I had a crush on who'd chosen someone else.

"Plenty," I said. "I had to pretend that I preferred to baby-sit and make money when all of my friends were out on dates. I knew what she would think, how she would look at me. She would point out her friends' children, say things like, 'Isn't Janet a pretty girl? She has such beautiful skin.' And there I was, with out-of-control acne that no stupid soap or cream was ever going to cure, knowing that my own mother saw me as flawed."

I paused to catch my breath.

"After Josh was born, my father told me that the attorney had arranged for me to have dermabrasion — a procedure to remove acne scars. Adoptive parents weren't allowed to provide birthmothers with special incentives, but the attorney was sure he could get it covered under medical expenses.

"Dad said, 'Your mother and I think that if you felt prettier, you'd have more confidence,' meaning that I wouldn't think I had to sleep with a guy for him to like me. I was all for it. Anything that would make me better looking and keep me in California longer. After weeks of antibiotics, the dermatologist said my acne was too active for the procedure to be worthwhile. That was that."

My head began to pound. I couldn't look at Barbara. I turned to stare at the bookcase across the room.

"I went home feeling uglier than ever. Is it any wonder I thought no decent man would want me? I was fucking doomed."

Barbara waited to speak until my chest stopped heaving. "That must have hurt."

I eyed her, resisting the urge to say, "duh," to cover the embarrassment of my exposure. "I hate when people feel sorry for me."

"I *am* sorry for you, for the girl you were, how hurt you were by your mother's words and actions. That's not pity; it's empathy."

I shrugged.

"I think you might be harder on yourself than anyone."

"That's probably true."

"I think you've set unreasonable expectations for yourself, based on what your mother expected."

"Okay." I looked at the clock on the table next to her and wished she'd call time.

"How do you feel about that?"

"Stupid. Why do I care so much? She never cared about me, who I was, what I wanted."

"Because you needed her approval, her love?"

I let my body droop. "Her love, Henry's, Josh's. All I've ever wanted is to make them happy."

"Making everyone else happy is not your job."

"I know," I squeaked.

"Your job is to be who you are. And people will either love

you for it or they won't. My bet is they'll love you. I do."

"My mother won't."

Barbara laughed. "You're a tough nut, but you're going to make it."

Session after session, page after journal page, I dredged through my memories and uprooted my grievances.

My mother wouldn't let go of the past. She beat me over the head with every wrong thing I ever did.

She was a stranger to me.

She didn't love me unconditionally.

She hid her feelings. And she kept me from expressing mine.

With each breakthrough, my load became lighter. I felt as if I were on the verge of discovering an important truth, something I'd known all along that hovered just beyond my consciousness.

She avoided difficult situations rather than dealing with them.

"Damn! Barbara! That's *me*! Josh was right."

I'd held my mother to standards that I myself could not meet, just as she had expected perfection from me. That didn't make Josh one hundred percent correct — much of what he'd said and done in recent years had been dead wrong — but he was right about one thing. As hard as I'd fought it, as much as I'd refuted it, I had been acting like my mother. I'd concealed my feelings, been ashamed of my son, and avoided every difficult situation. As hard as I'd tried not to, I had set conditions for loving my son.

This insight rekindled my anger toward my mother.

"Damn her! How the hell am I going to fix this?"

"You can't undo what's been done," Barbara said. "But you can start over, practice new behaviors that aren't like your mom's."

"I might be able to act differently with Josh from now on, but things will never change with her. She'll keep treating me and Debby and Bob and everyone else like she always has. It'll be a constant reminder."

"What if you could tell her how you feel?" Barbara said.

"Yeah, right." Even though we were talking more often, I still held her at arm's length to keep from getting hurt.

"Think how healing that would be. If you could tell her the truth, about even the smallest thing."

The next week, I couldn't wait to get to Barbara's office.

"I did it!" I said. "I told her how I felt."

As usual, I had called Mom on Mother's Day.

"Has Josh called you yet?" she asked.

"No. I doubt he will. Things aren't going well for us right now."

"What do you mean?"

"We had a fight. I don't want to talk about it."

"A fight about what?"

"Mom, I mean it. I really don't want to talk about it."

"Why not?"

I took a deep breath and spoke the truth. "Because it's Mother's Day and my son's not speaking to me and it hurts."

After a beat of silence, she said, "All right. So, how's Henry?"

"She heard me," I told Barbara. "It worked."

"Good for you," she said. "That was very courageous."

I waved my hand, dismissing her compliment and then smiled because I knew that this had been a huge step indeed. I began calling my parents more often, eager to test my new skill.

"This is getting really weird," I reported at our next meeting. "She's actually been nice to me."

"How so?"

"She asked me about my work and didn't say anything derogatory like she used to. Like how come I'm wasting my time in my own business instead of working for a big company. She said she misses me. And I really think she does."

"What did I tell you? We can't change others, but if we change, they have to if they want to stay in our lives."

I remembered one of my parents' visits, a few years before Josh reappeared. We'd had a few friends over and one of the most liberal had taunted my mom for saying that she thought Dan Quayle would make an excellent president. She'd seemed to take it in her stride. The next day, I asked her if she'd had a good time that night.

"I always have a good time with you, Denny."

Suddenly, I felt driven to find some good in my mother.

I rummaged through my scrapbooks. Memories swarmed as thick as flies in summer: birthdays, when Mom always made a cake and prepared whatever we wanted for dinner, and Christmases, with dolls and bicycles beside the tree.

I remembered the days when I'd come home from school and find Mom at the sewing machine, working on a new dress or skirt for me. She'd have me try it on to set the hem, and I'd squirm and giggle every time her fingers brushed my ticklish knees. "Oh Denny, you're so silly," she'd say, which made me giggle harder.

I pictured us huddled around the box of kittens after my cat gave birth in my bedroom closet one Mother's Day. One of my favorite memories was when she and her best friend took me and my best friend, Linda Sue, on a day-long boat trip to Catalina Island to celebrate our graduation from eighth grade.

"Girlfriends are very important," she told us. "The closest thing to family you'll ever have. Aside from your parents, sisters and brothers that is."

There was plenty of proof that she had loved me, as many good days as bad. Yet it was the times she'd disappointed me — and the times I believed I'd disappointed her — that stuck.

I thought about my parents' hopes for me, dreams that surely had been dashed when I'd gotten pregnant, dropped out of college, run off with Don, bounced from one chancy boyfriend to the next, and stabbed randomly at careers before finding my calling. I pondered Henry's hopes for Jeff, his concerns when Jeff had strayed from the safe and conventional path, and the anguish he'd felt, not knowing for ten years

whether his son was okay. Jeff had reappeared at around
the same age I had been when I'd settled into a mainstream
married life with Henry. Had my parents breathed the same
sigh of relief?

Once Jeff had finally made contact, I was terrified that
he might still harbor resentment from the days when I had
failed as his stepmother. But from the moment our eyes met,
I saw that the past was no longer an issue. It was clear that
he had grown, sorted through his hurts and his own mistakes,
and arrived at an understanding that had allowed him to move
on. Without saying a word, Jeff had freed me from the guilt
that had held me captive since the day he'd left home. His
forgiveness allowed me to begin to forgive myself.

"There's another clock." I told Barbara, referring to the
black and gold monument that hung in the background in
almost all the pictures in my early scrapbooks. My parents had
offered it to me some years before, and I'd hung it over the
mantel in our dining room. Antique value or not, seeing the
damn thing everyday made me feel ten years old.

"Do you want to smash it?" she asked.

"No," I smiled. "But I'm going to take it down. Maybe I'll
sell it in a garage sale."

That night I went into the living room to remove the clock.
Henry was watching a nature program about the hundreds
of homeless domestic cats that inhabit the Coliseum ruins in
Rome.

The unspayed females have at least two litters a year, the
narrator said, which they will nurture to maturity and live with
as a family indefinitely — unless they are separated for more
than a day or two. They showed film of a mother cat hiding her
kittens in a crevice of the ruins and going off to hunt for food.
When she returned, her babies were missing, moved by another
mother cat who had found them alone and taken them to her
own litter in a safer location. The original mother searched
relentlessly for her kittens, calling out to them and repeatedly
returning to where she had left them. A few days later, when

she happened upon her offspring with the other mother and kittens, she did not recognize them. She walked on by and eventually gave up the search. Their birth connection was gone.

"I saw her on the street a few times," Aunt Em had said of Sarah Agnes. "Sometimes she'd pass by the school yard and the other kids would point and say, 'That's your mother.' She never acknowledged me. Or any of her children, from what I've heard."

The mind can do almost anything we ask of it. The body is more difficult to fool.

My period had started every single time I saw Josh, whether it was due or not — as if my uterus spontaneously combusted every time I knew I was going to be near him. During the nine months that Josh and I were estranged, my hormones ran out, my periods stopped and my doctor pronounced me officially in menopause.

Chapter 26

SECOND CHANCES

Josh called six days after the September 11, 2001 terrorist attacks on New York and Washington, D.C.

"Hey," he said — his old greeting, but softer and more tentative.

"Hi." My body buzzed with sensations I'd forgotten: breath shallow, stomach sinking, heart pounding. I collapsed into the nearest chair.

"I've wanted to call you for a while," he said, and then paused.

"I'm glad you're calling now."

"Life's too short. I'm sorry for what happened and I want to try again."

Sorry. Finally, the single word that would have fixed things so many times in the past.

I let out a sigh. "I want that, too, Josh."

It had been nine months since he'd hung up on me; nine months since I'd heard my son's voice. And another year before I would commit to seeing him again.

I moved at my own pace, as I had attempted to do when we were first reunited, this time without feeling pressured or guilty. I'd worked hard — in therapy and on my own — and I was almost there. I no longer cared whether I was good enough, only that I felt ready.

Even after making significant progress on my issues with my mother, I had yet to address what had transpired with Josh, acknowledge my mistakes, and forgive him for his. Although our three-year break had been necessary, it created yet another gap in our history. He was still a stranger, as my mom had been despite having raised me. If that were to change, I would have to reveal myself, trust him to be accepting, and hope that he would open up to me as well. I would have to get past the hurts he had inflicted and look at him through the eyes of the loving, truthful, fearless self I had rediscovered, the eyes of the mother I was meant to be.

In 2002, Henry and I made the trip from California to Arizona to spend Thanksgiving with Josh, Jennifer and the kids.

I was as unprepared for my reaction as I had been the day the registry called almost seven years before. Josh had to work Wednesday afternoon, so he asked if we would stop by the trucking terminal on the way to their house. The apprehension I'd managed to contain during the two-day drive mounted as we climbed the stairs on the side of the building and opened the door. Down the hall, I saw a burly, middle-aged man filling out paperwork at a desk.

He glanced up at us and then called out, "Josh, you've got visitors."

As we entered the office, Josh came around the corner and my heart swelled with an almost lustful longing I thought I'd never feel again. He had aged but was still handsome, with his crinkly-eyed smile and cleft chin. The man who was my baby opened his arms to me. His embrace felt like yet another chance.

He shook hands with Henry, invited us to sit, and introduced us to the truckers who came and went from the office. For the next fifteen minutes while we chatted and joked, I couldn't pull my gaze from him, soaking in every little move, every word he spoke. Suddenly, I remembered how much I loved him, how whole and right being with him made me feel.

For the next four days, I basked in the attentions of my grandchildren: Gabe was already two when I met him for the first time; Naomi and Nick had transformed from toddlers into second and third-graders while I'd been gone; and sweet and sassy Katie was in the throes of adolescence. Yet I found myself taking every opportunity to wrestle free of them and seek out the company of my son, for one more reassuring touch on the arm, another laugh, a few private words.

"You and me, we're going to be okay," he said.

"Yes," I said. "The worst is behind us."

Not long before that trip, I had been helping Leanna and her sister-in-law, Linda, go through the belongings that Mr. and Mrs. Daniel had left behind. Valeria had died five years before, and Willard the previous July. Among the boxes of photos and slides, I found a picture of John and me. We were standing behind the table that held our engagement party cake, young and vibrant, smiling, with our arms around each other.

I'd never expected to see that face again and it sent a jolt to my heart. I spent the next week drowning in thoughts of what might have been and finally came to see that photograph as a gift, for me and for Josh. Having proof that John and I had once loved each other brought me peace and ultimately allowed me to let go of my anger.

During our Thanksgiving visit, I gave Josh a copy of the photo.

"There are two things I've always wanted to give you," I said. "A copy of your original birth certificate: the one with my name on it and the name I gave you. Someday when California finally opens its closed adoption records, I'll be able to do that. The other thing is a picture of your father."

Josh took the photo from my hand and I watched as he stared at the faded color image.

"Wow," he muttered, his face contorted with the same mix of unidentifiable emotions as when I'd given him the baby bracelet during our first visit. "I haven't searched for him yet," he said. "I don't know if I ever will."

The next several years weren't easy. I learned that many of the stories Josh had told me when we first met were laced with half-truths and some were outright lies. His run-ins with the law had been more serious than he had led me to believe. He had, in fact, been forced to work some of them off as an informant. He had never been in the Israeli Army. Because he could not prove he was Jewish, he had only been allowed to serve as an administrative volunteer.

When I asked why he'd told me he'd been a soldier, he said, "I thought it would impress you." Like his early religious outpourings, he had taken his best guess at who his mother might be.

I watched Josh make some unwise decisions and slough off any responsibility when his actions backfired. Try as I might, I could never convince him that time spent with his children was more valuable than continually showering them with gifts. I saw his financial situation worsen and his relationship with Jenn grow increasingly toxic. After eight years of marriage, they divorced.

In twelve years of reunion, Josh tested my tolerance again and again, yet I never stopped loving him. I didn't approve of everything he did. We disagree with regularity. But we can share our thoughts and feelings honestly and openly, without endangering our bond. We were no longer strangers. We are more than okay.

What happened shouldn't have... not in 1929 or 1970 or 1991. But it did, and we must all live with the outcome. As I loosened my mother's grip on my soul and fostered a more benevolent outlook, I came to believe we all did the best we could. My grandmother might not have had options, or might not have felt like she had, any more than I'd believed that I could buck the system and keep my child. Understanding my mother's history helped me recognize that she too had done her best. I no longer thought of Josh's adoptive parents as the enemy; surely they had done what they thought was right. Most of all, I believed that Josh was doing his best, given the cards he had been dealt and the choices he'd made — as am I. Having that faith is the only way I know to come to terms with the past and let go of the pain.

My mother didn't die from the world finding out that I had an illegitimate son. She died suddenly from an embolism two weeks after major back surgery. By then, I had made my peace with her, an accord that didn't require her participation, simply a shift in my own heart. Barbara was right, of course. If

I hadn't done the work, I would have been forever haunted by regrets.

I never asked Mom why she'd left her hometown so abruptly. Somewhere along the way, I'd let go of the need to confirm my suspicion — that she too might have gotten pregnant, hidden away, and relinquished her baby. Whether or not our family's cycle of loss had skipped a generation would remain a mystery.

One of the last times I saw my mother, I found the courage to ask what she remembered from her childhood. She said she didn't remember her father at all, and her mother only vaguely. She had no early memories of her brothers and sisters. Her life with the Nelsons had been good, she said; she'd had everything she needed and felt as if she belonged.

Then she said something else.

"I think children should never be separated from their mothers, but it doesn't always work out that way."

Our eyes met for a second before she looked away. There was no way for me to know exactly what she meant and I didn't care. It was the most honest and meaningful thing she'd ever said to me and I came to treasure it, like a rare and perfect jewel.

A birthmother I know once referred to relinquishment as an amputation. Losing a child, she said — or a mother for that matter — is akin to having a hand cut off. And reunion is like having it surgically reattached. Sometimes the hand can be reconnected successfully. The blood flows easily and the nerves are in sync. Sometimes it's not quite right. It's awkward or clumsy or even painful, and you hang on, hoping it will get better with time and practice. Even if the sharpest pain subsides, sometimes a constant dull ache remains. You start to wonder whether you were better off with just a stump, and the vague memory of what you lost lingering just below the skin.

Finding my son reawakened the wound that time had numbed. Embracing that second chance to be his mother became a reminder of what my own mother hadn't been for me. Those scars are still present, sometimes still come to me in dreams, but I know that facing them was the key to resolving my problems with my son.

Josh has yet to search for his father or his relinquished children. I hope to meet my lost grandsons someday. If that is to be, my wish is that the same sense of belonging will be there — the one that Josh and I shared in the beginning, and that I experienced with Naomi on that bathroom floor in Pensacola when she was two. And I hope that our connection will be stronger than the suffering.

A stump isn't better, I've decided. Living fully, loving even at the risk of hurting, is. Motherhood taught me that.

EPILOGUE: 2011

In 2005, my husband and I made a pre-retirement move to Southern Arizona. Our decision was definitely influenced by my ties to the area: my recently widowed father was still here, as well as my sister and niece. My son and his family lived nearby and they celebrated our decision.

I enjoyed about a year of seeing my son and grandchildren regularly before Josh left Jenn and moved two-and-a-half hours away for a job transfer. My weekly visits with Naomi to help with homework and take her to dance lessons came to an abrupt end.

Josh reconnected with Naomi's mother, much to Naomi's delight and my chagrin. It only lasted a few months before Marissa left, once again abandoning her daughter. Josh met a new woman and married for the fifth time. That relationship has been as tumultuous as all the others.

Living near Josh didn't bring the increased closeness and understanding I had hoped for. Instead, he seemed to become increasingly angry about what he believed he'd missed by not growing up in his family of origin. His demands for what I "owed" him became intolerable. When I set a new boundary, he threatened to deny me access to Naomi.

"You don't deserve to be a grandmother since you weren't a good mother to me," he wrote in an email.

At the same time, he cut off Naomi's visitations with Jenn, the only mother she had known from age three to near 11, and the step-siblings she had come to love and embrace as her true family.

What had always been a "long-term project" became a no-win situation, a hazard to my own sanity, and I felt compelled to put our relationship on hold until I saw some changes in Josh's attitude and behavior. I spelled out what I needed if we were to reopen communications. He made no effort to comply. Instead, he ramped up his threats, which primarily involved ruining my reputation with friends and calling my father to demand some sort of justice for how poorly his life had gone.

"Someone has to pay," he said.

It never occurred to him that his own father deserved a share of his rancor. Josh still hadn't attempted to locate him.

Josh didn't act on any of his threats. Eventually, he entered therapy, which had been among my requirements. As a result, he has been diagnosed with a serious psychological disorder. Thankfully, he is receiving treatment.

While I am certain that his relinquishment and adoption played a part in his affliction, I have finally let go of the guilt I carried after learning that he hadn't necessarily been "better off" without me. I've accepted that I can't undo the past and that I can't fix my son.

Josh and I haven't spoken for three years. I don't know when or if we'll ever see each other again. But I will never shut that door. Not as long as there's even the slightest hope.

I still see my local grandchildren regularly. Despite lengthy separations, my relationship with Naomi — now fifteen — has endured and thrived. When we get together it's always as if no time has passed.

Perhaps she is my true second chance.

About the Author

When Denise Roessle became pregnant out of wedlock in 1969, she inadvertently joined the ranks of the million-plus young women who fell prey to the Baby Scoop Era—a time when relinquishing their newborns for adoption was the socially-accepted solution to erasing their sins and filling an increasing demand for adoptable infants.

She was told to move on with her life, assured that she would forget and have other children she could keep. She finished college, married, and became a professional copywriter and graphic designer. But she never had more children. And she did not forget.

After reuniting with her grown son in 1996, Denise began writing on this more personal topic. Her articles have appeared in national adoption magazines and newsletters, and she continues to be active in the post-adoption, adoption reform, and birthmother support arenas.

For more information, visit **secondchancemother.com**

Red Willow Books

www.RedWillowBooks.com

Red Willow books are by authors who respect the craft of writing.

When you purchase a Red Willow book, you are truly supporting the author, as all Red Willow authors receive 50% of the royalties.

For more great books like this, visit RedWillowBooks.com where you can sign up to receive advance notice of new releases.

Made in the USA
Lexington, KY
30 June 2012